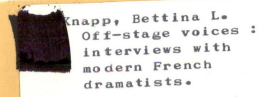

Knapp, Bettina L.
Off-stage voices :
interviews with
modern French
dramatists.

# Off–Stage Voices

## Interviews with Modern French Dramatists

Off–Stage Voices

Interviews with Modern French Dramatists

by

Bettina Knapp

edited by

Alba Amoia

The Whitston Publishing Company
Troy, New York
1975

# TABLE OF CONTENTS

## PREFACE

The first point of interest in this gathering of interviews is their diversity. Even when they speak about the theatre, which is not always the case, the persons interviewed appear sometimes not to have the same medium in mind. No doubt, this is due in part to the fact that the theatre has non-verbal, as well as verbal, aspects and that, among other things, directing and acting are involved, not just writing. But this is not the whole story: here and there, one may discern signs of the disorientation of a composite genre, and perhaps of its dissolution.

At times, contrasts emerge from the diversity, either in dramatic conception or in judgments about a dramatist. Blin despises Claudel; Barrault admires him. Unlike others, Rezvani has no passing compliments for Beckett. To elicit some significant disagreements or agreements, the interviewer has asked similar questions, in particular about Artaud. In the last two decades, Artaud has been turned into a kind of hero, or, if you prefer, sacred cow. Some of the persons interviewed have risen to the bait, others not.

The practitioners of an art are not necessarily scholars. Furthermore, there is the matter of deciding who influenced you and how: the border between fiction and intellectual autobiography is hazy. Finally, an artist may be afraid of deflating his originality if he acknowledges

an influence. Whether this is the case when Arrabal claims
he never read Artaud, I don't know. (I recommend the following trick: deny likely influences and invent an un-
likely one.)

Savary wants to get rid of dramatists, but a triangular
battle does not develop systematically between directors,
authors and actors. Failing this, one can at least pick
up a few echoes of the quarrels, jealousies, and instinctive
stabs in the back, which enliven the Parisian ring, in the
domain of the theatre as well as others.

I was thankful to Mrs. Knapp for abandoning, in her
scene with Arrabal, the self-effacing and admiring role
which, as an interviewer, she was expected to play. I wish
she had also asked Vauthier "when his megalomania first
began." But he had taken the precaution of having with
him a kind of spiritual bodyguard. The latter talks about
Vauthier's "search for the sacred" and Vauthier remembers
the number of curtain calls in Paris, Berlin and Zurich.
For someone who enjoys comedy (I do), this may be one of
the high points in the series. In the interview with Savary,
the director says that he believes "in kindness, in gentleness in the theatre," and then that he staged *The Raft of
the Medusa* in such a way that the spectators would have
the impression that dead bodies were falling on them.
Michel attacks conformist thinking, but what he says about
"our society" ("manipulation," "alienation," etc.) illustrates a conformist kind of criticism.

Some traditional themes and value words recur in the
series. There is a show of piety toward ancestors: nobody calls Shakespeare a dud or Racine a bore. "Life,"
"reality," "truth," "love," "human," are still used as
respectable passwords. Genet, who is often mentioned in
these interviews (Amidou says he is "inhuman," but
quickly makes amends), might have sung another tune if
he had not remained in the wings, but he would probably
have contributed to another theme: the "sacred." "Poetry"
and "music" also recur as value words, in the Romantic

and Symbolist tradition. The use of the same word does not necessarily point to the same conception or practice of dramatic art. Someone may praise a play for its "truth" or "poetry"; and someone else may criticize the same play for its lack of "truth" or "poetry."

It seems to be widely agreed among the participants that the theatre should not just be amusing, but critically revealing. A few of the persons interviewed are also concerned about practical results. There is at present no way of checking what effect, if any, a play may have upon the practical behavior of the spectators. For all we know, a play reputed to be "uncommitted" might produce the effect toward which a "committed" play would strive in vain.

It appears at least reasonable to assume that the diversity of plays, which is echoed in these interviews, does not favor a cumulative effect: the plays are implicitly critical of each other. Besides, in a society which feeds on haphazard and fast-changing slogans perhaps more than on stolid myth, it is difficult for the dramatist to pin down the enemy. There is also the fact that a play will be variously interpreted, as these interviews testify. Finally, the theatre depends on subsidies and publicity: it has to become an accomplice of the social system which committed dramatists wish to undermine. One might ponder in this respect a suggestion of Rezvani: eliminate professionalism.

By nature, interviews are closer to the theatre (logic of misunderstanding, comedy of errors) than to criticism. However, in this particular series, we find not only role-playing and story-telling, but a remarkable amount of sober reflection. With great patience, Bettina Knapp has managed to gather a variegated and substantial harvest.

Robert Champigny

# INTRODUCTION

Every age has had something new and exciting to offer the world, whether in the domain of the arts or of the sciences. In the theatrical field playwrights are forever gripped with a desire to reveal the fruit of their search, the depths of their feelings, the portent of their discoveries—*truth* and *reality* as they see it—in dramatic form.

French theatre throughout the centuries has been particularly beguiling. It has encompassed, synthesized and exteriorized both spiritual and physical aspects of man and life. Its range seems to have been infinite, its variety spellbinding.

In the Middle Ages, for example, liturgical drama in the form of Passion, Mystery and Miracle plays held audiences enthralled. On merrier occasions satires, farces and slapstick comedy aroused guffaws and giggles from wide-eyed spectators. The Renaissance gave birth to a more cerebral, philosophical and historical group of plays which were performed, for the most part, in schools and colleges. The 17th century, France's classical era, witnessed the emergence of perhaps the most remarkable theatre of them all: the psychological drama as created by Corneille, Molière and Racine. Once an apogée has been reached, a decline is inevitable. The rather mediocre social and sentimental dramas of the 18th century attest to this fact. During the Romantic Era, the pendulum swung sharply in the direction of love, melodrama, intrigue of all

types, supplanting the more earthly and realistic plays of
the preceding century. In due course, a variety of new
theatrical genres arose: Naturalist, Symbolic, Impressionistic, Surrealistic, Intimist drama.

A strange phenomenon occurred with the birth of
Naturalist theatre. The reign of the *metteur en scène*
(director) was ushered in. It was André Antoine, the
founder of the Free Theatre (1887), who became the inspiration, the guiding force of his troupe, responsible for
its productions, and for the successes and failures of the
theatrical enterprise. After Antoine, other directors won
fame, not always establishing their own companies, but
inevitably stamping their productions with their own original and personal touch: Paul Fort, Lugné-Poë, Jacques
Copeau, Louis Jouvet, Sacha Pitoëff, Charles Dullin,
Antonin Artaud, and contemporary figures such as Roger
Blin, Roger Planchon, Jean-Louis Barrault, Jorge Lavelli,
and Jérôme Savary.

After World War II a spirit of disenchantment permeated
the French theatrical world. Existentialist theatre, as
viewed by Sartre and Camus, looked upon life as an absurdity, meaningless--an agony. Post-war dramatists such
as Beckett, Genet, Ionesco and Vauthier made a mockery
of formerly held notions: idealism, purity, progress, religion, social structures, etc. They experienced that
excoriating feeling--metaphysical anguish. They tore
aside the mask which they believed had hidden man's true
nature and revealed on stage beings more monster than
man.

A *tabula rasa* to some extent occurred in the theatre
during the 1950's and 1960's. Formerly held social,
philosophical and psychological values, which had done
little or nothing to help or to save man during the holo-
caust, were theatrically destroyed. Dramatists annihilated
the very principles and structures upon which plays had
been based: plot, character, atmosphere, rational sequences, understandable relationships between protagonists, linear concepts of time and space, discursive style.

Beckett, Ionesco and Vauthier, the creators of anti-literary theatre, went so far as to reject the very idea of empathy. They devaluated language and did away with the usual meanings of words and rhythmic patterns. For Ionesco, language was transformed into an object; words were brittle, hard and painful, particularly when bandied about in a series of violent interchanges. Beckett's words seemed like a series of extractions, liberating forces, uttered with pain and giving rise to endless ramifications in terms of meaning and feeling. Genet's language was rich, baroque and became wedded to the image-dazzling, blinding, disquieting and forever shimmering. Vauthier's protagonists (or antagonists) expressed themselves frequently in highly poetic renditions, at other moments in screams, groans, lamentations and cries.

Drama proliferated in the 1950's and 1960's. A host of playwrights emerged (Billetdoux, Arrabal, Michel, Dubillard, Gatti, Obaldia, Weingarten, Carrière, Rezvani, Atlan, Borel, Worms) and novelists who turned to the theatre every now and then (Duras, Sarraute, Pinget), bringing to the fore a new and boundless realism, for themselves and for their audiences. Labels were attached to their endeavors in an attempt to understand the fantastic and frequently irrational world they conjured forth in dramatic form: the theatre of derision, of the ridiculous, of nudity; circus, street, panic, guerrilla, image, silence...

Contemporary man as viewed by these modern French dramatists has become a Narcissus-like figure looking into a pool at his own image. Instead of finding himself beautiful, as in the ancient myth, he finds himself to be revolting and sick and capable of every kind of corruption. He is a being suffocated by poisonous gases emanating from his own mind, soul and flesh. This is the basic fact about man behind the superficial falsity of his unreal and misleading beauty. To face corruption in the soul and see beyond it will, it is assumed, purge man of his aberrations and set him up whole again.

Every culture has its own form of purgation. The

great cultures of the past had noble means which did not debase man and rob him of his dignity. Though the bloodiest of crimes and most barbarous of deeds were enacted in the trilogy of the House of Atreus, purgation was the result of the traditional and exalted dramatic ritual in which the whole populartion participated; it was in the end a healthy and unifying force. Today, man daily hears threats of universal war and these potentialities are awesome. The playwright, however, reduces the volcanic to the minute and stages events in commonplace settings, because though the events are big man is still very small, dwarfed by the events.

Modern purgation is an individual matter. It may occur, as our playwrights, directors and actors suggest in this volume, through debasement and suffering, through satire, the farce, sado-masochism, poetry, solitude, blood— but with the hope of rising above it into health and harmony. Suffering or the inflicting of it, watching the spectacle of pain and torture or enduring it, seem to pervade our culture. One might say that ours is an age in which humanity will have to hold hard to remain human.

*

In this volume of interviews on modern French theatre, I have asked directors, dramatists and actors to discuss their concepts concerning their art, their creative life, beliefs, times contemporary culture and the world in general. Each of the individuals interviewed had *carte blanche* to express his or her most intimate ideas as freely as' each saw fit: objectives, anguishes, loves, hatreds, personal disciplines, needs and desires for fulfillment.

The Interviews with Directors, which constitute the first section of this volume, begin with Roger Blin's exposition of his work in the domain of the theatre. Blin was a member of Antonin Artaud's theatrical troupe. He acted the role of one of the Assassins in Artaud's theatrical rendition of *The Cenci*.

It must be recalled that Antonin Artaud's ''Theatre of Cruelty'' sought to do away with the traditional theatre, whose nuclear elements were words, well-made plots, psychologically oriented and rationally understood characters. Rather, ''A true theatrical work disturbs the senses in repose, liberates the repressed unconscious, foments a virtual revolt...and imposes both a heroic and difficult attitude on the assembled collectivity.'' Artaud viewed the theatre, as had the people of antiquity, as a ritual whose purpose was to stimulate numinous or religious experience within the spectator. To achieve this end he sought to expand the spectators' reality by arousing the explosive and creative forces within man's unconscious which, he believed, were more powerful than rational consciousness in determining man's actions. By means of a theatre based on myths, symbols and gestures, the play for Artaud became a weapon to be used to whip up man's irrational forces, so that a collective event could be turned into a personal and living experience.

After Artaud left France for Mexico, Roger Blin became both actor and director on his own. Blin brought extreme integrity, vision and artistry to all of his productions. Some of his most notable productions are Samuel Beckett's *Waiting for Godot* (1953), and *Endgame* (1957), Jean Genet's *The Blacks* (1959) and *The Screens* (1966).

Jean-Louis Barrault, when speaking of the theatre, refers to it as a bride, and the play in which he performs or which he directs as an act of love. A student of Charles Dullin, secretary to Antonin Artaud, member of the Comédie-Française, director of the Théâtre de France (1959-1968), mime and film actor, his passion for the theatre has not diminished throughout the years. His direction of plays by Claudel, Anouilh, Calderón, Giraudoux, Kafka, Chekhov, Vauthier, to mention but a few, brought him international fame. Barrault is a devotee of ''total theatre,'' a spectacle in which dialogue, monologue, pantomime, and choreography work harmoniously together, a theatre which mirrors man's entire existence in terms of his thoughts, emotions, rhythms, facial expressions, anxieties, etc.

**Roger Planchon, director of the Théâtre de la Comédie in Lyons (1952-1957) and since 1957 of the Théatre de la** Cité at Villeurbanne, was a disciple of Jean Vilar, of Erwin Piscator and of Bertolt Brecht. He concentrates on social and political aspects in the theatre. His production of Marlowe's *Edward II* aroused great controversy because he did not treat this monarch merely as a puppet and pederast, but as the protector of the arts, an innovator who tried to fight the powerful by gaining the sympathy of **the people.** Molière's *Georges Dandin,* as viewed by Planchon, was not only a cuckold, but a symbol of class struggle.

Georges Lavelli, Argentinian-born, won his reputation **in France in 1963 with his production of *The Marriage* by** Witold Gombrowicz. Later he directed *Yvonne* by this same Polish playwright, Obaldia's *The Agricultural Cosmonaut,* Vauthier's *Medea,* etc. Lavelli's is an eclectic approach. He is inspired and aroused anew with each play he directs. Whether it be Claudel, de Obaldia, Arrabal or Copi, Lavelli searches for the drama's inner meaning, enlarges upon it, exaggerates it if necessary, so that the impact upon audiences will be even more dazzling, frightening and imaginative.

**Jérôme Savary and his troupe, The Great Magic Circus,** are joy incarnate. It is the drole, the satiric, the fantastic, the grotesque which he brings before his audiences. His work in the theatre, for the most part, is free and inventive. Like in the *commedia dell'arte* of old, the plotline is sketched before the performance, but the approach to it changes every evening in terms of dialogue, action, interpretation, atmosphere and points of view, which depend exclusively upon the audience's mood and the troupe's frame of mind.

\*\*

I have chosen a cross section of contemporary dramatists to be included in the second part of *Off-Stage Voices*. Their works have been very loosely classified under the following headings: dramatists of the theatre of the absurd (Robert Pinget, Fernando Arrabal, Jacques Borel); poetic and imagistic theatre (Jean Vauthier, Marguerite Duras, Roland Dubillard, Romain Weingarten, Nathalie Sarraute, Jean-Claude Carriere, François Billetdoux, Liliane Atlan); socially-oriented dramatists (Armand Gatti, Georges Michel, Gabriel Cousin); humorous and farcical theatre (Jeanine Worms, René de Obaldia, Rezvani).

\*

    The world Pinget conjures forth in such plays as *Dead Letter* (1960), *Architruc* (1962), *The Hypothesis* (1966) is one of mystery and progressive anguish, tinged with black humor. Pinget's name is frequently associated with that of Beckett, not only because of their friendship, but because they are preoccupied with the same problems. Beckett's translation of Pinget's radio-play *The Old Tune* (1960) was startling; it transformed the sought-for incoherent dialogues between two old men, the drama's heroes, into a pathetic, poignant and highly lyrical work. Pinget's characters or anti-heroes, as they are referred to, seem to emerge from an indefinite area and realm, from an elemental world, despite the fact that they are simple and prosaic types. His travelers, coachmen, domestics, postmen, etc. belong to no specific time or place. Each is a victim of his solitude, of his absurd existence on earth. Because of Pinget's derisive humor and his highly developed sense of the burlesque and of carricature, a world of irony, cruelty, irritation and uneasiness unfolds before the spectator.

    Fernando Arrabal introduces his readers and viewers to a ferocious realm filled with gnomes, monsters, deformed and rejected creatures--those who dwell outside of God's universe. Arrabal, the creator of the Panic Theatre, underscores the ceremonial and ritualistic aspect in his drama. Arrabal's anti-heroes are for the most part either children or adults who have never evolved and who behave, think and feel like children. In such plays as *Fando and Lis* (1964) and *Oraison* (1958) the reader is charmed at first by the pseudo-innocence of the protagonists. Slowly, their juvenile approach to nature, love, or relationships of any kind, inspire terror. In *The Labyrinth* (1961), *The Automobile Graveyard* (1964), **And They Put Handcuffs on the Flowers** (1969), *Sky and Shit* (1972), an utterly evil, brutal, cruel and hideously grotesque world, stemming directly from the author's unconscious, opens up for spectators to observe. Abnormal on all levels, Arrabal's characters are tortured beings, either because of their physical or spiritual ugliness or because of their overwhelming fear of facing life and death.

Jacques Borel came to the theatre rather late in his career. Novelist first, (*The Bond*, 1965; *The Return*, 1970), critic and poet, he wrote his first play *Tata or Education* (1972) on the request of the French radio. *Tata* is a drama in which all sentimentality, tenderness and love have been banished. Comic and dramatic violence seem to have replaced softer emotions, as Borel deftly penetrates the inner world of a child brought up by two monstrous beings—a mother and an aunt—each stifling him as best she can and in her own perverse way. Despite these two inscrutable and pitiless feminine forces, a kind of incandescent humor arises from the grotesque and even mythical nature of the multiple situations offered the viewer.

**

Jean Vauthier is primarily a poet who uses the theatre as a vehicle to express himself. He brings to the stage dense and tortured conflicts in which his brilliant imagery, with its symbolic overtones and intricate rhythmic effects, serve to give the story its compactness and its momentum, its depth and darkness in which situations are pushed to the extreme. Vauthier's intention is to break down those barriers of custom and habit in social man, as well as the formal, traditional walls separating actor and audience. Once the social and dramatic conventions are breached, the spectators are free to engage in a complete emotional experience, brought about by a visceral empathy between themselves and the figures on stage. Some of the themes in Vauthier's plays (*Captain Bada,* 1952; *The Character Against Himself,* 1956; *The Prodigies,* 1959; *Blood,* 1970) are the following: the poet vis-à-vis himself, women, society, and God. Questions are posed in an attempt to answer anguishing problems. What is the poet's reality? How much can the poet give of himself? How much pain can he bear? Vauthier's protagonists have all reached a high degree of decomposition before the dramas open; they are separated from society and have no true relationship with it or within any group. Even when cast as lovers or as wife and husband, the characters always live alone--in isolation. They are constantly at war with each other and sexually antagonistic. Vauthier's attitude toward his religion is ambivalent. He is haunted by his God, hating Him and adoring Him at the same time, willing to annihilate and resurrect Him within his being. In their struggle to find peace and order, his characters experience spiritual pain, indulge in self-torture such as flagellation, striking and receiving blows, and trade insults until their souls are crucified and bloodied. After such extreme torment, Vauthier's "poets," who are despairing and who meet with an agonizing death in *Captain Bada* and *The Character Against Himself,* become whole again and are able to create and find their basic reality in *The Prodigies.* In the later plays they experience grace; their component parts have been fused together; the ego, broken to pieces, has been restored on a "higher plane." Revealed now is the poet in man—the only worthy condition in the eyes of God.

Marguerite Duras, known chiefly in the United States for her film *Hiroshima mon amour,* is one of the most versatile of women writers in France today. Equally at ease in three mediums--the novel, the drama and the movie scenario--her literary creations are unique. They are sensitive probings of the human psyche written in a quasi-detached, slow-paced manner, and infused with a highly charged personal poetry. Duras' characters are never drawn in depth, once and for all; they are, rather, made up of a complex of interwoven images, of beguiling sensations and impressions. The events recounted in her dramas (*The Viaducts of the Seine and Oise*, 1960; *The Musica* (1965); *Entire Afternoons Spent in the Trees*, 1965) are clothed in an atmosphere of awe and mystery. Her prose, hypnotic in its effect upon the reader, is an exquisite blending of the Oriental's extreme control and his "inwardness," and the Occidental's ebullience and his "outwardness." Themes occur and re-occur against impressionistic backgrounds; time is experienced objectively versus subjectively; an external event or strange encounter, like the irritant placed in an oyster, induces the happening that follows; the individuals struggle instinctually to puncture the suffocating isolation they experience; sanity and insanity; reality and fantasy, etc. Marguerite Duras' plays cannot be "cerebrally" appreciated or understood. They are more like personal emanations that seem to flow like giant waves splashing strange and haunting images onto the pages or the stage. Alternating bone-sparseness with cascades of words, the author awakens the reader's sensations and draws him to her fertile nomadic world.

Roland Dubillard became known as a playwright with the production of *Naïve Swallows* (1961). Dubillard's **drama offers no situations, no characters, no overt passions,** no linear time. It is a poetic theatre which is based on language and, paradoxically, at the same time attempts to do away with it. His plays rest on a glorification of the "banal," on a series of platitudes which become absolutely meaningless in themselves but take on a reality of their own after their destruction. Nothing on stage then seems either real (in our sense of reality) or secure, except for the fact that conversation is taking place. Yet conflict does arise in the bizarre realm he conjures forth for the spectator. To be on stage and to talk indicates a *presence;* the topics discussed constantly refer to something or someone who is elsewhere, either in the unconscious realm or in some past or future event, and thus refers to an *absence.* Conversation, as conceived by Dubillard, does not permit closer association between people; on the contrary, it acts as a source of conflict and misunderstanding and as an escape mechanism. Dialogues amount to monologues, as each person withdraws ever more powerfully into his own enclosed world of fantasy, absorbed and tortured by metaphysical questions centering on life, death, flesh and spirit. Yet *Naïve Swallows, The House of Bones* (1962), *The Beet Garden* (1969), *The Crabs* (1971) are also endowed with moments of extraordinary hilarity when puns, gags, repetitions, satire and slapstick comedy come to the fore, further baffling and disconcerting the spectator and at the same time beguiling him.

Roland Dubillard acted in Romain Weingarten's first play *Akara* (1948), which, though performed only three times, was hailed by Ionesco as "one of the first important plays of the new theatre." *Akara* breaks with traditional theatrical concepts not only in terms of vocabulary, but in the very ideation of the protagonist. *Akara* features a Man-Cat who, according to Weingarten, represents the novel, "the different"—the individual. He dies at the end of the drama because he is powerless in his confrontation with the *status quo.* Weingarten's theatre (*The Wet Nurses,* 1961; *Summer,* 1966; *Alice in the Luxembourg Gardens,* 1970) rebels against the superficiality and automatism of many human relationships. *The Wet Nurses,* a clownish escapade, derides the world of business, degrades the notion of married couples, points up the difficulties involved in passing from one stage of life to another. *Summer* involves audiences in the domain of the dream, a realm in which Weingarten invites men and women cats to portray their inner lives on stage. *Alice in the Luxembourg*

*Gardens* might be considered a modern view of mother-daughter relationships. What seems realistic or ordinary in Weingarten's theatre emerges as something fantastic, disjointed, violent and frequently cruel. The flow of images emanating from the unconscious of his creatures seems like an endless series of revelatory commentaries upon man's desires and thoughts which--if one refuses or fears to face reality--might have been better left unsaid.

Nathalie Sarraute's precise, penetrating and extraordinarily imagistic style was first revealed to the public in her volume *Tropisms*. "Tropisms," around which Madame Sarraute constructs her plays and builds tensions and conflicts, are described by her as "undefinable movements" existing within each human being; they are at the root of words people utter, the gestures they make, the feelings they display. Madame Sarraute further declares that the zone in which these "tropisms" flourish "is dangerous and insalubrious," an entity unto itself, part of neither the conscious nor the unconscious worlds. *The Silence* (1963) and *The Lie* (1966) were radio plays first, then performed on stage. The plot of *The Lie* is minuscule. Indeed, it consists of an insignificant fabrication, a game played by a group of friends. One person is supposed to lie and the others are required to guess the author of the lie. The liar, or the suspected liar, however, provokes profound emotions within each of the friends, making for an intensely dramatic situation. Nathalie Sarraute's dialogue sounds like a series of murmurs or uninterrupted inner conversations in which the banal becomes beguiling, the rhythms and musical qualities hypnotic. Certain critics claim that Nathalie Sarraute's view of life is pessimistic: her characters, though pleasant on the surface are aggressive and materialistic--parasites frequently. To place a moral judgment on her characters would be to limit her endeavors. Her protagonists defy limitations. They merely act and react, consciously or unconsciously, to whatever situation arises.

For Jean-Claude Carrière, poetic dialogue is of prime

importance. His play, *The Memory-Aid* (1969), has no plot.
It concerns a woman who enters a man's apartment and
does not want to leave it. The audience knows from the
very outset of the drama that she will remain, that she will
impose herself upon him. Suspense, if there is suspense,
is based on detail: the variety of maneuvers she uses to
win his affection, the changes which occur in both characters as relationships alter. The spectator interprets
the nuances as he sees fit, projecting upon them whatever
pleasurable or painful points of view are stirred within
him.

François Billetdoux's characters utter the faint and
anguished cries of men and women whose illusions have
been shattered by the brutal forces of life which envelop
them. Billetdoux introduces audiences to human beings
searching to realize their dreams and aspirations, to fix
and to hold on to something solid, and by so doing to give
themselves faith in living. All is in vain. For Billetdoux's characters, as they emerge in such plays as *Tchin-
Tchin* (1959) or *Then Go to Törpe's* (1961) and *The Widows*
(1972), life is a difficult struggle between how they wish
to live and how they actually live. At times, Billetdoux
brightens his bleak world with light touches of humor.
Even the droll, however, leaves a sting. It merely masks
the dissatisfied yearnings of a life his creatures cannot
face and from which they are forever trying to escape.
Billetdoux, a master of orthodox theatrical technique,
fashions his plays with skill, leading us forward to a
climax and a final *dénouement*. His style is taut and rapid,
at once romantic and realistic, prosaic, yet with the coun-
terforce of bold and tender images, frightening silences,
periods of delirium. Billetdoux never manipulates his
creatures; he lets them glide and talk willynilly, responding
to their inner compulsions. He tries to remain objective,
an outsider peering in, a doctor studying a patient, a
botanist fascinated by the thousands of small lines and
hollows in a piece of vegetable. Yet in spite of his efforts
at detachment, Billetdoux's compassion and humanity are

readily discernible.

There are writers whose sensibility and depth are such that they seem to bear within them the weight and burden of humanity's problems. Such a dramatist is Liliane Atlan. A victim of persecution during World War II, empathizing with those who met their end in German concentration camps, her plays (*Monsieur Fugue*, 1967; *The Messiahs*, 1968; *The Little Carriage of Flames and Voices*, 1971) resound with the poignant cry of a woman who is searching desperately for an answer to life's problems and who has found it in her God and in her heritage: the Bible and the Kabbala. For Liliane Atlan, the theatre is a mystical experience--an initiation into a deeper level of Self.

*** 

Armand Gatti is a socially and politically oriented dramatist. For him, the theatre is not a form of amusement nor is it simply a pleasant distraction. It is a stimulant to action, a force designed to liberate audiences from established notions, enabling them thereby to acquire new insights and meaningful experiences. Gatti's theatre is shorn of constricting theatrical conceptions inherent in the classical psychological theatre with its rational development of personalities, plots and climaxes. Nor does it follow the lines of the avant-garde theatre which deals so heavily in personal symbolism and mythology. It is a thematic and socially oriented theatre with roots in the work-a-day world. Gatti's plays, *The Imaginary Life of the Street Cleaner Auguste G...*(1962), *Chronicles of a Provisional Planet* (1962), *The Second Existence of the Tatenberg Camp* (1962), *V for Vietnam* (1967) etc. reveal also a profound interest in dramatic structure. His views on this subject closely follow the patterns set by modern science and mathematics, which have shattered former conceptions of space and time. Gatti, in his plays, has abolished clock-time by creating a non-linear drama with "multiple stage life." Characters not only live in several worlds at once (in various geographical areas), but simultaneously in different time sequences in the past, present and future. Audiences are given a prismatic view of the spectacle unfolding before them. They see the protagonists through their own eyes, through the eyes of the protagonists themselves during various phases of their existence, through the eyes of those who come into contact with the protagonists. Nothing in Gatti's theatre is static. Everything merges and swirls, propelled by its own dynamism--by life itself.

Georges Michel is well known in Paris, thanks to the support given him by Jean-Paul Sartre who published his first play, *The Toys*, in the existentialist review, *Modern Times* (1962), and prefaced his theatrical piece, *Sunday's Walk* (1967). Angered by the *status quo* and rejecting an avant-garde which, as far as Michel is concerned, has become a rear-guard, this socially oriented author wants to set the world aright by dealing directly and concretely with reality. His dramas, such as *Aggression*, are not traditional thesis plays, nor are they works dealing in dreams, fantasies and personal symbology. Using the most advanced theatrical machinery and devices at his disposal, this explosive young writer dramatizes social problems and collective anxieties which haunt both him and his generation: war, famine, racism, delinquency, etc. His plays are designed to question, provoke and shock audiences.

Gabriel Cousin's plays (*The Barker and the Automaton*, 1961; *The Drama of Fukuryu-Maru*, 1965; *Journey to the Mountain Beyond*, 1966) reveal an intense preoccupation with problems confronting his generation. Perhaps the most important influences on Cousin were Berthold Brecht and Antonin Artaud. The former led Cousin to discover a new, socially oriented theatrical climate and to discern and dramatize man's views, preoccupations and conflicts. Artaud taught Cousin how to use the stage technically, to create a "poetry in space" by concentrating on the actor's bodily motions, stage sets and accessories and viewing these as a series of animated hieroglyphics or signs. Cousin envisages an ideal theatre resembling, in certain respects, a circus or a Greek amphitheatre in which the stage can be used vertically on several levels as well as horizontally, a theatre with multiple movable stages, making simultaneity of action possible. As for the dramatic elements of the play itself, Cousin uses a Greek chorus, the physical presence and movements of crowds, mime, music, song and dance. To implement the play he employs a full panoply of mechanical devices: filmed scenic sketches, amplified sound, etc. All these techniques, Cousin maintains, must be used to create a unified spectacle, which is the play. Cousin's theatre is not didactic. It does not try to solve any problems. It defines and denounces the various tragic forms of man's existence.

****

Jeanine Worms' intention is to penetrate man's (and woman's) inner world, to exteriorize its farcial and tragic aspects and to present these on a platter in a series of one-act plays. Her language as it emerges in *The Night* (1968), *The Store, The Good Example* (1971), *Later* (1972), etc. literally explodes on the stage. Words are manipulated like solid objects; they are thrown, bandied about, pushed to the extreme, creating a series of whimsical and highly poetic situations.

René de Obaldia is a dramatist gifted with an incredible sense of humor, and a bitter and sharp feeling for satire. Indeed, even the most distressing themes--the possibility of atomic attack in *The Unknown General* (1964), the sexual attraction of a middle-aged man for a twelve year old girl in *The Satyr of La Villette* (1963), space travel and an overly mechanized and industrial society in *The Agricultural Cosmonaut* (1965)--are handled with pith and joy. René de **Obaldia** is also fascinated by language *per se* and the horrendous misunderstandings and conflicts to which it frequently gives rise.

Rezvani's dramas are bitter commentaries on modern life. They are not lugubrious, however, since acidulous humor and provocative language stress the farcical elements in man and the life he has created for himself. His play, *Body* (1970), a one-character drama, features an attractive businesswoman, a kind of half-female Women's Liberation type. As the play opens, she dons a vaporous garment and begins to talk in loving and endearing terms to a box. Moments later, she draws from it what looks like a long, limp piece of pinkish rubber. This thing's name? Body. Body has no eyes, no mouth, no sex—certainly it is a projection of the woman herself, as identityless and faceless a creature, psychologically speaking, as the blob of rubber she fondles. Laughter, pathos, shock and enchantment await the spectator in this farcical escapade created to deride certain aspects, groups and beings of 20th century civilization.

\*\*\*\*\*

The third and last section of *Off-Stage Voices* is devoted to actors. Marie Bell and Michel Etcheverry were associated with the Comédie-Française, a unique institution that has been a working theatre ever since its founding in 1680 by Louis XIV, that is, for over two hundred and ninety years. Whether at Versailles, the Tuileries or Chambord, whenever a gala event was scheduled, the Comédie-Française, or the House of Moliere, as it is also called, was asked to enliven the occasion. The Comédie-Française went through some trying times during the course of its history. The most turbulent period occurred during the Revolution. On one occasion, on November 14, 1789, during a performance of Marie-Joseph de Chénier's *Charles IX*, the actor Talma, a republican, quarrelled with a fellow artist, Naudet, a royalist. A duel was in order; sides were taken and blood was shed. The Comédie-Française also played a particularly brilliant role in the 19th century: for example, Hugo's *Hernani*, the first play of the newly grouped Roman-

tic school, was presented on its stage in 1830. Famous
actors and actresses of the Comédie-Française (Rachel,
Mounet-Sully, Sarah Bernhardt, Constant Coquelin, etc.)
brought international fame to this state-subsidized theatre,
which stands out as the only group in the world which
chooses its own repetoire, recruits its own members, trains
them to perfection, according to a definite code and a strin-
gent schedule, eliminating the unfit as they appear, and
promoting the talents of the gifted.

****

Amidou was chosen by Roger Blin to perform in Genet's
*The Screens*. Blin trained Amidou, relative novice to the
acting profession, for the lead part, permitting the actor's
natural gift to come to the fore. To portray a character
in a Genet play is a difficult task. Each of his plays
exudes the brutality of man at odds with the world--the man
who lives alone, misunderstood, a pariah. Believing themselves compressed by cardboard walls of illusion, some of
Genet's creatures smash against whatever appears to con-
fine them, desperately trying to make contact with the
"real" world. They seek to reach and experience the
depths of every emotion and in so doing plunge into a
morass of sordidness and shame, going ever more deeply
into those recesses where others are not courageous
enough to tread. Hidden beneath a mask representing control, lie bundles of violent emotions and muffled and strident laughter.

Daniel Ivernel, both theatre and film actor, is eclectic
in his outlook. He has portrayed all types of creatures:
traditional and unconventional, rogues and kings, lovers
and misogynists, in both classical and modern plays. He
is an actor who is guided by his emotions, inspired by
every individual role. He has no set point of view, except
a profound desire to infuse breadth, depth and life into
the character he is portraying. He has taken Hamlet's
advice to the Players seriously:

Be not too tame neither, but let your own dis-
cretion be your tutor: suit the action to the word,
the word to the action; with this special obser-
vance, that you o'erstep not the modesty of
nature: for anything so overdone is from the
purpose of playing, whose end, both at the first
and now, was and is, to **hold**, as 'twere, the
mirror up to nature; to show virtue her own feature,
scorn her own image, and the very age and body
of the time his form and pressure.

\*

But now, let us listen to the Directors, Dramatists
and Actors speak out for themselves!

DIRECTORS

## ROGER BLIN

Roger Blin is one of France's finest directors and actors.
He directed the premiere productions of Beckett's *Waiting
for Godot, Endgame, Krapp's Last Tape* (acting in these
plays as well) and Genet's *The Blacks* and *The Screens.*
Blin was born in 1907 at Neuilly-sur-Seine, a Paris suburb.
He was brought up in a bourgeois and devoutly Catholic
household but, after attending parochial school and the
Sorbonne, he left home to begin a bohemian existence, a
life without restraint. He became an atheist and remains
one. He refused to join any political party or literary
group, although he maintained close ties with many surrealists. Blin met Artaud in a Montparnasse cafe and they
became good friends--the young actor played one of the
Assassins in Artaud's production of *The Cenci.* Slowly
Blin's interests expanded. He wrote movie reviews and
then began to act in films and on stage; he directed; he
designed his own sets and costumes. A careful and pains-
taking worker, Blin has directed relatively few plays in
his life--he absolutely refuses to undertake a work he does
not love. Blin always chooses the hard road, never the
easy way out. When he began his acting career he had
great difficulty getting roles because he was a stutterer.
At this decisive point in his life he could easily have
become an outstanding painter, for he has substantial

visual talent (he still draws today, and continues to ex-
ecute the designs for his own productions). In describing
why he did not pursue his abilities as a painter, Blin
reveals the wellspring of his personality: "Had I no hands
I would have become a painter. But because I stutter I
had to become an actor."

Q.  Do you think Genet is a representative of a decadent
    society? Please explain.

A.  Yes, perhaps in a way. He was once part of a society
    in which anarchy, capitalism, and communism vied
    with each other for supremacy, paving the way for
    self-destruction. Genet was a victim of this society
    which he now seeks to destroy. In this sense, he
    could be called a representative of a decadent society.
    But now Genet has passed on to the opposite camp.
    He is against all order. He hates bourgeois society
    and is no longer duped by it. His brand of hatred is
    purely individualistic. He takes pleasure in it and
    experiences great jubilation, a feeling of revenge, as
    he looks out at society. But he does not try to cor-
    rect the society he denounces. He does not try to
    substitute one order for another since he is against
    all order. He owns nothing and yet he stays at the
    finest hotels. He can live in total discomfort and yet,
    when it comes to going downstairs to buy a small
    item, he will usually send the bellhop. Morally speak-
    ing, however, Genet is not decadent. His homo-
    sexuality is part of his make-up, part of his very life.
    He defends homosexuality as he defends the highest
    moral courage possible, the greatest sacrifice of which
    man is capable. This verges on the mystical. Genet
    is not decadent. He is human on all levels; human
    without being sentimental because his views on poverty
    and homosexuality forbid any sentimentality.

A.   Genet's plays have a deep effect on their audience.
This is often described as a "shock effect"—an
adjunct of the "theatre of cruelty." Would you describe Genet's theatre as shocking and cruel in
Artaud's sense of the words?

A.   Many people are shocked by Genet's plays. They are
frightened when confronted with a world they know
really exists--a complete world. Ionesco, for instance,
never stayed to see the end of *The Blacks*. As a white
man he felt uncomfortable; he felt he was being attacked; he sensed the great pleasure the Negro actors
took each time they insulted the whites. If people are
shocked by Genet's plays, they are completely dis-
armed by his other great quality—his ability to evoke
laughter, and laughter relaxes the spectator. If a
spectator is shocked by the obscenities he hears on
stage, he is won over by the sheer beauty and poetry
of Genet's language. Even those who feel they are
being mocked and ridiculed are struck by the "truth"
and burning sincerity of his poetry and are held by
a sense of "fair play." There are, of course, bigots
like Gabriel Marcel who turn away. Genet's brand of
cruelty is quite different from the type Artaud advo-
cated. Artaud's cruelty resembles in many ways religious cruelty as practiced by the Aztec Indians.
Genet's cruelty is more classical and is closer to
Greek theatre. This may seem strange in view of
the fact that Artaud was half Greek, his mother having
been born in Smyrna. Artaud's break with Greek
theatre may in part be due to his own strange personality as well as to the profound influence of the surrealist movement upon him. Genet was not influenced
by Artaud. He has read little of Artaud's work.
Genet's cruelty is simpler, more classical, more fatal-
istic--the cruelty gods inflicted upon men in those
days when gods were close to men. Genet feels deeply
that people are victims of society, and it is in illus-

trating this that his cruelty becomes most apparent.
Genet's asceticism is hedonistic. This is obvious in
his admiration of the body, in his sensual descriptions
and imagery. Genet's theatre is devoid of a goal, of
an ideal. His theatre is the expression of himself in
that it is constantly renewing itself, continually offer-
ing new series and stages of revolt. Genet's effective-
ness is based on that mysterious poetic phenomenon
without which everything would be meaningless.
Genet is the bold inventor of his own brand of meta-
phoric imagery, of the "coq à l'âne," the discoverer
of secret relationships between two things which seem
to have no rapport at all. Added to this is Genet's
brand of "madness" or "folly," of which Camus and
Sartre are totally devoid--that little thing which makes
for the poet.

Q.   How did you go about directing Genet's plays *The
     Blacks?* And how will you direct his new work *The
     Screens?*

A.   What I try to do when directing a play is to translate
     the author's ideas, his aesthetic that is, both visually
     and emotionally. I want the audience to feel the im-
     mense jubilation Genet felt when he wrote *The Blacks*
     and *The Screens*. It's the jubilation of a child who
     punishes others and at the same time punishes himself.
     Take *The Blacks*. It's anti-white, but don't think for
     a moment that it's a glorification of the blacks either.
     The play is purposely ambiguous--what with blacks
     acting out their ritual in front of a white audience
     which isn't white at all, but made up of blacks dis-
     guised as whites. Genet is not shedding tears over
     the fate of the blacks. He is showing humanity with
     all its passions, its hatreds, jealousies, and vices.
     He is trying to penetrate the inner core of man, to
     understand it. He is searching for man's motivations,
     really Genet's motivations. Each time Genet writes,

he tries to get to the bottom of things. This is the only way he can find himself and so liberate himself. The pen is his only friend and confidant. My role as director is to make this clear to the spectator.

Q.  *The Blacks* is an anti-white play set in a primitive mold, yet you had to work with "white" Negroes for the most part. Did this give you any **problems** during rehearsals? In other words, were your Negro actors truly "black?"

A.  *The Blacks* is an anti-white play. I did work with "white" Negroes—West Indians, Africans, Parisian Negroes. This mixture was necessary for two reasons: material and moral. It is almost impossible to find thirteen professional Negro actors in Paris. I used amateurs for the most part. I took the best of what I could get and I worked with them for two years trying to improve their diction—to make actors out of them. Genet wrote *The Blacks* for all Negroes the world over, from the blackest of Africans to the honey-skinned West Indian. The Negroes were slaves, victims of society—and it is to these that the play was addressed. There were many problems involved with such a production. The problem of accent for one—the rolling of the "r." More serious, however, were the difficulties I encountered with the "white" Negroes living in Paris. They were well brought up Negroes, assimilated Negroes who were shocked by Genet's language. They did not want to be taken for savages. And yet, one did not have to scratch too deeply to discover that they had suffered the tortures of racism and persecution, the immense pain of being considered inferior. Fundamentally, they agreed with every word in the play, with the spirit of the work. And keep in mind that *The Blacks* went into rehearsal at a time when many African countries were seeking independence. For these actors, then, the piece took on great meaning. Even the most assimilated Negroes felt a deep craving for independence, to expel their oppressors. Other problems arose within the cast. The two actress- es from Martinique (the one who played the African Queen and the one who played the White Queen) hated each other. I was not aware of this at the beginning. One afternoon, after a matinee, I went backstage and smelled the odor of incense. I was surprised. I dis- covered that the White Queen was burning this incense to ward off the evil spell she accused the Black Queen of casting upon her. The Black Queen, she maintained, aimed the jettatura in her direction and willed her to forget her lines. The Black Queen's witchcraft was present in her on-stage acting, in her secret, symbolic and ritualistic gestures. Since most of the actors in the French production were amateurs, I was able to mold them, for I was dealing with raw material. In the English production I was dealing with professional actors who knew every trick of the trade and my task was far more difficult. Though they were admirable actors, their approach to *The Blacks* was highly emo- tional. This piece should be played without any sentimentality. That's why I decided--and this is not indicated in the text but is my own invention--to trans- form the general laughter at the end of the play into a savage dance lasting a few minutes, after which would come the minuet.

Q.   Did you encounter any difficulties in the text itself?

A.   Genet's style is unique. His sentence structure is archaic; it sounds like eighteenth century prose. At times, his writing is also precious. Genet's sentences are long, full of repetitions. It's poetry, and the actors must speak quickly, always keeping in rhythm with the lines ... the tempo changes; it's like counterpoint. Insolence and violence are Genet's supreme qualities. He shocks his audiences. He wants to. Yet he is never vulgar. What Genet despises and what he constantly fights against is a shallow and empty style. He hates rhetoric.

Q.  Does he ever find himself falling into this shallowness of style?

A.  Yes. We all do. Genet writes slowly. He labors over each sentence, each word. I worked with him on *The Screens* for a month in Italy. We went over the entire play very carefully. We purified the text . . . eradicated all those parts which did not properly belong . . . dramatized it.

Q.  In other words, you are to Genet what Jouvet was to Giraudoux.

A.  I detest Giraudoux. His theatre is the most abominable of all.

Q.  Genet's characters have been described as existing in a hall of mirrors. The characters have no center or essence and are only reflections. Is it possible for one actor to achieve this sense of multiple identities? If so, how do you go about working toward this result? What specific directing techniques do you use to evoke this feeling?

A.  The actors who played in *The Blacks* were, unfortunately, not sufficiently well-trained to bring out the myriad subtleties of the text, and so many "reflections of reflections" were lost. Of course the special use we made of the mask, the changing of vocal pitch, the sets, the lighting effects, and the stylized acting (the slowing down and acceleration of speech) added to this willed multiplicity. But these "reflections of reflections" present in Genet's plays are limitless, and even the author himself gets lost in this labyrinth.

For those who can see, many paths and chambers have
been opened in this endless hall of mirrors by the text
and the actors' interpretation of this text. There comes
a point, however, when the actor becomes impotent,
unable to correct what Genet himself failed to clarify.
A theatrical miracle occurs during a Genet production;
the author wants everybody to believe what he says.
This audience credibility, however, must be shattered
every now and then.  As a result, it becomes even
more credible.  The chain can be broken when an
actor winks at his audience or an unexpected literary
allusion is interpolated into the text.  The magic
spell the author and actor cast upon their audience is
now **broken,** but this very rupture increases the extreme tension of the play.  For this reason Genet,
without realizing it, approaches Brecht without, of
course, possessing the latter's didactic attitudes.  He
goes further than Brecht.  Though Brecht fails in
achieving this rupture, this very failure constitutes
a victory for him, because he is still a poet no matter
what he does.  But Brecht does not succeed in destroying  audience  credulity,  nor  the  ever-present
theatrical magic.  In spite of all his attempts at anti-
magic, he creates a continuous, theatrical universe.
It is extremely difficult for a dramatist and a director
to prevent a spectator from being fascinated by a man
he sees on stage who is holding a flower and who
speaks to him, or by another whose eyes are blackened
by makeup and whose face blazes with light.

Q.   How do you create the decors for the Genet plays?

A.   I strive for total realism.

Q.   What do you mean by that?

A.   Take a telephone, for example; place it on a table on
     stage.  That's all right.  But I want the telephone to

be able to eat, to talk, to have a life of its own. It must be an animate object. The prop must be a composite of what you see and what you have seen. The decor must be alive, move and breathe. It must be human. Take a street. The street most frequently placed on stage today is the street you see every day. If you reproduce it on the boards as such ... well, I call this stupid realism. But the street you see at night when you are drunk—you see it in a different way. You are wobbly. The street turns, it assumes weird shapes, it's alive. What do you see in the street now? How do you see the street? This is true discovery. You are perceiving reality; for the first time all bonds and restrictions have been broken. Objective reality has been dislocated. You now perceive a far deeper reality. That street has become flesh and blood for you.

Q. How did you bring this out in your stage sets for *The Blacks?*

A. The sets were simple. They were made up of iron bars covered over by asbestos. The asbestos made the iron bars look more pliable. It was a stark and yet soft set. From the orchestra the decor looked like a giant sculpture. With proper manipulation of the lights, it assumed different shapes, different colors and moods. It reflected and participated in the action of the play.

Q. What will the sets be like for *The Screens?*

A. As the title indicates ... the sets will be made up of numerous screens which will be brought on stage from the left, from the right, and from the back. The screens will be placed on three different levels. Their appearance and disappearance on stage will blend with the general tempo of the piece. They will be part of the play, while remaining dramatic entities unto themselves.

Q.   When one talks of Genet, one always mentions the
     "ritual," the "ceremony" in his plays. What kind of
     rituals are there in *The Screens?*

A.   There are four rituals in *The Screens*. The first cere-
     mony takes place in a bordello where Mass is being
     said...a very sacred Mass. The prostitutes are
     garishly dressed. There is an old Arab woman who is
     walking along. She is so thin that she is made only of
     clothes. She has practically no body. The second
     ritual starts when the Arabs begin to draw on the
     screens. They draw everything they have done to
     help the revolutionary forces. Since they have burned,
     tortured and slaughtered French poeple, the screens
     will slowly be covered with an eye here, a leg there,
     a gaping mouth, a nose, an arm... All this is done
     before the audience. This will show how the Arabs
     pay tribute to their dead. The third ceremony intro-
     duces us to the colonials. And we watch them as they
     pin medals on manikins. This medal-pinning contest
     is to be played in rhythm with the picture-drawing of
     the Arabs. This is how Genet points up the idiotic
     **efforts of the settlers in contrast with the important**
     work being done by the Arabs. The fourth ritual be-
     gins when a French lieutenant is struck by a stray
     bullet. Before he dies, his soldiers will pay tribute
     to him. They stretch him out on stage. Each in turn
     stoops over and farts in his face. "Un petit air de
     France," they say. "Respire bien l'air..." In
     the original version of the play Genet has the soldiers
     drag the lieutenant off stage for this ritual. But after
     we worked the play over together, I felt the entire
     scene would be clearer and more forceful if the cere-
     mony took place on stage. This play is a culmination
     of everything Genet has done. All his past themes
     have been woven into a solid network. It's like a
     **modern tapestry with all its brilliance, flashes, discor-**
     dant and swiftly moving colors... a tapestry pos-

sessing both artistry and depth.

Q.  You've indicated that the decor must take on an animated life of its own.  Is this best achieved in a
proscenium stage or what we would call an open
stage?  Do you like to work with sets or with set
pieces only?  In what sense does the actor himself
set the stage?

A.  Everything depends on the play.  I was very pleased
with the sets for *The Blacks*.  I always work closely
with the set designed.  I like working with people.
I usually tell the decorator what I have in mind and
we carry out our ideas together.  I designed the tree
for *Waiting for Godot*.  Sets on stage must take on a
life of their own.  One cannot be limited by them.  The
twenty-five centimeters separating a table from a
chair on stage can be made to look like ten centimeters if the decorator so wills it.  In Japanese
theatre a small piece fifty centimeters high can represent a small mountain.  And the spectators will
really believe they are looking at a mountain.  It
makes no difference to me whether I use a proscenium
stage, an arena stage, or even the type Artaud had
in mind—that is, where the audience would sit in
the center.  Naturally, it's no good if the stage is
too small and the actors cannot move around freely.
But if one is too fussy and too exacting concerning
the type of stage he wants, few plays would be produced these days.  If there is sufficient space (a
stage about seven by eight meters square) and the
visibility is good, that's all that's needed.  A beautiful studio never made a painter.  Van Gogh never had
a studio.  Actors do set the stage.  Their gestures,
without resorting to miming (that is where perspective
is diminished or enlarged as when one walks up a
flight of imaginary stairs), their voices if used subtly,
their acting—all figure in the stage set.  The director's

work must remain invisible. The more it is effaced,
the better. The director's greatest moments of joy
are experienced when he watches his play unfold before him without recalling for one moment the difficulties he encountered in its production.

Q. Do you ever find your role as designer conflicting with
your role as director or as actor? What do you feel
**the relationship between designer, director, and actor
should be?**

A. In France, a director or an actor finds a play which
captures his fancy. Then he tries to get a producer
or some financial backing. He then looks for a theatre
and a set designer. I personally prefer an architect
or sculptor to assist me in creating the sets for my
productions. I hate painters as designers of sets. I
like to work with people who have ideas and who
serve the text. Some producers choose plays for
certain stars. Not I. I always refuse to direct a play
which doesn't enthrall me. I like to discover the play
myself and also create the lighting effects myself.
My choice of actors for the plays I direct depends
upon those I can find at the time—that is, those who
are at liberty. I do not direct a play the way a German director does. The German director (a man between fifty-five and sixty years of age with a head
which looks like a violin) reads the play he has been
asked to direct. He spends several weeks (away from
the theatre) writing down in detail all the stage directions. He returns to the theatre with three-hundred
pages of notes. He then sits down in the orchestra,
talks into a loud-speaker, and directs the actors
according to what he has written in his manuscript.
Every sigh, every facial gesture—everything has been
noted beforehand with the utmost care. There is no
leeway. I proceed differently. First of all, I never
write anything down beforehand. I'm on stage all of

the time. I show the actors how I would like a certain scene to be played, but I never impose my ideas nor do I ever explain the ''true'' or ''fundamental'' meaning of the play as such to the actor. I usually draw upon a metaphor taken from daily life, enlarge upon it, and this is how I explain the scene or the play to the cast. Sometimes I let the actors feel their way through a part even though I know they are on the wrong track. After a while they themselves realize they have reached an impasse. Then we rectify the mistakes together. When I see an actor acting out a scene spontaneously and differently from the way I conceived it, I may suddenly realize that the actor is right and that I am wrong. A good means for discovering the right way to play a scene is by poking fun at it—ridiculing it. Such mocking relaxes the actors and permits them to perceive subtleties and hidden meanings by the very absurdity of certain situations. It also prevents the actors from being overly timid. Some of the actors in *The Blacks* were very timid at first. And timidity is contagious and can ruin a production. An actor must have freedom to express himself, but this freedom must be controlled. A play must breathe and live a life of its own.

Q. You have directed and acted in the plays of Beckett. What are the major differences between Beckett and Genet? Would you describe them as roughly equivalent authors? Beckett's use of language is much more sparse than Genet's. Is the work on stage with the actors vastly different when you're working with Beckett from when you're working with Genet? Who do you feel is the greater playwright?

A. These playwrights are vastly different. There is an exuberance, a baroque quality in Genet's use of language, whereas Beckett draws his musical and rhythmical effects from his very reserve, his puritanism.

Yet, these two authors have some points in common. Both Genet and Beckett are poets who aspire toward a certain type of classicism; both are subjective playwrights who try to express themselves with the same degree of sincerity; both search for verbal and rhythmic effects which are a far cry from the routine, from reality as we know it. It is difficult to point up the differences in directing techniques; I have only directed one Genet play, *The Blacks*. I directed and acted in *Waiting for Godot* and directed *Endgame*. *The Blacks* took me two years to complete; *Waiting for Godot,* four years. Beckett was unknown and Genet already figured in the public eye. I found myself drawn to these works and compelled to bring them to life. I cannot say who is the greater of the two playwrights. They are both solitary men who make little effort to have their works produced and who avoid publicity like the plague.

Q. What do you feel the theatre of the future will be like? What place in this theatre do you feel Genet will have? Beckett? Ionesco?

A. I am not a prophet. Genet, Beckett, and Ionesco have been influenced by their times. They cannot possibly remain aloof from fascism, anarchy, captialism, and man's exploitation of man. It is impossible to have a theatre today which does not reflect these problems, which is not tinged with blood. Genet is still going through a sort of "first stage"—a revolt which is in itself both positive and negative. He is trying to open up new worlds for us—that's why his plays explode. They are like dynamite, like fireworks possessed of great beauty and poetry. Genet offers no solution to problems, no new forms to replace the old, no goals. This is because he feels that all order, all organizations are the beginnings of new constraints. Genet has not yet said his last word. Some see his

work as saintly, others as anarchical. Genet wants us
to see and believe in his sincerity. Beckett is far
less communicative, far more reserved than Genet.
What people consider to be Beckett's negative side
(his fear and love of death) is compensated for by his
humor, his tenderness, his prudishness. We are confronted with a positive personality —a man who fought
indignities. In World War II he was a liaison man
between the French Maquis and the R.A.F.; he was
also a nurse for the Red Cross. He is a man who
chooses his path of action and proceeds accordingly.
I was struck by this character trait. Pozzo in *Waiting
for Godot* is an extraordinary portrayal of man's exploitation of man. Man's cynical, his horribly brutal
side is here pointed up by Beckett. These satirical
scenes are tremendously powerful. Parallels can be
drawn between his plays and his novels. In both cases
there is a lessening of action, a motionless quality
present. Beckett is becoming more and more reserved
and enclosed. In *Waiting for Godot* we are introduced to four mobile characters; in *Endgame*, three
of the four characters are immobile; in *Krapp's Last
Tape* there are one-and-a-half characters (one character
and his ghost); in *Happy Days* there is one motionless
character who is slowly sinking into the sand and one
invisible character. Where can Beckett go from here?
It is hard for me to conceive of Ionesco's theatrical
future. At the beginning he introduced us to a type of
poetic theatre—an absurd theatre. He is becoming
more and more of a moralist these days. Perhaps
Beckett will one day be able to communicate with the
outside world. Perhaps Genet will become a devout
Catholic. One never knows.

Q.  Beckett, Genet, and Ionesco are all dealing with the
anxieties of our day, and yet they approach these
anxieties from different points of view: Beckett in a
naked language with an empty stage; Ionesco through

the disarticulation of language and a stage overflowing with things that overwhelm his characters; and Genet by a more or less naturalistic stage with human beings who are larger than life. Do you feel that all three of these **approaches are legitimate?** Is one necessarily truer or richer than another?

A.   Genet, Beckett, Ionesco and Adamov are four sincere playwrights. They are individualists and have found no single school. Adamov, a man without a country, used to have a lot to say concerning surrealism, his fear of the police, his homelessness as a man in exile. When we were with Adamov we used to feel as though we were in the presence of a Kafka who knocks the wind right out of you. Adamov tried to explain the world as he saw it. His political views have limited him theatrically. His plays have become thesis plays in which Adamov, the individualist, the man riddled with anxieties, has disappeared. One cannot say that the work of Genet, Beckett, or Ionesco is "richer" or "truer" than that of the others. They are all poets in their fashion. Their approaches to the theatre, though different, are legitimate. Each in his own way has tried to denounce an evil—whether it be the evil of living or the evil of society. The three then, in this respect, are playwrights of their epoch and reflections of their times. They are modern writers, as opposed to Claudel, for example, who is like a monstrous mushroom living in a feudal world. His plays, written in a marvelous language, are the living incarnations of something which has long since disappeared—they are like goiters, like gothic fibromas. Claudel is a defender of the most reactionary forces, of bondage and stupidity.

**

Q.   Someone said that *The Screens* is the first play, since

Shakespeare, with a "universal view" of man.

A. Just the opposite is true. Genet—in a poetic, burlesque, exaggerated way—shows the mechanism of colonization and rebellion. He does not put the colonists and the Arabs on a par—he is, beyond doubt, on the side of the Algerians. But the ambiguity of the play stems from Genet's equating colonization and rebellion. Ommou expresses Genet's ideas perfectly:

> The lords of yesterday will tell the lords of today that nothing must be protected so much as a little heap of garbage... Let no one ever throw out all her sweepings... One never knows—keep a little mudpile in reserve in a corner.

Genet himself preserves poetry—a permanent, anarchical virus. If there is any rapport with Shakespeare it is in Genet's baroque style. The crudities and vulgar phrases are part of Genet's language, as are the most elegant constructions.

Q. Is *The Screens* a political play?

A. Of course, in a way. But Genet is not really concerned with social order—he is against any established government. Genet told me, "This play is not an apology for betrayal; it is an aesthetic theatrical experience."

Q. But *The Screens* is historically accurate?

A. Genet's Algeria is real. Even his poetry is like that of the Arabs. But, at the same time, each character speaks in his own voice, and in Genet's. This language is free and baroque at the same time.

Q. What is the relationship between the living and the dead?

A.  I don't think I need elaborate on what Sartre and others
    have said about Genet's obscure thoughts concerning
    Christianity, the after-life, mistakes, and redemption.
    But this place where living and dead meet is not a
    Christian paradise—it is, rather, a no-man's land where
    reconciliation can happen.   Genet told me that he
    would like *The Screens* to be an homage "to death
    considered as an action," to "a wanted death...
    voluntary... a voluntary termination of the greatest
    love, life."   This may be clearer if I quote from a
    letter Genet sent me:

> ...may this particular event— or its presen-
> tations—... act upon thousands of Parisians,
> without disturbing the world order and yet
> bring about a poetic, fiery release so strong,
> so dense that it would illuminate the world
> of the dead as well as that of the living and
> those to come (but that's less important).  I
> am telling you this because this feast, so
> limited in time and space, and which is ap-
> parently intended for audiences, is of such
> a serious nature that it is also intended for
> the dead.  No one must be turned away from
> the feast.  The feast of the dead must be
> beautiful: those watching you blush from
> the experience.  If you stage *The Screens*
> you must work toward this unique feast.  And
> those elements which are not part of the
> feast must also succeed so that whatever
> separates us from the dead will be tran-
> scended.  One must, therefore, try to steer
> actors into the secret depths, not through
> finesse, but by making them accept dif-
> ficulties, step by step, imposed on them by
> their gestures which will have no relation
> to those used in everyday life.  If this kind
> of life is shown on stage, it is because I

see the stage as a place which is closely
related to death. All liberties are possible:
the actors' voices must spring directly from
the larynx—such music will be hard to find.
Their make-up will encourage audacities.
No longer having social responsibility, the
actors will develop a responsibility of
another kind.

Q.  What is the relationship between the combatants and
the whores?

A.  The bordello is a sacred place.  There human beings
achieve the greatest shame.  During the rebellion,
whores were considered less than nothing, disdained
by all.  It was precisely at this time that the ceremonies in the bordellos reached their greatest complexity and became extraordinarily meaningful.  The
men spent long hours watching Warda pick the dirt
from her teeth.  Later that ceremony was repudiated
as the Algerians pushed for war.  Still later the combatants came to the brothel just to "tear off a piece"
between two skirmishes.  The whores had to adapt to
the changing times—and the ceremonies fizzled out.
During this time the whores were accepted as Algerians: there was only one common enemy, the French.
Warda alone tries to preserve the shame of the bordello.
Thanks to her, its sacred nature will endure.

Q.  Did Genet attend many rehearsals?

A.  He did not want to become too involved. He was afraid
that if he enjoyed them, that would keep him from his
work.  Also, he has not been well.

Q.  What does Genet think of Artaud?

A.  I don't know how familiar he is with Artaud's writings.
Artaud, however, would have despised Genet because

of Genet's homosexuality. Genet, on the other hand, would have been moved by **Artaud's** personality. I don't think they ever met, nor do I think that Artaud's ideas have influenced Genet's work; they have affected his personality. Genet was influenced by Cocteau—by the bric-a-brac of his poetry, just the kind of stuff Artaud could not stand. In *The Screens* there is a precious quality that has become part of Genet's style, of his subtlety of thought.

Q. What do you think *The Screens* is about?

A. Genet told me that it was an homage to death through beauty. An attempt to transform fecal matter into something of beauty—to transform suffering into beauty. But *The Screens* is not an apology for treason. Saïd is a hollow hero. He is a hero insofar as he appears to be a small heap of necessary garbage which must be carefully preserved no matter what social order one may wish upon the world.

The above interviews were published in *Tulane Drama Review* (vol. 7, no. 3, March, 1963) and in *The Drama Review* (vol. 11, no. 4, Summer, 1967).

## JEAN-LOUIS BARRAULT

*Interviewer's Note:*

Jean-Louis Barrault and Madeleine Renaud left the Comédie-Française to form their own troupe in 1946. They
chose the Théâtre Marigny as their new home and gave
successful productions of plays by Marivaux, Molière,
Racine, Musset, Claudel, Feydeau, Giraudoux, Sartre,
Anouilh, Gide and Cocteau, among others. The French
government, by official decree dated August 22, 1959,
turned the direction of the historic Odéon Théâtre de
France over to Jean-Louis Barrault. The Barrault-Renaud
company paid a nominal rental for the theatre and received
an annual subsidy from the French government, but the
direction of the Odéon Theatre was wrenched from them
after the May riots in Paris in 1969. The homeless company
nevertheless continued performing in various theatres
and countries. Dedicated to their art, Barrault and Madeleine Renaud constantly renewed their repertoire and their
performing methods, with such psychedelic productions as
*Rabelais* and *Ubu on the Butte.*

Q.   Your extraordinary performance of Faulkner's *As I
     Lay Dying* brought your talent to the attention of
     Antonin Artaud. What effect has Artaud had on your
     work as an actor and director? In what sense do you
     feel Artaud is still a vital force in today's theatre?

A.   Artaud has influenced me. His view of the theatre

was totally *inner*. He was a mystic and visionary who seemed to be able to penetrate beyond facades. He reached right into the core of things, of people, and of situations. He taught me to do likewise. He never intellectualized. He despised the cerebral actor, the didactic director. He felt his way into plays. My attitude is similar in that I don't "intellectualize;" I act. I am not a philosopher—I despise abstractions about the theatre. To *act!* This is of import.

Artaud's concepts are certainly very much alive today, in terms of the visceral theatre which seems to be flooding the world. It is as though the outer world were impinging or imposing its dicta on the inner man. In the Living Theatre, the Theatre of the Ridiculous, the Panic Theatre, the Gorilla Theatre...they all attempt to move—even to bludgeon the spectator into participation. Artaud used these methods in the early thirties and even before in his **Théâtre** Alfred Jarry (1926)—a bit differently of course; nevertheless, the seed was there.

Q. You have written an essay on the "actor as an athlete." Could you please tell us how you feel an actor should be trained for his art? What training do the actors in your troupe receive?

A. Acting is a profession and strangely enough, it is not a profession. In France today, training is experimental. An actor should be supple; naturally, he should learn the art of diction, of breath control, of using his body and face—of exteriorising his emotions—but training is not enough. It's a question of working together, as a group, of using one's imagination and heart, of being sensitive to the play one is acting in—of listening to the author and the characters he conjures up before us.

The theatre is a question of instinct. After spending many years in the theatre, an actor or director develops a sixth sense. He possesses his *métier*. There are no fixed rules, no definite theories. Acting is flexible, as is interpretation. One must feel one's way into a part—using one's sixth sense as guide and mentor.

Q. Has the work of Stanislawski influenced you?

A. Yes. In terms of "sincerity" and "honesty." Each part one portrays must be approached with sincerity and honesty. I was not influenced by Stanislawski's style.

Q. You produced Ionesco's *The Sky Walker*. Do you believe his theatre remains vital today? Many critics maintain that his best work is his early plays?

A. His theatre remains vital because it has something to say —it has a message. I don't agree that Ionesco's best works are his earliest. One can speak in terms of evolution as far as Ionesco's dramas are concerned. His talent, which has by no means diminished, has grown more profound with the years.

Q. The "Theatre of the Absurd" seems to be passing out of existence. What kind of theatre do you think will replace it?

A. I don't believe that the theatre of the absurd is passing out of existence. Certainly absurdity is not disappearing from life. Life is still absurd—even more so today—as far as I can see.

Q. Vauthier's play *The Character Against Himself* takes over two-and-a half hours to perform. It is a one-character play and you played the Character. Did you identify with this man who tried to recapture the inspiration of youth but who failed miserably and painfully in his attempt?

A.   It is hard to draw the line between *imagination* and
     *identification*.   I imagined the person I was trying to
     **bring to life—he lived within me for many, many months.**
     Perhaps there was some unconscious identification
     with a man who tried so desperately and so poignantly
     to relive his youthful experience—that night when he
     wrote his first play.   The inspiration of youth is so
     sincere, so moving... The identification, if there was
     any, was really unconscious.

Q.   Your seasons often varied from the avant-garde to the
     classical.   How did and does your company cope with
     such divergent material?   Could you share with us
     specific exercises, improvisations and training tech-
     niques?

A.   The styles were very different.   It takes two or three
     years for an actor to become accustomed to working
     with others—as a unit.   At the end of the period the
     troupe as a whole develops its own style.   The actors
     in our troupe are very supple and can adapt to most
     any type of play in a short time.

Q.   What are your rehearsal techniques?   Do you block a
     play before rehearsals?   Do you use improvisations
     and études?   Do you let the actors go their own way?
     Do you read the play a great deal with the cast (as
     Vilar did)?   Do you direct on your feet or from a book?

A.   I first read the play to the actors.   Then I describe the
     play and the entire spectacle as I see it.   We then sit
     around a table for about a week and discuss the play,
     the characters in the work, the personality of the
     actors who will portray the roles.   I then cast the
     play, basing my decision on the personality, tem-
     perament, voice, demeanor, ability and penchant of

the actor. This step is extremely difficult and delicate. We then rehearse on stage and I direct from a
written *mise en scène* which I have already worked up.
The cast learn their parts. These early rehearsals
last about two weeks and then another two weeks are
spent "disobeying" the original *mise en scène* I
created on paper. After more work, the play begins to
speak to us, the play commands us. Our vision of
the entire production changes little by little. The
**play comes to life. The characters have been created
and the "mayonnaise," so to speak, has taken. The**
period of preparation for a play is about six weeks.

Q. Do you find "emotional recall" a valuable tool for the
actor? How do you use it?

A. Yes, it can certainly help in the creation of a character. But imagination more than a "souvenir" is
important—although, we might say that it is a blending of both.

Q. Was it you who suggested to Claudel that he shorten
*The Satin Slipper* from four to three *journées?*

A. Yes. The fourth *journée* was written in a completely
**different style. And, furthermore, the play was entirely**
too long.

Q. How did you and Claudel work together? Playwright-
Director?

A. Admirably. He has an acute sense of the theatre. We
always got along very well and he appreciated the way
I produced his plays. I might say, he was thrilled
with the finished work.

Q. What was his reaction to opening night of *The Satin
Slipper?*

A.  It was a terribly exciting experience for him.  He was
    beside himself with joy—ecstatic.  His reactions were
    almost   child-like.     He   was   surprised   by   his own
    genius.  He could not believe he had written the play
    he was actually seeing.  It was as though there were
    two   Claudels   at   that   moment—as   though   he   were
    double; the author had vanished on opening night—the
    spectator-Claudel   was   all   agaze,   as   though   he   were
    viewing something new and fresh, hearing and seeing
    beings he was unaware of having created.  He was in
    a state of suspended animation.

Q.  How, when and why did you first decide to produce
    Claudel's works?

A.  I decided to begin producing his works in 1937.   I
    admired   him   intensely.     In   fact,   I   think   he   is   the
    greatest playwright of the 20th century—on a par with
    the   greats   of   French   theatre—Corneille   and   Racine.

Q.  Jacques Lemarchand of the *Figaro Littéraire* wrote
    that Beckett's *Happy Days* was a masterpiece and
    that   the   production   was   "unforgettable".     How   did
    Blin feel or see this play—how did he direct it?

A.  First of all Blin understands Beckett.  He has a feel-
    ing   for   that   silent   and   uniquely   sensitive   writer.
    **Madeleine Renaud, who starred in the play,worked with**
    both   Beckett   and   Blin   for   two   months.     Actress and
    director penetrated the text and by work and by sheer
    magic of the art of acting and directing—a half buried
    woman   shared   her   anguishes   in   a   tête-à-tête   with
    hundreds of spectators viewing the play.

We   wish   to   thank   the   editors   of   *First Stage* and   **Drama
and Theatre** for permission to reprint in part the above
interview from *First Stage* (Vol. 3, no. 4).

## ROGER PLANCHON

*Interviewer's Note:*

Roger Planchon is a socially oriented director. He is as much at home in a classical repertoire (Shakespeare, Moliere, Marivaux) as he is in modern works (Brecht, Adamov, Vinaver). He is also the author of several plays, including *The Delay*. The social, political and economic situations of his characters are of greater interest to him than are their psychological problems.

Q.  Your Théâtre de la Cité is in Lyons?

A.  **We play at Villeurbanne, a working-class city outside of Lyons.** Our audience had never gone to the theatre before. We try to stage the best modern plays, as well as revive the great classics: Goldoni, Shakespeare, Gogol. Our audience knew neither the modern nor the classical works. We are trying to create a theatre to fit local needs which are, or course, really more than local.

For years I thought we had to be enriched by experience. But now I think there's an excess of information. I am cutting myself off voluntarily from all links and ties. I want to do only those plays which can be staged in France and are based on local stories. This is the true way to reach greater breadth. I do not want to write or do plays for export.

Q.   What do you think is the relationship between writer,
     director, and actor?

A.   I'll tell you a story—this will be the simplest way of
     answering your question.   When I wrote my first play,
     *The Delay*, I had already been working in the theatre
     for twelve years.   When I came face-to-face with that
     blank piece of paper, I realized that all my theatre
     experience was no help to me here.   The dramatist's
     problem—filling that paper—had nothing to do with
     the director's problem.   And when I found myself on
     stage acting, I discovered I didn't know how to direct
     the play.   I am unhappy with my staging of *The Delay*.
     An author is the last one who should direct his play.
     A director must say "this part is good" and "this
     part is bad."   He should be objective.   The author
     feels that the director is being unfair to the play;
     seemingly without a thought he sacrifices whole
     chunks of it.   However, the director must be unfair to
     the play in order to build something solid from it.
     The *mise en scène* must be built like a pyramid: the
     basic things first.   The author is unable to separate
     "basic" from "non-essential" in his own work.   I
     was torn to pieces while staging my own play—I am
     the director who wrote a play but didn't know how to
     stage it.
         As for acting, well, I find this much easier.
     After all, a director directs me.

Q.   How do you get your actors?   How do you direct?

A.   Some actors have been with us for years, others are
     **here just for the season, and some job-in for a single**
     play.   We have no strict rules—it all depends on the
     needs of the company and the play.

As for directing, I don't like to sit around a table and read. I block a play very quickly—in two days sometimes. Frequently I change scenes later. Sometimes I change the blocking three or four times without having the actors recite even one line of the text. I let them improvise. After reworking a scene three or four times I call the actors together and ask them which way felt best. By my work is not arbitrary—there is method to all this. The actors are put before objects or other actors. A picture takes shape in my mind, and I work from this image. Once the play is fixed and definitely on its way, we sit down around a table and I explain the roles. Then I ask the actors to take the stage and do what they want; little by little we tighten the play. Finally, after each actor has improvised, experimented, explored the role, a synthesis takes place. I give the most important explanations—psychological, ideological, etc. —a week before opening.

Q. How long do you rehearse?

A. Unfortunately, only six weeks, eight hours a day. I would like to rehearse three months. But we have money problems—our subsidies are insufficient. Lack of money and staff also prevents us from using costumes, sets, and props right from the beginning. I would like very much to do this.

Q. What is the difference between the Villeurbanne and Parisian audiences?

A. The Lyonnais audience has never gone to the theatre and, therefore, theatrically nothing astonishes them. Whatever we do, they think, "This is the way it's always been." In Paris we always create a scandal. I have done more than ten plays in Paris, and each time people leave during the performance, slam doors,

scream, etc. But the Lyonnais public doesn't know
or care that our production of *Tartuffe* is different
from that of the Comédie-Française. What they want
to "know" is the play itself. It's not that the people
of Villeurbanne lack critical faculties—it's just that
these are directed to different areas, to content.

Q. Your production of *Tartuffe* started an uproar in **Paris.**
Why?

A. *Tartuffe* can be interpreted in many different ways; no
one knows how Molière saw the play. Right after
Molière's death, directors saw *Tartuffe* as an evil
atheist and thought the play an attack on the Catholic
Church. Then Coquelin of the Comédie-Française
came along and presented Tartuffe as a very pious
man. This, of course, corresponded to Coquelin's
violent anti-clericalism. For Coquelin, Tartuffe was
the perfect example of the good Christian who wanted
to kill and devour everything and everybody. Jouvet
felt that Tartuffe was a double personality: a Christian
saint on the one hand, and a "man" with all the
sensual drives on the other.

Our interpretation was different because we
weren't interested in whether or not the play was **pro-**
or anti-Catholic. We were interested in the psychological aspects of the work. I found Orgon's attitude
to Tartuffe very strange. Actually, Tartuffe is not
the aggressive one. Orgon gives everything to Tartuffe
who, of course, accepts it all. It was not Tartuffe's
idea to marry Marianne—it was Orgon who proposed
the marriage. Orgon also wants to disinherit his own
children and make Tartuffe his heir. It is Orgon who
gives Tartuffe the strongbox (Tartuffe has no idea
it even exists). Perhaps one could argue that Tartuffe
leads Orgon on; but from the point of strict morality—
and I am a moralist—the one who acts is the guilty
man. Orgon was an important man, a friend of the

King.  He met Tartuffe in church, brought him home,
fed him, clothed him, etc.  For the past three hundred
years these actions have not been understood. Critics
have called Orgon stupid—but a man's actions cannot
be explained away that easily.  Orgon is not stupid,
but profoundly homosexual.  It is obvious that he
doesn't know it—the play would fall apart if he were
conscious of it, if he simply tried to sleep with
Tartuffe.  Our production focused on this relationship between the two men.  Understand that, we don't
make Orgon effeminate; he doesn't go around kissing
Tartuffe in the corners.  But we bring out his homosexuality in other ways.  Do you know what Orgon's
last words to Tartuffe are?  ''Ah! Le voilà donc
traître''—the language of passion, Racine's language.
And Dorine, Orgon's servant, tells her master that he
has more affection for Tartuffe than he would for a
mistress.  All this is very striking!  The play doesn't
change over the centuries, but our understanding of
it does.

Reprinted from *Tulane Drama Review* (Spring, 1965).

## *JORGE LAVELLI*

*Interviewer's Note:*

The Argentinian theatrical director, Jorge Lavelli, arrived in Paris in 1960 for a six months' stay, the recipient of a government grant awarded to professionals not to study *per se*, but rather to help them to broaden their horizons. After the six months elapsed, Lavelli remained in Paris— and still practises his art there today.

In 1963 Lavelli won the Prix des Jeunes Compagnies for his production of *The Marriage* by Witold Gombrowicz. He also directed plays by Tardieu, Ionesco, Arrabal and Pirandello, among others. Each production bears his personal stamp: the stress he places upon the ritualistic elements in the theatre which he looks upon as a ceremony, his special attitude toward gestures and intonations, and the usage of empty spatial areas on stage. Lavelli's work is precise, rigorous, sensitive and truthful—a *cruelty* in a sense, since he *considers truth a cruelty.*

Q.   Can you tell us something about your early days in the theatre?

A.   My theatrical life began in Buenos Aires, my native city. I went to drama school there and trained as an actor. I played in several plays by Brecht, Chekhov and some Argentinian authors. Later, I began direct-

ing plays. It seemed to suit my temperament. Before
I came to Europe I directed a small group along with
some friends of mine. It was like a theatre workshop.
Once I came to Paris, I concentrated on directing.

Q. You directed *The Council of Love*, a play which created
quite a sensation in Paris because of what certain
critics called its sacrilegious content.

A. *The Council of Love* is an exciting play. It was written at the end of the nineteenth century (1894) by
Oscar Panizza, a German national of Italian origin.
Later on in his life he moved to Switzerland, where
he became a Swiss citizen, and then on to Paris. He
studied medicine and became a physician in 1880,
specializing in mental diseases. He only wrote one
play, *The Council of Love*, which was not produced
during his lifetime. He was also the author of political
tracts and some anti-religious pamphlets. Panizza
suffered deeply from religious conflict throughout his
life: the Catholicism of his father was always at war
with his mother's Protestantism. This entire emotional
upheaval which he knew so well and had been so
deeply entrenched within him is manifest in his play.
As for his other works — though he enjoyed quite a
reputation in literary circles, he found it difficult to
have his political works set into print.
  *The Council of Love* was published in Zurich.
As a result of its publication, Panizza was condemned
by the German courts (during the reign of William II)
and sent to prison for one year. This year in prison
certainly accentuated what was already a noticeable
weakness and contributed to his mental breakdown.
Panizza died in the insane asylum in 1921.
  *The Council of Love* was practically unknown in
Europe until 1961 when a group, interested in Panizza's works, published (Pauvert) it along with some of
his poems. The edition was confiscated. A law suit

ensued and was won with great difficulty. I heard
about this play shortly after my arrival in France.
I was struck by it for several reasons. First of all,
the author was not, what one commonly calls a traditional dramatic author. He did not know — or he
knew them poorly — the theatrical conventions. He
wrote his play, therefore, with great abandon and
freedom. His play is unorthodox. It could be considered a type of dialogued novel. For example, the
atmosphere he wanted to **create** – the ambiance in
which he sought to drench his work — was far more
important than the dialogue. **The story itself,** which
takes place in several different tableaux, is not conceived in a classical manner: there is twice as much
space devoted to scenic suggestions — these are
frequently implied — as there is to the dialogue. In
some ways *The Council of Love* can be compared to
the XVIth century Spanish 'autosacramental' theatre.
At that period they enjoyed a similar type of freedom
with respect to the structure and construction of a
dramatic work — it was not built up in a Cartesian
manner. Furthermore, *The Council of Love* is a personal work, a testimony really of the author's anguish,
his turmoil, his doubts, the problems all sensitive
individuals encounter, the questions each thinking
person poses for himself today as well as during
Panizza's time. In this play which takes place in
Paradise, in Hell, and at the Palace of the Popes
during the reign of Alexander VI and the Borgias ...
the author created a climate which corresponded to
his own soul state.

**Heaven was described by him as toppling, deca-
dent, no longer able to function positively.** God
(Christ) and the Divine inhabitants are like sticks of
old furniture, impotent, in a state of desuetude. As
for God's earthly vicar — the Pope — he lives in a
state of opulence, contrary to all Christian principles.
Heaven then is decadent and its parallel is seen on

earth — the people living in a state of **perversion. This** is the core of the play.

The story is very simple and actually highly moralistic — contrary to what certain critics have stated. The plot: the punishments sent by God to man. The Devil is the one to carry out the punishments and who causes debauchery on earth. Effects are achieved not only through the dialogue but by means of the characters themselves. For example, God on stage looks impotent. He totally lacks majesty and suffers from a pronounced catarrh. Debauchery takes place in the Palace of the Popes and here again the lavishness of the gestures, the make-up, the costumes enhance the ostentatious and lascivious climate. Chastisement takes on the form of sickness — syphilis. Syphilis is incarnated in a beautiful woman who lures men to her domain.

It is strange to think that this play, written almost at the same time as *King Ubu* by Alfred Jarry, did not have any influence whatsoever on its time. Today, one can hardly believe that such imagination, such an acute sense of the derisive, such *cruelty*, so dear to twentieth century authors, existed at that time.

Q. Did you use any special method or technique to direct *The Council of Love?*

A. I paid particular attention to the text, to the costumes, **to vocal intonations and to the tableaux, of course, in** general. I wanted to show the parallel that exists between corruption and impotence which results from abandon and opulence. The Devil is the most human of the characters. He was dressed in black. What made him outstanding, however, was his club foot and with all the symbolism involved in such a weakness. The reason he most closely resembles man is that he would like to be someone in his own right and not just merely obey or accept the orders, bargains and benefits offered by the Divine beings.  He has experienced oppression from his superiors and is very much aware of this state of affairs.

The play also possesses a medieval "Mystery"-like quality.  This climate stems from the theme as well as from the manner in which it evolves, how the events ensue dramatically.  I tried to underline this macabre, ritualistic side of the drama by means of pace and vocal tonalities.

*The Council of Love* was performed with few accoutrements though some people found it lavish and opulent.  We had very little money at our disposal. The costumes were quite extraordinary, yet they were made out of practically nothing.  Some of them gave the impression of extreme luxury.  The Angels' costumes, for example, were made out of feathers.  The ladies in the play wore great capes — very simple ones however — but with hoods which hid their faces each time they showed their profiles.  The Pope's courtiers wore clothes of brocade embroidered with gold thread.  The court women were bare-breasted. As for the decors, they were very few.  I rarely use built-in decors in my plays.  The sets serve to situate the various areas in the play: hell, the Pope's Court, etc.  Heaven, for example, was represented by a broken-down throne and as God sits on it, he very nearly topples over.  In this manner, he really has become incorporated into the decors itself.. into the *mise en scène*.

Music also plays an important part in the play. Actors and musicians are mixed together on the stage. You can't tell one from the other.  Sometimes the music is in counterpoint; at other instances, it creates a historical climate.

Q.   Can you give us some more details concerning the extraordinary costumes worn by your cast?

A.   It's very difficult to speak of such visual elements.
I'll try.   The costumes worn by those peopling Paradise were dirty white.   They resembled dirty rags,
tatters.   The Pope wore white; his courtiers, as I
said before, were dressed in gold brocade.   Syphilis,
played by a young girl, wore a color which stood
out — violently — from the rest: red.   She was the only
one to wear that color.   She was nude under a trans-
parent cape.   But her cape was quite unusual because
it took shape as she moved.   She could, therefore,
create the shape she wanted on stage.   When, for
example, she spread out her arms, the tableau created
on stage was that of a flower.   She wore very little
make-up in contrast with the others who had lots of it.
She exuded innocence; childishness, almost.   It was
this very aspect of her personality which made her
the very dangerous person she was.

Q.   You also directed Fernando Arrabal's *The Architect
and the Emperor of Assyria*.   When did you meet
Arrabal?   What was the genesis of this production?

A.   I met Arrabal right after I had won the prize for Witold
Gombrowicz' play, *The Marriage*.   I had heard of him
before 1963 but had never met him.   He seemed to be
impressed with my work.   As for me, I wanted to direct
his play *The Grand Ceremonial*.   Unfortunately, it had
been given out to another director.   I began directing
some of Arrabal's short plays at the Théâtre de Poche:
*The Communicant and the Princess*, etc.   This was four
years ago, however.   After that I directed *Picnic on
the Battlefield* for the Théâtre de Bourgogne.

   I consider *The Architect and the Emperor of
Assyria* Arrabal's finest play.   It's a type of résumé
of everything he has done up until this time.   There
are several important themes interwoven into the
fabric: for example, the impossibility man experiences
when trying to accept himself as he is.   This theme is

made obvious by means of the characters: their continuous attempts at metamorphoses ... their desire to
escape, to become something other than what they are.
Another theme is that of the Emperor who symbolizes
a decadent, rotting culture: a man who has never been
able to commune with nature, even to come into contact with it on the most superficial level. Nor has he
been able to experience God. His anguish lies in his
various attempts to become God. Such an attempt on
his part is in direct opposition with the Architect's
**domain:** the one who is master of Nature — a type of
pocket God. The theme of solitude is also intrinsic
to this play. No one can escape his own solitude:
even master and slave cannot reach each other. Both
the master and the slave in *The Architect and the
Emperor of Assyria* suffer from parallel feelings of
solitude. Each tries to leave the other in order to
escape his anguish but cannot do so. The fear of
being alone is so devastating, **so insurmountable, that**
they prefer to accept a kind of sentence to be united,
to continue together, rather than experience the in-
tolerable pain of loneliness.

Q. How do you treat language and vocal intonations when
rehearsing a play?

A. It depends upon the work. When directing a play by
Claudel, **Gombrowicz** or Arrabal, I play up the *text.*
I begin from the *word:* the thought emerges from the
word. I also try to discover a particular vocal point
of view, a type of equilibrium or harmony ... the same
kind one can find in a musical composition.

I am particularly interested in *forcing language
to explode on stage.* This may seem a bit bizarre.
But once language has been freed from its various
limitations (stereotyped definitions) it can arouse
certain feelings within the spectators' being. The
word can be accompanied by very special gestures — al-

together new and unexpected. In this way, the stage **space can be filled; it can be concretized, transferred** into a living and maleable element intrinsic to the play itself. Frequently, gestures and attitudes become far more important than words in putting over certain ideas or feelings.

In Jean Vauthier's play, *Medea*, I payed particular attention to the vocal qualities of this drama. I treated it like a musical score, setting up an equilibrium as well as certain effects between the strong and weaker moments in the play... between the soloists and the choruses. I tried to find an *immoderate* vocal attitude: sounds which would force word explosions on stage. Words took on different meanings, inuendoes, nuances, creating a whole new set of inferences, deepening the spectators' enjoyment, provoking his search into new realms within himself.

One must force out from the actor, as well as from the play itself, certain expressions, certain ways of articulating, of gesticulating — create a whole new inner atmosphere, a world through which the senses can flow forth freely. Such effects can be artificially achieved. For example, it would certainly be difficult for me to roll on the floor in a state of anguish or to raise my hands toward heaven in a supplicating manner when speaking, let us say, in a perfunctory or detached manner. My feelings would not correspond to the manner in which I was speaking. Yet, if I use artificial means in the very beginning (screams, unnatural attitudes, lighting effects, etc.) the unity, the profound personal truth of the character in question would emerge. One must try to tap one's spiritual resources, draw on one's reserves, nourish a text — create unity out of disparity.

Q. Some of the things you have just said (spatial concepts, immoderate vocal tonalities, gestures, etc.) are reminiscent of Artaud's way of thinking. Were you influenced by him?

A.   I have read his works.  People have told me that I
have been influenced by him when they saw the first
play I directed.  At that time, however, I had not yet
read his works.  Later, after having read his essays
and scenarios, I found his concepts absolutely fascinating.

Q.   What do you think of the Living Theatre, of Grotowski?

A.   I saw many of the Living Theatre's productions.  When
they first arrived in Europe, I found their methods
rather naturalistic.  Their production of Brecht, for
example.  Their contact with the continent has enriched them enormously.  I saw their first production,
*The Connection.*  The Living Theatre — and this is of
particular interest to me — is a fine example of everything that is immodest or unchaste in the theatre.
The actors in this troupe are frank and sincere...
perfectly truthful in their way of looking upon art as a
communical project.
     I have only seen Grotowski's production of
*Akropolis.*  I was not very impressed with it.  There
was something about his attitudes, his concepts,
which failed to touch me.  Few of his actors ever
succeeded in transforming the rigid formalism basic
to his work, his structured direction.  Few perhaps
believe in his theatrical religiosity.

Q.   What are your impressions of Jérôme Savary's directing
methods?

A.   I like his work.  His approach is novel and infused
with a certain joy, humor and freshness.  One enjoys
the communal participation present in each one of his
productions.  A spectator enters right into the goings-
on all over the theatre — each person in the theatre,

whether standing, sitting, lying down or dancing about, is part and parcel of the spectacle itself.

Q. You mentioned earlier that when you direct a work by the Polish writer Witold Gombrowicz you play up the text. Could you tell us more about these productions?

A. Yes. I directed *Yvonne,* which he wrote in 1935 and *The Marriage* which he finished in 1947. I consider Witold Gombrowicz one of the finest writers of our time — certainly one of the most fascinating. And he's another example of a man whose knowledge of the theatre is very scant and yet whose every word is dramatic. He is a writer of imagination — of instincts.

    *The Marriage* is a type of autobiography. In this play he develops a theme which is dear to him and which he has treated in his essays and in his novels: immaturity in youth and a kind of corruption and decadence on the part of the adult. *The Marriage* is a dream-like play; rather a nightmarish one. You can feel the fact that someone is trying to relive his life, to discover the person within him, the one who haunts him. Throughout the work he views the characters surrounding him — his family; his father, a type of King swindler; his mother, a prey to hysteria; his fiancée, a prostitute of sorts. All of these characters — the most aggressive as well as the most oppressive — parade before his eyes ... those of a dreamer.

    The play is constructed in a very special manner: as though it followed the pattern of certain Shakespearian tragedies. Derision and certain tragi-comic notes are pushed to the extreme and span the entire work. The play itself is written like a type of choral symphony ... a march, a tragic one. This was accomplished by means of Gombrowicz' writing style: its extreme freedom as well as the rapports which he established between the characters he created. His play is a kind of synthesis of the best of contemporary theatre since Jarry's time.

There was but a single basic set in the play even though several different areas were elicited. This set included several carcasses of cars and trucks. Such materials were quite novel for the time. These cars were incorporated right into the dialogue, the costumes and the general climate of the play. For example, the old crates gave the impression of former wealth and grandeur, faded beauties, rotting and corrupt elements so basic to the play. The characters did not wear masks but they were highly made up. They wore wigs which also incorporated themselves right into the costumes as well as into the décors: rags which underlined the decadent climate which drenched the spectacle. The music, which was also a very important factor in this production, was composed at the same time as was the *mise en scene*.

The play then was treated on various levels: the visual (costumes and decors), the tonal (harmonies created through vocal intonations as well as the musical accompaniments); the rhythmic (the evolution of the various areas in which the play was enacted). In this manner, the spatial areas on stage as well as above it were filled, thereby creating a climate based on *distance* and *formation*.

We wish to thank the editors of *Yale/Theatre* for permission to reprint the above interview (Vol. 3, No. 2), 1971.

## JEROME SAVARY

*Interviewer's Note:*

Jérôme Savary is the originator of a very special brand of theatre. He sees the theatrical production as a feast, a celebration in which both audience and actors enter into full communion. He has directed Fernando Arrabal's *The Labyrinth,* Cervantes' *The Wonder Show,* his own *The Raft of the Medusa,* etc. Savary calls his company The Great Magic Circus and the critic Gilles Sandier, writing for *Arts,* has described his productions as "orgies," as "authentic ceremonies," as a theatre which has returned to its "sources: the temple and the bordello."

Q. What was your training in the theatre?

A. Not the usual. I received a musical education. I studied percussion, harmony, the trumpet and the piano. I also studied graphic arts. I went to the Ecole des Arts Décoratifs in Paris.

Q. Were you influenced by anyone or anything in particular?

A. It's difficult to say. I rarely go to the theatre. Perhaps what really influenced me was the Théâtre des Nations where I met directors like Victor García, Jorge Lavelli, Jean-Marie Serreau. They stimulated me. The entire place fascinated me. I began working

with Serreau as a set designer. I soon realized, however, that this field was absurd. Then I became a
director.

Q. Why should stage design be absurd?

A. I don't believe in sets. I have no faith in the designer's function in the theatre; nor do I believe that the
musician has a special function there. All these
divisions are out of date and no longer valid. Nor do
I believe in dramatists. "Playwrights are nonexistent,"
lament those critics and directors who are aware of
the mediocrity of present-day productions. But how
could there be any? How could anyone who really
has something strong and sincere to say want to
say these things in a play today, in this kingdom of
condensations and puns? Who would be crazy enough
to give his blood and his soul to wholesale grocers,
menopausal *grandes dames,* or **students** still too
naively enthusiastic to understand that the theatre is
to contemporary culture what Chiang Kai-shek is to
China? Today, a man of the theatre must be a complete man. He can have a specialty, of course, but
he must work with and be part of the group. The only
**written** plays I have ever directed were Arrabal's *The
Labyrinth* and Cervantes' *The Wonder Show.* The
**other spectacles** were either written by me or developed
as collective projects with my troupe. I believe in
theft: I steal other people's texts. We take a little
Cervantes, a little Shakespeare, a little Molière and
place bits in our productions here and there ...

Q. Can you give us some details about *The Labyrinth?*

A. Arrabal and I had written a play called *The Boxes.*
He then asked me to direct *The Labyrinth* for him
and he gave me carte blanche. The cast originally
consisted of five characters. I added another five:

a goat, chickens, etc. In Paris, the production was unorthodox. In New York, however, we changed everything to such an extent that we finally omitted Arrabal's name from the program. We changed actors constantly — mostly for financial reasons — and we ended up with an international group. Some of our actors spoke their lines in French, others in English or Spanish. We set up a series of platforms and riggings **so that we could have many small acting areas** and could center on one or several of them at a time by means of lighting techniques. I directed this performance with drums, a few horns, a microphone; when I wanted a certain person to stop performing, I would sound the drum. The result was quite extraordinary.

Q. What do you mean when you say that the theatre is a feast, a joyous occasion, a festival?

A. I believe the theatre to be a communal project, a celebration. The theatre is a form of expression which will become more and more of a necessity. Society today is becoming more and more mechanical and scientific. Religion has little or no importance any more. People just seem, perhaps for these reasons, unable to talk to single individuals. The theatre is an excuse, a way to force people to communicate — to destroy the walls which make them live their inner existences alone. The theatre is not and should not be a literary form of expression. Today, we are returning to a more primitive theatre of passion, of communication. A theatrical celebration can take place anywhere: outdoors, indoors, in a garage, a stable. The difference between a performance and a feast or celebration is that the former is presented for others, the latter is something in which everyone participates.

Q. How do you choose the members of your troupe?

A.  I am opposed to selection, so I do not choose them.
    Those who want to join come to see me.   They are
    not professional actors — they have other jobs.   There
    is nothing quite so sordid as a professional actor.
    As soon as one has achieved this status, one has
    succeeded in cutting oneself off from the outside
    world.   My performers have not been deformed by
    literature or the theatre.  Many of them are fine musi-
    cians, others are acrobats, and so on.   When they
    come to me, they remain a part of my troupe as long
    as they want.  We sign no contracts and there is no
    obligation.    Incidentally, my actors are not paid
    unless there is money in the till.   They accept our
    working conditions or they leave the company.   We
    work only eight months a year.   We work very hard
    during that period and must rest afterward, to renew
    ourselves, to dig deep within our beings.  While we
    are preparing a production, we discuss the work, and
    our discussions sometimes become quite violent.

Q.  Do you ever perform in theatres?

A.  I do out of necessity but I don't like to.   It depresses
    me.   Seeing people lined up before us in seats watch-
    ing the curtain go up or down just saddens me.   I am
    a firm believer in magic, in the creation of atmosphere.
    To liven things up we use real fires, smoke of all
    types and colors, fireworks, animals in the theatre.
    Sometimes we use a little tree or a chair, but derisive-
    ly.    The problem with avant-garde theatre today is
    that it is absolutely intellectual.   You have to be
    cerebrally inclined in order to understand what is
    going on.  We, on the contrary, try to appeal to every-
    one: illiterates as well as the intelligentsia.   After
    all, today's society no longer reads.   The masses
    enjoy television, the movies, visual forms of enter-
    tainment.

Q.  What do you think of the Living Theatre, of Grotowski's
work?

A.  As I said, I am for communication.  The minute you
have a "superman" or a "supermystic" performing
before you — as does Grotowski — you create a barrier.
As for the Living Theatre, Beck created a type of
"prophetizing superman" who disdains his audiences.
This too destroys all sense of unity.  He didn't awaken
any feelings of participation within the spectator — on
the contrary, he created division.  There has been no
greater failure today, as far as I am concerned, than
the productions of the Living Theatre, rigid and purely
intellectualized productions.

Q.  How have the critics reacted to your work?

A.  They have been violently opposed.  Nearly all the critics came to our Great Magic Circus production.  Yet
few were capable of writing a word about it, of describing any part of it.  Poirot-Delpech of *Le Monde*
telephoned the critic of *Variétés*, the one who writes
all the reviews of circus, variety acts, etc., and asked
him to write something.  Our new brand of theatre
won't be accepted till the old literary type of dramatic
production dies.  Critics view modern theatre only in
terms of what they know — traditional theatre — and
they intellectualize what they see.  They are entirely
cut off from modern-day realities.

Q.  Since your plays are not written, do your performances
vary each night?

A.  Yes.  Perhaps.  Slightly.  The structure, however, is
the same.

Q.  Would you describe a performance?

A.   Our last performance was divided into two parts: the
     first part was structured and included some scenes
     designed to amuse people: vampires entered through
     the windows, we circulated among the audience, trap
     doors opened (we wanted to give the impression of
     great dynamism); the second part of the play was more
     imaginative.

Q.   How do you work on a play?

A.   Generally speaking, we first study the area in which
     we will perform: the windows and doors, wherever
     they may be, near the rafters or in the cellar.   We
     also study the theatre's surroundings: the exits,
     entrances, the courtyard, etc.   One recent production
     took place at the Théâtre Plaisance in Montparnasse.
     We set about — almost systematically — to destroy
     the theatre.   Once this was done, we installed a
     series of platforms and towerlike structures, all sorts
     of equipment for acrobats to do their stunts, small
     stages — a variety of acting areas. (We do not explain
     these things to each other.  I despise explanations.
     They remind me of a teacher who is trying to direct
     his students.)   We also try to construct a series of
     visual gags.   On one occasion we set up a trap door
     which opened — creaking of course — and a hand
     emerged.   At that moment a vampire flew in from a
     window in the rafters.   We had to find a way for our
     actors to fly through that window.   These are the
     technical problems with which we are faced.
          After familiarizing ourselves with the acting
     areas, we then discuss the various themes of the play
     we have in mind.   I introduce some of my own ideas
     at this point.  I am particularly interested in bringing
     out or in arousing man's *animal-like* nature.   When
     aroused, communication is surely to occur.   That's
     why we use screams, onomatopoeias, vocal intonations,
     grotesque ways of walking... This is how we begin

constructing our frame-work. In one production we began with a scene from Molière. We were dressed in seventeenth-century costumes. Nothing could be more classical than this. After two minutes, some of the actors began disrobing. They were wearing cave-men costumes: tiger skins, etc. Then they began jumping about, performing all types of stunts. I wanted to show the spectators the enormous differences which exist between so-called civilized man — the outer man who wears the mask of culture — and primitive man, or the inner man, standing before them. Moments later, other actors descended virtually nude from all parts of the theatre. They grunted, howled ... made all sorts of mad noises. A handsome youth, beautifully costumed, hung from the rafters for a long while, then began throwing kisses to the audience.

I believe in kindness, in gentleness in the theatre. These are universal qualities. Love too.

Q. Do the elements play an important part in your theatre?

A. Yes. This aspect of our work makes us really unique. We use lots of water, fire, and ventilators to make the spectators' hair blow. In one production we created a curtain of water. On another occasion, the doors to the theatre opened quite suddenly and all the spectators heard the sound of rain. They were convinced it was pouring outside. Seconds later, someone entered the theatre, took his overcoat off because he was certain he was drenched.

In one of our productions, *The Raft of the Medusa,* the entire play took place on water. The dramatisation was based on the horrendous historical event which occurred in 1816 when the frigate, the Medusa, sunk with four hundred aboard. A raft was quickly constructed. But it could hold only one hundred and fifty people. The suffering on board this raft was unbelievable. Food and water ran out and finally the people began eating the cadavres. Géricault's painting, *The Raft of the Medusa*, was inspired by this event.

Our cast consisted of forty-five men and fifteen women, all of whom wore algae on their heads and imitated the sound of waves and wind throughout the performance. I stood in the balcony directing the entire performance with percussion instruments — like a real orchestra conductor. In this way, I established the performances' rhythmic and tonal qualities, creating crescendoes and diminuendoes as I saw fit.

A fish net hung from the top of the balcony to the bottom of the stage. The audience could see the action only through this net. You must try to visualize the scene. The spectators sat below the fish net and had to look upward to see the activities which were enacted far above their heads. The actors were in a life raft. When the passengers began eating each other up — what a sinister story — they fell, all bloodied, on the nets. The audience of course had the impression that these cadavres were falling on them. You can imagine their reaction. At the end of the evening — since no one was left alive — the net was filled with dead bodies, blocking the spectators vision almost entirely and creating blackness throughout the theatre.

Q. Would you call your theatre symbolic?

A. Everything which emanates from the unconscious is symbolic. Those who do not react emotionally to our antics are cold and calculating people — certainly wrapped up in some intellectual framework. They refuse to let themselves go, to participate. They are incapable of enjoying life!

Reprinted in part from *The Drama Review* (T. 49, Fall. 1970).

DRAMATISTS

## *ROBERT PINGET*

*Interviewer's Note:*

Robert Pinget was born in Geneva in 1920. After receiving his law degree, he moved to Paris where he studied painting and became a fine artist (1946-1950). It was only after having traveled throughout Europe, going as far as Israel where he worked on a kibbutz, teaching drawing and French in England, that he found his real bent in the literary field. The author of several plays, *Dead Letter* (1959), *The Old Tune* (1960), *Architruc* (1961), *Here and There* (1961), *Identity,* and *Abel and Bela* (1971) as well as novels, *The Investigation* (1962), *Someone* (1965), *Le Libera* (1968), *Passacaille* (1969) etc., he sums up his profound literary preoccupations as follows: "One thing alone interests me: capture *the tone of a voice.* This tone is, in actuality, one of the components of my own voice which I try to isolate, then to objectify."

*****

Q.  Were you influenced by Samuel Beckett? Did he play a part in your intellectual and artistic growth?

A.  No. I had already reached a certain intellectual level before I even met Beckett. He did not play any role in my intellectual or artistic growth. He is a very good friend of mine. I did learn a lot from him, how-

ever, in the domain of the theatre: his working method
in particular; the extreme precision he brings to everything with which he comes into contact, and his *mises
en scènes* especially. I have worked for and with him
and he has worked for and with me. For example, he
translated my second dramatic work, *The Old Tune,*
into English, which was broadcast over BBC in 1960.
I translated Beckett's *All That Fall* (1957) into French.
My play, *Dead Letter,* was co-billed with Beckett's
*Krapp's Last Tape* at the Récamier Theatre in Paris
in 1960. We did the *mise en scène* together for my
play, *The Hypothesis* (1961), which was performed at
the Odéon.

Q. Would you say that your plays have undergone a type
of evolution, from the time you wrote *Dead Letter*
to your last theatrical works, *Identity* and *Abel and
Bela?* If your point of view has changed, could you
tell us in what way?

A. A type of evolution might be said to have taken place,
but in terms of the dramatic projection *per se;* that is,
the objectivization involved in the creation of a play
and the theatrical conventions with which the dramatist
must wrestle. As for the *tone* itself, which is of
utmost importance to me in the writing of both my
plays and my novels — this cannot really be discussed
or assessed in this context. To create the *tone* in my
plays is not something spontaneous. It imposes itself
on the drama after an enormous amount of work and
discipline, of the most classical kind. This discipline
includes all kinds of exercises: scales, for example,
and the infinite virtuosity implicit in the domain of
diction, elocution, the volume of a voice, its nuances —
in short, the mastership of the vocal organ.

Q. Could you go into a bit more detail in terms of the *tone,*
so vital a factor in all of your creative work?

A.   This tone about which I speak is actually one of the components of my own voice which I try to objectify. There is always a little bit of me in each of my characters; but each element is objectified to such a degree that it becomes a character within itself. The tone varies from one book of mine to the next. This is true because my search in this domain will go on forever. My lot is to choose, each time anew — because I would like to isolate one tone out of thousands which my ear must then record.

What is said or *meant* does not really interest me; it is the way it is said that does. And the choosing of the *way*, represents a large and painful part of my work. The subject of my novels or plays leaves me indifferent. My work consists in shaping it into a certain mould.

When I speak of *what my ear records*, it is indeed this spoken language or rather its non-codified syntax, espousing the least inflection of feeling, which fascinates me. This syntax which is always evolving and has always tried, from time immemorial, to better adapt our language to the demands made by the senses is, as far as I am concerned, the only one worthy of interest. I am not trying to codify it; this would be working against my interests, but rather to speak in favor of it. And I am doing this, not for any intellectual reasons, but simply out of egoism.

It seems to me in fact that artistic sensibility — mine, consequently — is worthy of being formulated as explicitly as possible; now, this can be accomplished only by means of words and a suitable syntax. I say this to reassure my readers. If they find poetical elements or psychological reality in my books — in short, anything besides verbiage — I won't be hurt at all.

A new point of view, a modern sensibility, and original composition can certainly be found in my writings, but I am not responsible for all this.   If

I become aware of these added elements as I advance
further along in my difficult métier, the fact still remains that it is the *voice* of the one who is doing the
talking, and that voice alone, that captures my interest.
Our ear is a recording device as powerful as our eye.
Now, I believe I can say that our normal tone, the one,
for example, we use with ourselves or with those close
to us, is a sort of composite of several tones — aside
from those we have inherited or find in books — recorded by us since our childhood. If it is interesting
to discover this natural tone in a letter, for example,
by oneself and after the fact, how much more interesting is it to analyze each of the component parts of
this voice, and from each in turn, to create a book.
I must explain something: I have never attempted to
render objectively, as on a recording machine, the
sound of a stranger's voice; I have enough work in
store for me trying to render my own. We find here, in
particular, one of the requirements of art which is
really nothing more than the ability to transcribe an
individual's expressions while not exposing those of
another.

I say the voice of *the one who is talking*, because
my preliminary work consists in choosing the one
voice which interests me at this particular time, and
isolating it. When I use the term preliminary work, it
does not really express what I mean: a kind of unconscious work which goes on during my unproductive
periods or after a book has been published. These
periods are more or less long and difficult to stand.
The tone I choose must first ripen; at this point it is
not really chosen, but rather imposes itself upon me.
If I still speak of choice, it is because the different
tones I have exploited up until now still sound in my
ear and I am always tempted to use them over again.
I do not use them from one book to another because I
feel — and probably wrongly so — that I have exhausted
each one of them. In any event, they bore me once I

have written them down. Because of my inactivity, the fact that I am not writing, not creating something, the temptation still subsists, and it is difficult for me to bear. I am, therefore, dependent upon this kind of ripening, during my slack periods.

It would also be incorrect to say that I find the exact tone right away. This has happened to me, but it is an exception. It is more of a tonality at the onset; or the confidence I feel in this particular tonality which slowly takes shape as my work progresses. In any case, the conscious realization of the accuracy of the tone — or of its approximative soundness is reached only on the last page. Even if I have only had the feeling of having touched upon the right note, here and there, in the course of my work, that encourages me sufficiently to continue.

Q. Your last play is entitled *Identity*. Could you tell us what you mean by identity? It is psychological or social identity? How does such a notion apply to your characters?

A. I am dealing with the identity of Mortin as the author, projecting himself onto the other protagonists in the play: the doctor, Noémi, who are, in effect, his creatures. Once these two characters have disappeared, Mortin's identity can no longer be reflected on to what were really mirror images of himself — and so it dissolves. Aphasia stems from such a void.

Q. You described the "movements" of your characters in *Identity* as both "mechanical and noble." Is this a means of underlying the contrasts existing between the idea one has of a human being and the relative objective reality of the situation in which he finds himself?

A.    Such "mechanical" movements may be one way of
accentuating the *artificial* (in the most noble sense
of the word) aspect of the dramatic play.

Q.    Could you tell us something about the *tone* you tried
to convey in *Identity?*

A.    The tone is not only essential to the play, it constitutes the work.    The tone or tonalities of the
various characters were discovered little by little:
the right accents, rhythms, all phases of this audible
instrument — and their unlimited manifestations in
the work-a-day world.

Q.    Abel and Bela are "two actors in the process of
creating a play." Did you have Molière or Giraudoux
— or even Pirandello — in mind, when writing *Abel
and Bela?*

A.  No.

Q.   Your sense of humor, so acute and penetrating in your
novels, is even more powerful in your theatre. Your
analogy, for example, between the **"well-made play"**
and a "seamstress' work" is wonderfully clever.
But how do you go about "constructing" your plays?
Intuitively?    Does the dream enjoy a role in their
genesis?

A.    At the beginning, it is really a question of chance —
*l'aventure*.    The arduous work involved in the actual
construction of the play slows down the impact and
flow of inspiration: in fact, it stops it short once the
structure itself appears set.    Difficulties arise with
the development of the various themes and how best
to set them forth.

Q.   How do you feel about modern theatre in France?
     Rezvani's or Ehni's political theatre, for example?
     or the aesthetic plays of Weingarten and Dubillard?
     Arrabal's Panic Theatre?

A.   I like only one kind of theatre — with a *text*. My only
     concern and interest lies with the dramatic rendering
     of this text and the infinite possibilities which the
     author, director and actors have at their disposal.
     (I mean specifically in connection with the form
     taken in terms of the oral expression.)

Q.   Would you like to direct your own plays?  What is the
     director's function in your opinion?

A.   Yes.  I have already started to direct my works.  It is
     an extremely difficult task because the director's
     function is to *explain* the play to the audience.
     The author, on the other hand, is usually satisfied
     when he creates something which will please him and
     in which he is able to express himself as fully and
     as deeply as possible.  The goals — a chasm to be
     breached!

Reprinted in part, in translation, with permission of the
*French Review* (March, 1969).

## *FERNANDO  ARRABAL*

*Interviewer's Note:*

Fernando Arrabal was born in Melilla (Spanish Morocco) in 1932.  Shortly after completing his law studies in Madrid, he moved to Paris where he has been living since 1954.  The author of six novels, he is best known for his plays, which include *Fando and Lis, The Automobile Graveyard* (1958), *Guernica* (1959), *Picnic on the Battle- field* (1952), *And They Put Handcuffs on the Flowers* **(1970),** *Sky and Shit* **(1972), etc.**  In July 1967 Arrabal went to Spain to be present for the publication of one of his works, *Arrabal celebrating the ceremony of confusion.* While at a gathering to autograph his volume, he dedicated **a copy** to his **seventeen -year -old** nephew and wrote: ''I — on God, the country and everything else.''  The nephew showed the dedication to his **father,** who informed the **director-general** of the Spanish press.  Arrabal was arrested at one in the morning on July 22 at Murcia, where he had gone for a vacation — less than twenty-four hours after he dedicated the book.  He was brought to Madrid (500 kilometers away) in a police wagon.  He was immediately put in solitary confinement for five days after which time he had to be transported to a hospital because **his dormant tuberculosis had been re-activated. A hate** campaign began in the Spanish newspapers.  The Catholic

newspaper, *ABC,* declared, "This act cannot remain un-
punished." Juan Aparicio, one of the founders of the
Falange, demanded that Arrabal be castrated for what he
had written. Arrabal's situation became a *cause célèbre,*
reminiscent in many ways of Federico García Lorca's
plight in 1936. Fernando Arrabal's trial came up in
September, 1967. He was acquitted and let off with a
fine.

Q.   Why have you chosen to live in France since 1954?

A.   It was really a question of chance. My life was chaotic, confused and painful. The political situation
in Spain in 1955 was not conducive to writing my type
of theatre. My plays must be given in a free country
and not in one in which the government has a strangle-
hold over everyone's thoughts and emotions.

Q.   Has there been a North African or Spanish influence
in your work? What writers influenced you?

A.   Though I was born in Melilla (Spanish Morocco), I did
not live there any great length of time; its influence,
therefore, was negligible. There has been and still
is, however, an **enormous** Spanish influence in my
work. But I must say in all frankness that I have
renounced my country and its influences to a great
extent — at least consciously.
      Kafka, Dostoyevsky, and Carroll have had the
greatest influence upon me. I am also fascinated by
science fiction, by fairy tales, and, of course, by
chess. But painting preoccupies me even more than
literature. I am fascinated by lithographs, engravings,
**woodcuts—the** type you find in travelogues or in
diaries. Bosch, Goya and Magritte have had an
enormous influence upon me. I draw myself. In fact,
those paintings on the wall, right in front of you,

were drawn by me and painted by a painter friend
of mine. Strangely enough, it is through the visual
that I am inspired to write. I first see my idea and
then I organize it dramatically. But I have no recipes,
no rules for writing. My style is classical — romantic
at times. I usually lock myself in my room and write.
But it is always from the visual — the image — that
my work takes root.

Q.  Why do your characters, for the most part, act and
talk like children?

A.  I think that my characters speak as they should, or as
I did when I wrote my early plays such as *Fando and
Lis* and *Oraison*, for example. Fortunately or unfortunately, I began writing when I was very young,
at 14. I expressed the world which lived within me
at the time. I was in my early twenties when I wrote
*The Tricycle*. I had just arrived from Spain. I had
never lived, either sexually or any other way. I was,
one could almost say, a retarded child in this respect.
My childhood was not only difficult, but horrible.
I never knew my father. My father was a lieutenant
in the Spanish army and was arrested during the
night when he was asleep, in 1936. I was three
years old at the time. My father was condemned to
death. He escaped in 1941. But I never saw him
again. My mother defamed his memory ever since
I was a child. She forbade us to pronounce his name.
He was unworthy of us, she said. My mother despised him and everything he stood for. Our household was a strict one: pro-Franco and ultra-Catholic.
I was brought up to hate my father. In other words,
**the political civil war was waged not only in the**
battlefield, but in my home and above all in my heart.

Q.  Critics have called your plays "cruel." Can you

explain this term? Is it the same kind of "cruelty" to which Artaud referred?

A. I don't know **Artaud**'s work at all. Perhaps my plays are cruel in the Artaudian sense. I don't know. I can illustrate my point of view best by relating the following anecdote.

In 1954 a friend of mine, Arroyo, submitted a play of mine — without my knowledge — in a contest in Madrid. I read some weeks later that I had won second prize. Several days after that I was told that I could not be awarded the prize because I had copied **Beckett's play,** *Waiting for Godot*. But I had never read Beckett's play nor had I even heard his name. I was even more indignant when I learned that the prize had gone to the conventional poet Becquer. I hate that poet. To make matters even worse I had confused Becquer with Beckett. You can imagine my anger.

Needless to add that since that time I have read Beckett's works. And I certainly see the resemblance. But I still have not read **Artaud's work,** *The Theatre and Its Double,* though I am familiar with its message. I believe, as did **Artaud,** in a physical and concrete theatrical language. It's really André Breton's fault if I haven't read **Artaud** because Breton condemned both **Artaud** and Vitrac. Breton always used to tell me that Artuad was a man who was always getting excited over nothing. He discouraged me from reading Artaud.

My plays are not cruel in the usual sense of the word. In fact, they are always filled with love. They are human and realistic works. The characters' very emotions and feelings compel them to act as they do. After all, how can one really know love without having experienced pain and hurt? If one person really loves another, he must run the gamut of all emotions and sensations. But my characters also know kindness — an immense amount of it. *Fando and Lis* is a modern version of *Romeo and Juliet*. In the play *The Two Executioners*, a type of melodrama, you have featured the conflict between the good and bad son. The good son, in my opinion, is the one who rebels against his mother; the bad son, the one who acquiesces to his mother's every demand. The last scene is the only one I cannot bear — it is excruciating — when the bad son (the good one in the play) wants the good one (the bad one in the play) to beg forgiveness of his mother.

Q. Is *The Two Executioners* autobiographical?

A. Yes. I have a brother who is an aviator in Franco's army. He is very reactionary, **very devout,** and represents all those forces I despise. I am the rebellious son. The mother in the play speaks just as my mother does in real life. I never see my mother now. She sends me telegrams, however.

Q. Outside of your **play, *Picnic** on the Battlefield,* which is anti-Korean war, are any of your other plays politically oriented?

A. No. I am not preoccupied with politics. I'm just against and afraid of war. I was afraid of the Korean war just as I am afraid of the war in Vietnam. But **perhaps my play, *Guernica,* could be considered po-**litical in some ways. It'a about an old couple who find their apartment in shambles, destroyed by the bombardments of Guernica. At this point they come face to face with the horror of their wretched lives, the suffering, the gruesome nature of events which overwhelm them. I might add, incidentally, that this play was in part inspired by Picasso's painting.

Q. I noticed a certain ambiguity in your theatre vis-à-vis your religion: a hatred as well as an attraction. Are you religious?

A. I was brought up in the Catholic faith. This has stamped me for life. I am very hostile, however, toward Catholicism. I blame Catholicism to a great extent for having made my life such an excruciatingly unhappy one. I am haunted as a result of my Catholic instruction by the idea of hell, of sin, of torture. I try to rationalize, to tell myself that these things are really impossible, a figment of the imagination; and yet, these fearful ideas return time and time again to haunt me. Maybe this is one of the reasons I am so attracted to the paintings of Bosch and Goya. We have something in common. Because of this agonizing fear I am forever tormented by nightmares: hell, fire, torture. Writing is perhaps a compensation, a liberation for me. I would like to be able to think clearly, in a well-organized manner, be Cartesian like my wife, who is a Professor of Spanish at the Sorbonne.

Q. Why does the theme of Christ's passion preoccupy you to such an extent? You portray it so cleverly in *The Automobile Graveyard*. Are you attracted by fables and myths in general?

A. I adore myths, fables, science fiction, children's tales. I am, therefore, also very attracted to the Christ myth. It's just like a melody you keep listening to and end by liking. If I had not been familiar with Christ's life and if I were to hear about it now for the first time, I would find it ridiculous. But my Christ is much softer and much more human than the Christ in real life. I softened the Christ fable in *The Automobile Graveyard*. When I wrote this play

I refused, at the time, to admit that it was Christ's
life. Now I admit it. The Christ in my play steals,
lies, is hypocritical and makes love. The Christ of
the fable is like a Martian.

Q.  Did audiences attack the parallels you drew between
Christ and the character Emanou in *The Automobile
Graveyard* as being blasphemous?

A.  Yes. In Caracas certain people considered my play
an act *"de agravio"* to the Sacred Heart of Christ.
They felt that Christ's heart had been offended and
mutilated.    The same reaction occurred all over
South America.    Not so in Sweden and New York,
where the reactions were normal. If my plays were
to be produced in Spain — and I'd love this — it
would probably cause a trauma in the heartbeat of
that country.

Q.  What does the word *Tar* symbolize in *Fando and Lis?*

A.  Well, first of all "Tar" spelled backwards spells
"Rat."   I realized this, however, only after I had
written the play.   I wrote this work when I was in
the sanatorium recovering from tuberculosis.    My
great desire was to leave the sanatorium.   I guess
that "Tar" stands for Utopia because life outside
of the sanatorium seemed ideal for me.   My only
thought was to get out.   Now I think that Utopia
exists in the sanitorium — but at the time Utopia
was outside of it.

Q.  Why are your plays continually impregnated with sado-
masochism?

A.  In *Fando and Lis,* for example, when Fando seems to
be hurting Lis — he really is not.   It's just that

Fando wants to live intensely and completely. He
wants to experience everything in the domain of
human existence. Incidentally, my wife's name is
Luce but since I pronounce the French ''u'' with
difficulty, I call her ''Lis.'' She calls me Fando.
But this play troubles me very much now. I think it
is too simple — **too innocent**.

Q. Why are your dramas always filled with sexually
obsessed individuals?

A. It's because many writers begin writing late in life.
I, on the contrary, began writing early in life. I
dramatized and wrote about all those things which
preoccupied me. When I began writing I did not feel
I was writing something of great import — I was just
writing for my pleasure, unburdening myself. I wrote
because I was compelled to write. When I arrived in
Paris, people told me that what I was writing was
important.

Now, I feel that sex is very important. It should,
therefore, be an intrinsic part of the theatre. Perhaps I am obsessed by the sexual. If I have to choose
between eroticism and **pornography**, I should choose
**pornography**. There is a big difference. Eroticism
is a hypocritical pornography. What's marvelous
about pornography is that no act is irreparable. In
*Solemn Communion* one of my characters makes love
to a dead woman on stage. Such an act created a
scandal even in Paris. Yet there's nothing harmful
in making love to a dead woman.

Q. What role does the dream play in your theatrical life?

A. A very great part. My plays are direct manifestations
of my inner world as revealed through my dreams. I
told you earlier that the visual — the dream — is my

starting point. The play, *The Labyrinth,* is an exact
representation of the nightmare I had during the time
when I was being operated on in 1956, during my
bout with tuberculosis. I saw toilets in this nightmare. This image occurred and reoccurred constantly.
People accused me of wanting to provoke, or of
dwelling on the sordid. I don't. My plays are real,
they are for the most part dramatized dreams. But I
do not insist upon showing every element of the
dream in my theatre. For instance, in Rome, the
director told me that it would be impossible to put a
toilet on stage. I didn't insist. They put showers
instead.

Q. What does the word "labyrinth" mean to you?

A. It represents a kind of caricature of the chaotic nature
of life pushed to the extreme. I believe that most
people live in a state of utter confusion. Yet where
there is no confusion there is no life. I am very
close to the labyrinth.

Q. Can you tell us something about your **play,** *Theatrical
Orchestration,* in which there is absolutely no dialogue? Is it a play which appeals to the visual sense
alone?

A. *Theatrical Orchestration* is a play which failed completely. The mobiles created for the play were done
by Alexander Calder and the play was directed by
Jacques Poliéri (1959). There was no **plot**; no
arteries. The play consisted solely of objects:
paintings, moving objects of all sorts, strange and
impossible contraptions and machines. Everything
seemed to me, at least when I wrote the play — and
this took an entire summer—to possess a Kafkaesque
quality: suspense, humor, poetry. When I saw the

play enacted before me, I realized that there was
absolutely nothing to it. The critics were right. It
is a work of no consequence.

Q.   **The** critic of the *Figaro Littéraire,* Jacques Lemarchand, stated that your theatre is situated mid-
way between the Marquis de Sade and St. Theresa
d'Avila.

A.   I am very flattered by such a statement. Sade was the
great persecutor of conformity, and St. Theresa
d'Avila had her troubles with the forces of the In-
quisition. Both were erotic. Saint Theresa said
some extraordinary things, as you know. She said
she felt the Lord driving himself into her deeply;
she spoke of the fire which invaded her being at
those moments, of the extreme pain and pleasure
she knew during these experiences.

Q.   Why do the three men in *The Tricycle,* who rob and
then kill a bourgeois, and are arrested for their crime,
remain totally indifferent to their lot?

A.   That's typically me. I myself am in a state of confusion and chaos for the most part. A distinction
between happiness and misfortune cannot be made.
We human beings are forever building systems and
structures for ourselves. Our lives are guided by
these fantasies. In my plays the characters are unaware of these systems, of these codes and ethics.
They know no morality. They wonder frequently
how they should act. I frequently ask myself the
same questions. Therefore, the men in *The Tricycle,*
bound by no rules or regulations, feel no remorse
nor any other emotion when imprisoned; it's just
another phase of existence which opens up for them.

Q.   What do you mean by "homme panique" and *"théâtre
panique"?*

A.  I am *"un homme panique."*   And this is no joke.
Perhaps I call myself by this name and I refer to
my theatre as a *"théâtre de panique"* as a reaction
to people's extreme desire to classify everything.
I do not want to be considered as part of the group
called "the Theatre of the Absurd" nor do I want to
be taken for a "surrealist." Some of my friends —
Topar, Jodorowsky, Stenberg — and I decided to
call ourselves "panic." Panic is to be understood
as meaning everything: like the great God Pan — All.
The *"homme panique"* also refers to one who refuses to take any risks or commit any dangerous act
or any heroic deed. Our *"théâtre de panique"* really
encompasses everything in life — it has no limitations.   Now critics have begun to talk in terms of
"panic texts," or they say that something is "panic."
It has now become something quite concrete.   In
fact, a Professor at the Sorbonne has written a book
on "panic."   People have already begun to formulate
theories concerning this group, and as soon as it
becomes as rigid in its doctrines as certain other
literary schools, we will destroy our "panic" group
and renew ourselves.

Q.  Did you undertake to study the psychology of the ugly
and the abnormal male in your *The Grand Ceremonial?*
Ironically you gave the name Cavanosa to your hero,
to a man whose life was ruined by an overly possessive mother, to a man whose sole pleasure in
life is to destroy what is beautiful in the world —
namely, the beautiful woman.

A.  Yes.   You are absolutely right.   But this play also
recounts the Beauty and the Beast myth.

Q.  Why is your theatre so ferocious?

A. Is it? People have accused me of cruelty toward cats also, of all sorts of things. I am sick — I am ''the great sick **one**.'' (I say this in jest **naturally**.) And since I am sick, naturally I hate humanity in general. My plays, therefore, are manifestations of these feelings. People have **said** so many things about my theatre. Let them all talk.

Q. What kind of a theatre do you prefer for your works: an **open-air** theatre, a theatre in the round, with or without proscenium, etc.?

A. The technical aspects of the theatre do not interest me at all. Nor does theatrical architecture interest me.

Q. Have you ever directed a play?

A. Yes. *The Crowning.* I directed it and wrote the music for it. The critics killed it. Yet it was an extra-ordinary play — but nobody understood it. I also directed *And They Put Handcuffs on the Flowers.*

Q. Do you come to rehearsals when other directors are preparing one of your plays for production? What is your rapport with actors?

A. Tragic. It's tragic because I'm never serious. I'll never be serious; or rather I'll be serious when I'm twenty centimeters taller than I am now. I am never present at rehearsals. I go to rehearsals only two or three days before the opening. When I arrive in the theatre the actors look at me and say: ''That's Arrabal?''

   As for the director, I tell him that he must create an extraordinary theatrical event, a magnificent cere-mony, **a real theatre of panic with its rituals and**

its rites, its initiations and sacrifices. He must
succeed in this even if he has to alter the play. Let
him violate the play providing the spectacle is a
delirious one.

Q. What about stage sets?

A. The sets vary with the play. Any kind of set is valid
whether designed by Rauschenberg or da Vinci providing it is a meaningful expression of the play's
moods, rhythms, and sensibility. Everything and
anything is possible on stage.

Q. What contemporary dramatist do you admire?

A. I hate them all. I'm jealous of every one of them.
But I must tell you that I have translated three of
Genet's plays into Spanish: *The Maids*, *Deathwatch*
and *The Balcony*. They were published in Argentina.

Q. Can you tell us something about your last sojourn in
Spain?

A. As far as politics is concerned, I can only enunciate
a series of platitudes or else speak in terms of good
common sense. I have always been against all kinds
of tyranny and dictatorships. Why I was provoked,
imprisoned, judged, and persecuted in Spain is
beyond my understanding. I do not want to talk about
it. But I keep thinking of the others who were imprisoned with me at the Carabanchel prison and who
are going to spend many long years behind bars for
acts that a civilized country can not condemn without
dishonoring itself.

Q. What did you think of Victor García's direction of *The
Automobile Graveyard* (1967) in Paris? The entire

theatre was remodeled for this play and turned into an actual automobile graveyard. Tons and tons of sets had to be brought into the theatre, filling two trucks (each 60 feet long). The spectators sat on swivel chairs in the center of the action.

A.  I think it was the ideal lay-out for my play, which requires the type of auditorium Artaud had dreamed about, but which was unknown to me at the time I wrote the play. On the other hand, Victor **García** is a "wise savage" who has a feeling for the sacred and for the sacrilegious. He adheres to my play like foam to a foot ... the point of a knife to a wound.

Q.  Why do you choose directors of Spanish extraction?

A.  I am equally enthusiastic about the works of Grotowski, Peter Brook and Julian Beck. In France there are three Argentinian directors (Savary, Lavelli and García); they understand my obsessions. We are Seneca's descendants; he was the first one to show the Spanish-speaking artist the road to exile.

Q.  I seem to detect a return to the purity and goodness of childhood in your plays — *The* **Grand** *Ceremonial*, for example. Is this true?

A.  I am certainly obsessed by the temptations inherent in purity and goodness; they fascinate me, even to the point of nausea. But climaxes are hot — with precipices and sharp curves.

Q.  Some spectators said that while watching *The Architect and the Emperor of Assyria* they had the feeling of going back in time — to the infantile stage, back to their beginnings. What do you make of that?

A. Certain spectators reacted in this manner; others, on
the contrary, claimed that the play depicted a world
to come. Still others looked upon it as science
fiction. The poet must — and this is inherent in his
art — provoke all kinds of reactions. In my opinion,
the work of art bursts forth from the author's own
confused innards with all of its fascination and
terror. This does not mean that I either defend or
provoke such confusion. I simply declare that such
a state exists. I even say that where there is not
confusion, there is no life.

Q. How do you account for the pessimism of *The Architect and the Emperor of Assyria?* Everything always
begins over and over again without any changes.
History then is nothing more than a predetermined
series of beginnings.

A. On the contrary. I consider my play optimistic — it
even has a happy ending. I think that it's a play
possessed of luminous roots, cases and vases.

Q. Is it true that you would enjoy eating a baby?

A. Baudelaire said that fresh nuts taste like baby brains.
I certainly do not want to commit any irreparable
act. As you know, I flee from both ashes (death) and
incense pots (church).

Q. When did your megalomania first begin?

A. I'm not a megalomaniac. But I sometimes use megalomania as a theatrical device. It enables me to stand
the horror which this body of mine — handed me at
birth — inspires, particularly during those moments
when I feel myself assailed by a sterile lucidity.

Q. What's the relation between your own sexual obsessions and the eroticism in your plays?

A. I am interested in eroticism and pornography — as
everyone else is. I'm not a **Martian.** I'm not at all
surprised that such themes appear in my theatre,
just as others **do.** Death. I shall never be able to
forget my childhood, which was suffused with a
tragic sense of life.

Q. Why are Religion, Death, and the Mother constant
themes in your works?

A. **What** astounds me is that Religion, Death and the
Mother are not constant themes in everybody's
writings — actually, they are. We hide in different
skins; the same skeletons viewed under variegated
trembling lights appear different, but are not...
basically.

Q. Do you regard the theatre as a language or as a scenic
vision?

A. You would think that dramatists today are faced with
a real dilemma that they must choose between two
formulas: Jouvet's — "the theatre is a dialogue,"
and Artaud's — the theatre is a combination of
gesture, movement and *mise en scène.* Personally,
I dream of a theatre where humor and poetry, panic
and love would be fused. Poetry is born from the
nightmare and its mechanism, which is excess. The
theatrical rite — the *panic* ceremony — must be looked
upon by the spectator as a kind of sacrifice. This
infinitely free type of theatre which I envisage has
nothing to do with anti-theatre or with the Theatre
of the Absurd. It's a vast domain, shrouded in ambiguities, and patrolled very carefully by the mad

hound which stalks the night.

Q.  How many times have you bet on God's existence in
the slot machine?

A.  I have not used the slot machine to bet only on God's
existence, but on many other things as well. I think
that the future is going to be made up of a series of
theatrical coups. Thanks to the slot machine, I can
set this mechanism in motion. It helps me see into
the future; it is presided over by chance and memory
(used as an accessory — i.e., the degree to which I
can make use of my intelligence or my senses).

Q.  Where will you spend your vacations from now on?

A.  I'll do my best to avoid Spanish prisons. Is that what
you wanted me to say?

Q.  What do you think of this proverb attributed to Confucius:  Twelve eggs and a little luck can bring you
thirteen little chicks?

A.  Confucius was already a *panicist:* he believed in
chance.

Q.  When do you think you will become a member of the
French Academy — or by default, the Spanish Academy?

A.  I don't know.  I would love to become a member of
one of those bodies; just to be able to give one of
these ephemeral "panic plays" or happenings there.
They lend themselves so admirably . . .

Q.  If you had to state in brief your personal point of

view about your theatre, what would you say?

A.  For me the theatre remains a ceremony: it's a feast
    both sacrilegious and sacred, erotic and mystic,
    which would encompass all facets of life, including
    death, where "humor" and poetry, fascination and
    panic would be one. The theatrical rite then would
    **be transformed into** *opera mundi,* like the fantasies
    of Don Quixote and the nightmares of Alice in Won-
    derland.

Reprinted in part from *First Stage* (Vol. 6, no. 4) and *The Drama Review,* "Auto Interview" (T. 41, 1968).

## *JACQUES BOREL*

*Interviewer's Note:*

Jacques Borel was born in Paris on December 17, 1925.
His father died shortly before his birth.  He spent his
childhood with his grandmother, and after the age of ten,
with his mother.  His early years were bitter and cruel,
not only because of the poverty he knew, but because of
the repressive nature of the parochial education he received.  Borel began writing poetry at an early age.  After
earning the usual degrees he started teaching English at
the lycées.  In 1925, he wrote his first novel, *The Bond*,
which won the much coveted Goncourt prize.  His second
novel, *The Return*, was published in 1970.

Borel is an outspokenly anti-structuralist and anti-
"new Wave" novelist.  In fact, he is against any kind of
school or grouping.  An arch individualist, he favors
"confession type" writing, which, he says, most people
disdain today, but which opens wide the hidden regions
within the soul.  Essayist, novelist and poet, he is also
a dramatist.  And this, despite the fact that he is "suspicious" of the theatre, wondering whether it does not
encourage a state of escapism.  Borel's first play, *Tata or
Education*, opened on February 15, 1972.  Some critics
likened his drama to *King Ubu* because of its cutting
edge and also its cruelty; others found it hilarious.  All

agreed on its profound ramifications for man and society.

Q.  Your childhood was painful. Can you tell us something
    about it?

A.  My life was painful, yet very simple and *ordinary*.  I
    was an orphan, really; and this is, of course, an
    important consideration.  My mother and I were very
    poor.  I worked hard and early in life to help her out.
    There is a certain amount of banality in life itself:
    the years of boarding school were very difficult; the
    lycée; my studies at the Sorbonne; and the jobs which
    I held all along.  I also taught English until 1967.
    My thesis was on G. M. Hopkins — the first disser-
    tation in France on this poet.  Then marriage.  Chil-
    dren.

         I always had a passion for poetry.  This was
    perhaps instrumental in my becoming a critic of
    poetry.  I write regularly for the *Nouvelle Revue
    Française* and for *Critique*.  I try to approach poetry
    from an "inner realm."  Yet, my critical faculties
    have been developed to such an extent that I have
    become very much aware of my own deficiencies, in
    terms of poetry.  I gave up writing poetry for this
    reason.  My first narrative writing was autobio-
    graphical.  I began my first volume in a state of de-
    spair at the age of 36.  It was published when I was
    40.  I was awarded the Goncourt prize for this work
    and, I must confess, it was like a thunderbolt.  I was
    horrified by the fact that my tragic life with my mother
    could have been turned into what I hate the most in
    this world — a best-seller.  A long silence followed.
    I tried to forget; to be forgotten.

Q.  Can you go into some detail about *The Bond* and *The
    Return?*

A.   *The Bond* and *The Return* are behind me now. They
contributed — as does all writing but not these two
works exclusively — to molding or modifying my outlook on life. Since I am still in the process of evolving, I really cannot talk to you about these works
themselves. I can, however, discuss my growth in
terms of my writing, my vision.

  *The Return* is really not a novel though people
have called it that. It is a type of lengthy and breath-
less meditation in which a personal history — with all
of the apparent narcissism inherent in this kind of
writing — has been, hopefully, overcome; and where
the destiny of a being confronts, obscurely, a distant,
ancestral forest of myths. These novels were conceived as a type of autobiographical "summing up;"
*The Bond* and *The Return*, as Parts I and II, and *The
Fascinated Ones* "would" be the third. I say "would"
because I may perhaps yield to the very profound and
lancinating temptation of cutting up or shattering the
**mould.** In fact, even before finishing *The Fascinated
Ones*, another large volume, *The Journal of Ligenère*
(Ligenère is the fictitious name for a real and fright-
ful place), will have been published - in January 1973.

  I absolutely did not plan on writing *The Journal
of Ligenère* with publication in mind. I never even
thought of such a possibility when I started it. I'm
afraid I'm really not a "writer." Perhaps writing is
an escape? In my case, however, it is a question of
an authentic journal which I have kept regularly for
nearly twelve years, during the period when I visited
one of the most disinherited and neglected places
in the world — the psychiatric hospital where my
mother has been agonizing all this time. The inter-
vals between my visits, the memories of so much
suffering, of such injustice and misfortune (hers,
that of others, of all people) continue to haunt me.
After having experienced this kind of pain, one's

views of the world are completely upset. Such an
upheaval is certainly obvious in my writing — whatever the current styles. Dostoyevsky was born as a
result of *The House of the Dead*.

What can I say? You will perhaps better understand my feelings if I quote King Lear, when he
tears off his clothes and cries out on the moors:

> Is man no more than this .... Thou art the thing itself:
> unaccommodated man is no more but such a poor, bare,
> forked animal as thou art.
>
> Off, off you lendings! Come, unbutton here!

I obey nothing else. Yes, everything in life
speeds by so quickly today. To lay *bare* (perhaps
this is already a death knell), to strip off all alibis
(isn't literature or at least a certain type of literature
an alibi?), all veils, by writing. Yes, that's it, I
believe. To accomplish this cutting open from the
very beginning, no matter how embryonic the attempt
may be, and even if the end product fails .... This
is what I attempted in *The Bond* and even more so in
certain chapters in *The Return* — in terms of the
death of illusions, of myths. This type of approach
has been my constant command and has increased in
intensity and depth with time.

How can this kind of writing be labelled "nar-
rative," particularly if one is absolutely bent on
honesty and veracity? How can one not challenge
writing itself? An author must try to go still further
even if it means going to the extreme, that is, of
sacrificing, of even killing writing itself. That's
what my *Journal* really is.

Now you see that it is much more than a "doc-
ument" or a "testimony." It is a meditation on pain
*and* writing: on an experienced pushed to the extreme
— not abstractly conceived nor willed, nor even
deliberate, but rather linked to the very breath of
another being, born from the most unsharable contact

with the most cutting of agonies. My amazement and my indignation **vis-a-vis** myself *and* my writing stemmed from the fact that I was unable to understand how my writing (far from being smothered within the embryo or choked up within some kind of feelings of nothingness emerging from one's own inanity in terms of the primordial wound, the incomprehensible and mortal wound of living), had become, at least for a while, more vigorous and more motivated.

You understand now why writing which "uses" situations and experiences seems meaningless to me — though the temptation of seeing an autobiographical "summation" through to the end is great — and why this kind of expression fills me with a kind of shame, revulsion and horror.

I have frequently repeated two of Kafka's phrases which once again come to mind. Both of them appear in *Meditations on Sin, Suffering, Hope and the True Way*. The first: "There is no having, there is only a being, a being who longs for the last sigh, for suffocation."

To write books, to pile them up, to create a **"work,"** to dream of taking one's place in the history of literature, is to orient oneself not toward being, which is what I had believed for so long (Rilke's "To sing is to be"), but rather toward having, to realize that writing (the anguish of writing, the anguish of living — and nothing can separate these two in my mind) can one day become the source of having and constitute having itself.

The other Kafka phrase: "Nothing is real except the light that shines on a grotesque face as it withdraws, nothing else." It seems to me that we are confronted with this unbearable "face" today and we must cope with it, we must come to grips with it. It is on this level that the voice within me indicates the very area where my "work" is to come into being

— without it there would be nothing but ruin, an inability to finish, a hopelessness which comes from a feeling of having reached the very edge of a terrible abyss, before which one is not yet able to rebel (or else, it's the same ceaseless, unanswerable questioning) and from which one knows that no withdrawal is possible any more.

Q. Why and how did you begin writing for the theatre?

A. When I was young, I dreamt — as do many others — of being an actor. It seemed that I had the "voice" for it. I even took some courses in acting, but it was obvious that I was not suited for this profession. You can succeed as an actor only if you know how to make people laugh; I only know how to make my children laugh!

I really don't believe I like the theatre. After the publication of *The Bond* the French radio asked me to write a play. I said no, because I was certain I had no talent for writing and, furthermore, I had no desire to write for the theatre. There is not one dialogue in my novels — and this despite my ability to record voices, thoughts, inflections, as though I had a recording machine implanted within me, noting everything down, and with *terrible* precision. I really don't like dialogue in novels or other forms. Dialogue: to listen to others in life, to the most insignificant details and despite Nathalie Sarraute's *tropisms*. Yet, the unconscious wager... I wrote my play, *Tata*, in one fell swoop — in two weeks.

Q. Who is and what is Tata?

A. The aunt in my story. Let me quote something I wrote about *Tata:* "*Tata* is the sad story of a young man, Charles, killed by kindness." He is a "child of sin."

He is just going on 18 years of age; but his mother,
Josèphe, and his aunt, Albine, treat him like a child,
and keep him locked up in a home isolated from the
world.   They wash him, comb his hair, dress him.
They are always there, day and night.   They never
leave him out of their sight.   For Albine — Charles
must be saved from the sin to which Josèphe had
succombed long ago.   Charles, however, seems to be
playing a game; his reading of the books by the
Countess de Ségur, which he found hidden away some-
where, encourages him to create a most unusual
fantasy world.   Equally unusual is the form his rebellion is to take.

I would like to quote a statement made by one of
the critics concerning this play: "This farce of un-
paralleled violence is highly dramatic .... The author
has recourse to a gigantic caricature, to an imaginary
creation, analogous to King Ubu's universe.   He
places the "cocoon-like" family unit on trial.   The
theme of this farce is simple: a woman has made a
mistake eighteen years ago.   The fruit of her sin,
Charles, has been brought up in a cottony, anesthetic-
like universe by his mother, and particularly by his
aunt, Tata, one of these monstrous women for whom
nudity — even Christ's nudity on the cross, is a
mortal sin.   Jacques Borel's merit comes from the
fact that he has accepted the enormous ramifications
of such notions with all of their logical consequences.
A woolen sweater will clothe the crucifix above
Charles' bed.   Only the head of Christ will be visible.

Tata: You see how flighty even bishops and
           priests can be.   When the young girls go
           to confession and see this ... how can
           you expect people not to expose them-
           selves on the beaches? ...

Alas, in spite of the fact that Charles wore diapers
until he was 7 years old, despite the fact that he was

isolated from his neighbors, from the world, from
life, that his only outside contact were the novels of
the Countess de Ségur, he grew. Ignoble nature took
hold of him. With Borel's terribly subjective logic,
Tata draws an analogy between Charles and her cat
whose carnal lust she has succeded in destroying
by "operating" on him herself, and bravely with a
scissors, and transforming him into "an angelic
companion." What will Charles' fate be?"

Q. Is *Tata* autobiographical?

A. Jean Vauthier in a radio interview wanted me to admit
that it was. He probably believed that it was. He
certainly is not the only one who thought so. But I
say it is not. I am neither castrated, as Charles is,
nor am I an exhibitionist as he turns out to be; nor
even an illegitimate child. But it is true, as it is
with many young French children within the last
century, I did read the novels of the Countess de
Ségur. According to modern psychiatrists, her vol-
umes are filled with sadism. In Sartre's magazine,
*Modern Times*, there was a fine article on the so-
called "edifying," aristocratic and very Catholic
Countess — author for nice children. Certainly her
characters are, to a great extent, at the root of my
farces. I have tried to mock the "wise" and com-
placent. This does not imply that I am not *also*
trying to settle my personal accounts in this play, as
in my novel *The Bond*, with my own religious and so-
called well-meaning education.

Q. Do you go to rehearsals or to the theatre in general?

A. No, because the theatre fills me with an oppressive
feeling of futility, almost in the Pascalian sense of
"diversion." I prefer to read the few plays that are

meaningful to me by myself. To have a silent tête-
à-tête with them, as one does with all books. I
was asked to attend the rehearsals of *Tata*. In fact,
I was almost forced to go. I did make a few suggestions.

I "saw" Tata, I heard her, I seemed to know her.
I was vaguely disturbed, because no actress could
really incarnate her properly — there **are** always differences. Nevertheless, Tata played by Denise Gence,
one of the finest actresses of the Comédie-Française,
was truly remarkable. My only suggestion was to
insist upon the chatty side of the character, the
voluble, the "Marquise" side of Tata. She is one of
those beings who drowns everything out — all truth.
She levels everything under the flow of her innocuous
verbiage. I think that this kind of person is well
known to the psychoanalyst.

I also begged the director not to play Tata in a
realistic way. Perhaps certain scenes or episodes
*may* appear realistic no matter how mad they are, but
to play them this way would lead to error. Madness
or the *dream* is the culminating point of my play.
Of Charles' poetic reveries, with his imaginary
friends. And *not* realism.

Q. What about the actors?

A. I had a good time with them. It was a milieu I did
   not know. We had lunch and dinner almost every day
   together. Even in life, actors are astonishing. We
   really never know when they stop acting — perhaps
   they are not even aware of it. That's why they are
   so fascinating.

Q. What dramatists have influenced you most incisively?

A. The only ones I really love are the Greek tragic

dramatists. That's really theatre: the confrontation of man and destiny. Shakespeare also. But even in Shakespeare there is a deteriorating relationship between man and destiny, and the sacred. And that's why he is so modern. Jan Knott was right to insist upon this point in *Shakespeare, Our Contemporary.* Finally, Racine: he's the only one probably, at least in *Phaedra,* who is able to place man — in terms of the sacred — face to face with his destiny.

My play, therefore, may seem to be only an "incomprehensible" caricature. Or perhaps, the times warrant such notions — because everything that is sacred has gotten the hell out of the theatre. If I have written a modern play without realizing it, it's because I am part of my century, subject to the same anguishes, sensitive to derision. And now to explain myself: I can take the mockery Freud made of Sophocles' great Oedipus myth.

Q. What about novelists?

A. Outside of Dostoyevsky and Tolstoi, I really don't like fiction. I only like autobiographies, which are frowned upon today, particularly in France. It's like introducing a little truth into the lie. The Rousseau of the *Confessions* or of the *Reveries,* or Proust... These are examples of autobiographies.

Q. Why did you call *Tata* a moralistic and didactic play?

A. Because it is a jarring farce. We can find a common denominator between Molière in this respect, and *Tata.* Both are satires of a certain kind of education, so destructive in so many cases: bourgeois, Catholic, puritan. This kind of education is on the way out, although it still exists in certain Latin countries; but the reaction today (a logical outcome) is at the opposite poles — and is equally oppressive.

Q.  You have specific ideas concerning comedy.  Can you
    elaborate on these?

A.  Each time I think of the theatre, it's in terms of comedy
    — clownish things.  Cruel farces, in a half dreamlike
    style.  A play in which madness is the pivotal point,
    which makes one laugh until it tears your heart out —
    until it becomes unbearable.  No, not Ionesco-type
    comedy.  It would be more Molière-type humor.  I
    remember when I was a child, I cried when I saw
    *School for Wives*.  I have wanted to write something
    about this play for years.

Q.  Since you are a novelist, would you consider yourself
    part of the "new wave" group alluded to by some as
    the *école du regard?*

A.  I hate the word and the notion.  "New wave" sounds
    like a TV ad for a toothpaste or some gadget — newer
    and brighter.  I despise so-called schools or groups.
    These groups are a French phenomena perhaps — the
    product of pedants.  Why *école du regard?*  Why a
    school at all?  Kafka was alone.  Bernanos.  Céline
    was alone.  Baudelaire.  Nerval.  Faulkner.  My
    answer to this question is contained in my second
    novel, *The Return*, where I describe the house in
    which I once lived, piece by piece, object by object.
    In an implacably precise manner.  And yet, it's the
    opposite of the *école du regard*.  Objects do not in-
    terest me.  Nor do they move me.  People do.  I'm
    perhaps very much isolated these days.  This may be
    unfortunate or it may be for the best.  I hate technique
    for technique's sake.  Pascal and Claudel said the
    last word on this subject.  So did Rousseau.  I abhor
    those who smirk at **Solzhenitsyn**.  Is it he or they who

are the bourgeois? Because *his* art is not like tooth-
paste — ''newer and brighter.''

Q. Are your characters logical? Irrational? Symbolistic?
or shadows? How could you describe them?

A. All characters seem to me to be both logical and irrational. We can look at the terrible logic of the
insane — namely the paranoics. It's when the irrational disturbs everything, creates a state of chaos,
that I'm fascinated. All characters are symbolic and
real, physical and shadow-like. If a character were
conceived only as a symbol, it would not hold together. If Don Quixote were merely a symbol, he
would have vanished a long time ago. The same can
be said for Hamlet, the Brothers Karamazov, and
Faulkner's characters. I would like to believe in
the reality of my characters. Little by little I come
to realize or experience the deep crevices within
their personalities, the disquieting, dangerous inner
world.

Q. What about modern directors, like Lavelli? Dramatists
like Arrabal?

A. I live like a hermit, in the country, with my wife and
five children. I rarely go to the theatre or to the
movies. I must admit, however, that I'm very impressed with Lavelli's *mise en scène* and also with
Arrabal's theatre. Arrabal's novel, *Baal Babylone,*
touched me very deeply. I told you about my passion
for autobiography, even if it's half imaginary, because
of the dangerous depths to which it leads the reader
and the sudden aperture into the most vertiginous
depths. I have a passion for confessional literature.
Adamov is greater as an autobiographer than he is as
a dramatist. *Man and Child* is truly remarkable. As

far as his plays are concerned, they can be interpreted any way — the way the wind blows.

Q.  What are your future plans?

A.  I've been asked to write some plays and probably will.
    And yet, I'm still "suspicious" of the theatre. I keep
    thinking of it as a type of escape mechanism.

## JEAN VAUTHIER

*Interviewer's Note:*

Jean Vauthier was born in Liége, Belgium, in 1910. His father, an engineer who specialized in bridge building, travelled to Russia, Portugal, and throughout France and Belgium. In 1920 the family settled in Bordeaux, Madame Vauthier's native city. Following the regular course of study at the lycée, Jean soon began to write poetic essays, paint, and develop a love for the theatre. In 1933, he enrolled at the Ecole des Beaux-Arts; five years later, he set out to earn his living as a journalist and illustrator. He devoted his spare time to painting and writing, and at night he worked at various jobs in the theatre.

In 1951, Vauthier's play, *The Impromptu of Arras,* was produced by André Reybaz at the Festival of Arras and a year later, Reybaz directed at the Théâtre de Poche in Paris *Captain Bada* which was awarded the Ibsen prize. In 1953, Gérard Philippe directed and acted in *The New Mandrake* at the Théâtre National Populaire. Jean-Louis Barrault produced *The Character Against Himself* in 1956 at the Marigny Theatre and that summer Jean Deninx directed Vauthier's adaptation of *Romeo and Juliet* at the Festival of Blois. *The Prodigies* opened in 1957 at the Staatstheater in Kassel, Germany, and was directed by Max Fischel. Four years later, Georges Vitaly produced *The*

*Dreamer* at the Théâtre La Bruyère in Paris. That same
year marked the completion of Vauthier's movie scenario
*The Abysses*. *Blood* was produced in 1970 at the   TNP
and in 1972, an adaptation of Marlowe's *The Massacre of
Paris* opened at the new TNP in Lyons and was directed
by Patrice Chereau.

Q.   How were you first drawn to the theatre?  What was
     your first play?

A.   An  intellectual  climate  has  existed  now  for  many
     years which prevents one from speaking simply, even
     if it is only to say "hello." I am incapable of this.
     You are asking me to reveal my innermost secrets:
     this is much more trying than it appears to be, be-
     cause, I must confess, unfortunately, of the difficulty
     I have in collecting my ideas: I can only give them
     life.  Not only does an evil demon flood me with a
     feeling of immodesty when I probe into my intimate
     thoughts, but I do not like to pretend that analysis,
     in general, interests me, and because of this, I have
     become  incapable  of  commenting  on  a  play  after
     having written it. This is a bit restricting.
         Thank God I know exactly what to say to actors
     and how to sweat in order to make a text become ef-
     fective,  so  that  the  spectator,  at  certain  moments,
     will rise ever so slightly from his seat, and no longer
     be  capable  of  controlling  his  breathing.  After  all,
     isn't  it  reassuring  to  know  that  neither  Molière  nor
     Shakespeare  ever  wrote  treatises  on  the  theatre  or
     philosophical  works  based  on  the  ideas  of  great
     deceased  philosophers.  To  each  his  own  domain.
     Once  again,  what  is  really  special  in  my  case  and
     very  disturbing  to  me  is  that  a  car  washer  knows
     better how to comment on the theatre than I do. But
     let's try anyway.
         I think that what drew me — my first impulse —

toward the theatre was the esplanade of the basilica
at Lourdes. It was a place for pilgrimages. I was
ten years old at the time. 40,000 people assembled
on the esplanade. There they responded to a priest
who was talking — whose voice carried without the
help of electronic devices— by merely opening his
mouth wide and turning it skyward. He gave so much
of himself in his loud shoutings adressed to the Holy
Virgin that he would dart forward and leave the earth.
He was alone, in the sun, standing upon acres of
land.

I accompanied the stretcher upon which my paralyzed brother was lying. The crowd applauded violently when every now and then a paralytic tore himself from his stretcher and knelt before the host which
had just passed before him. All of this, every year,
had a profound effect upon me. But later, the prayers
said in common were carried electrically. As far as
I am concerned, priests holding a microphone before
them have disavowed part of their function. The one
who, years before, had shouted out and had left the
earth was the noblest, the most respectable, the most
genial of actors I have ever known. All honors go to
him whose name I do not know.

My life? I really cannot say. It was a daily
struggle against a lack of money and, later on, against
suspicion. I wrote at night during my adolescent
years and later on too. Courage and virtue, erecting
their monuments about me, stirred me to write. I am
innocent. I mean by this I was really not responsible
for the potential courage and effort which came forth
from me later on. The difficulties, and this is true
for many artists, appeared only later on, in stages,
and not as a united and profound front. First, I bat-
tled with myself, then with others, unable to see
problems arising. I was convinced only of the sacred
nature and the rapture of human genius as bequeathed

to us. To put it more precisely, I had thought, and
for a long time in an obtuse way, that it was only a
question of mastering myself each day, of acquiring
and of producing. Could I have suspected that great
actors work poorly unless forced to, that money regu-
lates the destiny of works, that audiences, even
intellectual ones, are frivolous, that great causes
are tantamount to madness? In brief, that every day
reality exists? My best recipe was probably not
knowing all this.

There is one play that I wrote in one stretch;
since then I reworked it and began it over again:
*Captain Bada*.

Q.  Are you Parisian, from the north or from the south of
France?

A.  Certain relatives on my father's side were Belgians.
My mother, on the other hand, came from the south of
France, from Bordeaux. Perhaps this makes for contrast. I feel I come from the south of this country.
But what difference does it make? What is essential
is that I have given only a third of what I want to
give — and we must die. But there is still time ...

Q.  You seem to be tortured by the question of religion.
This seems most particularly true in *The Prodigies*.
In that play are you both attracted and repelled by
religion?

A.  Am I really tortured by religion in *The Prodigies?*
The character Marc could raise such a question.
He swerves from pitiable hatred to love; and this is
achieved through humorous as well as tragic means.
But Marc's conversion remains suspect. He *pours*
himself into religion. One should remain skeptical
concerning the solidity of his conversion. My friend,

Claude-Henri Rocquet, is sitting with us. Let him speak.

R. It is true. I have already noted how religious anxiety explodes in certain of Vauthier's plays. But I prefer using the word "sacred" to that of "religion" or "mystique." A feeling for the "sacred," in my opinion, appears in Vauthier's works by means of "hollows." These "hollows" permit things to stand out in relief. The notion of profanation plays a part in his work. A word Vauthier sometimes uses when talking is "scoffing" *(bafouement).*

A. This word does not exist in the French language.

R. That does not matter. Vauthier's heroes until now are "scoffed-at-heroes," and it even happens that they, in turn, scoff at what they respect — deep down in their souls. To scoff is to add adoration to profanation ...

A. A religious anxiety is not scoffed at in my play, *The Prodigies.*

R. No, but your work, until now, strives to paint a world where diverse types of "scoffings" reign. Vauthier is interested in the world of the Sacred. This world is martyrized, scoffed at. Now, religion is the opposite extreme of "scoffing." Certainly, the anxiety experienced by Vauthier's characters — between "Scoffing" and "Praying" — comes from him and, therefore, represents certain aspects of himself. Mrs. Knapp, and rightly so, asked **Vauthier** in what way **he** **was** "both attracted and repelled by religion." Vauthier answers that he sees nothing higher or more beautiful, more real, than Christ, and if he does not implore his help, it is because he feels

himself to be unworthy of Him.  I believe that in a
world suffering greatly from gangrene and in which
the existence of apostles of a higher cause is barely
permitted, Vauthier thinks that one must exist, touch,
win practical victories, attract a cluster of powers
toward a zone leading to the soul.  One of Vauthier's
greatest sorrows is the state of neglect in which
contemporary theatre finds itself.  Directors employ
all their efforts to slanting his works, to making them
impure, and thereby pleasing audiences; but only
part of the impurity present in his plays is due, perhaps, to sudden outbursts in his frantic attempt to
rise above, to struggle against the "diabolical," to
gather strength in order to begin his work of combat.
I believe Vauthier began to realize this program with
*The Prodigies*.  **This play shows the "wretchedness"**
**of   intellectual   pride   and   vulgar   voluptuousness.**


Q.   Critics have mentioned the fact that your "poetic and
     symbolic theatre" is reminiscent of Rimbaud and
     Baudelaire's works.   Would you say this is true?
     If so, in what way?

A.   I admire them profoundly.   But when I was writing I
     was unaware of undergoing any such influences.   It
     is correct to say, however, that the great enthusiasms
     of youth leave profound impressions upon the ad-
     mirer.

R.   In my opinion, one can compare Rimbaud, Baudelaire
     and Vauthier.   Forgive me for quoting myself but
     during a public lecture (a "debate") devoted to *The*
     *Character Against Himself* and organized as a result
     of the Barrault production of this play, I got up and
     said that "...if Rimbaud is a mystic in a savage
     state, the Character in *The Character Against Him-*

*self* is a mystic in a civilized state." These words pleased Jacques Lemarchand of the *Figaro Littéraire.* It is true that Rimbaud's words "Purity, purity, dangerous misfortune ...." could very well be the cry of Vauthier's *The Character Against Himself.* And, on the other hand, the effort deployed by Vauthier's characters to become ennobled to the point of being able to experience an arch-angelical vision of the world can be found in Rimbaud. Baudelaire also searched for the sacred. He is also the poet of the *cité,* of the city. If Rimbaud searched for an exotic and paradisiac vision of life, Baudelaire establishes his vision in the very interior of the city. And neither does Vauthier flee from reality: he is one with the modern world. Against what does the Character struggle? Against erotic magazines found daily in the kiosques. In Vauthier's *The Character Against Himself,* one again finds Baudelaire's city world. It is striking to note that The Character tries to experience the notion of the divine by fighting with simple, modern, every-day objects. The mediocre and banal in this play serve Vauthier's purpose. I repeat: it is through them that he can express himself.

Q. What was your attitude toward the Jean-Louis Barrault production of *The Character Against Himself?* Were you present at the rehearsals? Were there any problems involved? Do you feel that Barrault did justice to the interpretation?

A. I feel that Barrault never acted with greater genius than he did when he played *The Character Against Himself.* The critics wrote: "We again find the twenty-year-old Barrault, the one who acted in *Hunger,* in *Numance,* in *As I Lay Dying ....*" Barrault lost seven kilos during rehearsals when he worked with

me.   During the performances he was always in a
state of extreme tension.  I found it natural to require
the maximum from him.

Q.   Did Barrault realize the great amount of effort necessary to portray the role of the Character before rehearsals began?

A.   Not completely.  We lived tragic weeks and months.
He fortunately possesses a heroic temperament and
a sporting conception of his work.  What frequently
bridled him, as far as his artistic life was concerned,
were his terrible commercial imperatives, the insufficient state aids.  You realize how dangerous these
obstacles can be in the career of a director and
interpreter – and can reduce an author to a tenth of
his power.   So far as Barrault was concerned, we
knew that a well-filled house was necessary if a
beautiful and difficult work such as Claudel's *The
Satin Slipper* could be given.  But in spite of a well-
filled house, deficits still appeared.   That is why
facile plays, traditional **successes**, preceeded and
followed Claudel.  We all know that a worthy theatre
can exist only if supported by Maecenas or by the
State. ''To support'' means: to make good all deficits.
Barrault approached the difficult role of The
Character in *The Character Against Himself* tranquilly,
as though he were making his way toward the enemy
camp.   But once caught in the vice of the first rehearsals it was as though death had made its way on
stage and was observing the imprudent one at close
range.  Plays are usually sustained by the text.  Now,
this was not the only thing which counted: the Echo
had to be permitted to live; one had to know how to
be silent and watch the things around one come into
being, yes, to listen to the echo.  This text swarming
with breaks had to be spoken with twenty different

virtuosities – not for only a few minutes, but for
two hours and forty minutes. In most of the traditional plays we know there are "peaks," a few
great scenes (and sometimes only one) when the
actor approaches his maxima: after which there are
zones of "repose." Besides, the director conditioned
the actor's comportment. And the sonorous quality
of the recording either permitted or did not permit
the actor to respond and justify his acting. He had
to stay on stage without casting the slightest shadow
of insincere acting. He had to also become truly
physically exhausted – if he didn't, the unsteadiness
necessitated in certain scenes would remain in the
domain of artistic fiction. Now, fiction was almost
always used, but at this anticipated moment, beauty
required the act to be real. And so, Barrault tottered
because his strength was really faltering. And at the
end of the performance, he said to me back stage:
"Did you see, did you see? I was really unsteady,
I was going to fall." A doctor was giving him in-
jections at the time. Ever since the first rehearsals
we felt a mixture of love and hate for one another.

I felt that it was right for Barrault to exhaust
himself. My whole life had been nourished by examples of voluntary exhaustion – from an excess of
devotion to my art. I did not feel that felicitations
were in order. To congratulate the interpreter, I felt,
was to attempt to debase his honor. He was doing
his duty: does one dare congratulate somebody for
being honest? Would not this suppose that he might
not be? I thought, therefore, only about one thing:
to gather together all the imperfections I found with
his work and bring them to the attention of the interpreter. I would forget none of them in this way,
his devotion would attain its logical norm, that is to
say, it would be total. Each intonation, each vocal
nuance was worked on ... It had to be that way.

Can you imagine Bach or Schumann neglecting something; or their interpreters forgetting a single note?
Are there any enduring monuments or exceptional
lives which are not completely themselves, without
scoria?   And isn't it an admitted fact that the sacrifice of life has been frequently practiced for the sake
of the work of art?

   *The Character Against Himself* was a success.
In Paris there were twelve curtain calls nightly.   At
the Berlin Festival, with Barrault acting the Character, the curtain went up **thirty-seven** times.   In
Zurich, **twenty-seven** times.   I remember with a smile
how anguished we were during those last hours.
Even after the basic cuts had been made, it appeared
that another fifteen minutes had to be cut.   There was
little time to make these cuts; the hours were counted.
I knew that if this quarter of an hour were omitted,
the play would lose its internal cohesion.   As the
moment for the sacrifice was about to take place — I
fainted.   This fainting spell saved everything.   Barrault was delighted.   Then I too could grow weak
physically?   He gave me back my fifteen minutes.
After that he was in a state of jubilation.

   I seem to remember that during one rehearsal he
was on the verge of striking me — and I him; at least
pushing each other around.   He gripped me tightly
around the neck.   I was ready for all rash acts; effort
is frequently expended in a fit of rage.   We loved
each other.

   At that time, I still had some family left, a **house**
in which my paralyzed brother lived, a garden, my
dog, an old servant.   Many years had been lost, but
pathetically so, in a kind of glory.   I had exhausted
myself with the trips I made from Bordeaux to Paris
which took seven hours.   I had made one hundred
and fifty of those trips.   What time was wasted!
I have never retrieved these losses and consider

myself somewhat degraded. I no longer possess what
upheld me at the time: the places of martyrdom no
longer exist for me, the lair and the love, the great
mass of difficulties. My mother is dead. My brother
also ... the servant ... the dog...

Q. How would you sum up both Bada's and George's attitude toward and problems with women?

A. Your question makes me realize even better how much
man's need for woman is more a sign of their weakness
rather than their strength. Women are complex beings;
Georges in *The Dreamer* is a timid type. To conclude
from this that his timidity is disguised homosexuality
would be foolish. If Georges abandons his poetic
conscience and his throbbing poetic obsession (which
makes for his vulnerability), he would become a great
woman chaser.

R. Recently you agreed that the roles of Alice (*Captain
Bada*) or of Laurette (*The Dreamer*) are female counter-
parts of masculine characters. The latter is not
capable of giving sufficient love. And the feminine
character does not really understand the masculine
character — and he, in turn, does not make the necessary effort to try to be understood. One notices with
Vauthier that, up until now, the woman is an obstacle
to the male's dream: she is negative; and only becomes positive when identified with the dream of the
masculine character. The woman in *The Dreamer*
certainly plays a part, but attains prestige only because she remains inaccessible in the hero's mind.
Georges prefers to return the wife to her husband—that
is to say, to the exterior world.

Vauthier's characters are tightly bound up with
a state of childhood. Such a state of affairs may be
interpreted in two ways: on the one hand they are

psychologically immature — and this reference to
childhood reveals itself in the work and heart of
most creators to a greater or lesser degree. They
have an emotional need for their mother. This tendency also reveals a nostalgia for purity. Rimbaud
refused to become an adult — or, at least, when he
reached this state, he refused to remain a writer.
One can say that Vauthier's characters require women
to know how to cradle their dreams. But the adult
woman, the woman-woman, places man in a position
where he must also assume adulthood and from that
time on she is a menace to man's childhood.

Q.   You make use of the painter's colors and the musi-
     cian's notes in your theatre. Would you then call
     your theatre a meeting ground for the arts?

A.  No, no...

R.   In Vauthier's plays there are, obviously, unconscious
     references to the art of music and, at the same time,
     the characters in his works speak of their need for
     music (and this to the point of its becoming an obses-
     sion); finally, music is used again and again in the
     very workings of the play itself. Mrs. Knapp is right
     in asking this question. Vauthier's plays are *seen*
     (as a painter sees) in a precise fashion. Vision as
     much as concept is essential in the creation of his
     plays. One must, because of this, remain faithful to
     these elements when staging the play. And this must
     be carried to the extreme and include all the elements
     usually considered as mere accessories. For ex-
     ample, in *The Character Against Himself*, the locale
     has already been constructed and the play can func-
     tion only if this locale is able to restore the author's
     vision. His Character reacts to certain given things
     and these reactions would be false were these certain

things to be neglected.

A.  This is one of the reasons for my difficulties. A great
    **number of directors, perhaps** because they are not
    rigorous enough in their approach, settle for the fol-
    lowing: "I shall create something very personal out
    of this rich text." Music? I think I'm a menace to
    the person who does not like music. He will find it
    more difficult than others not to become base and
    solemn.

    Music was an important force in my life. I used
    to go to concerts in Bordeaux. Then during my child-
    hood and adolescent years, the family piano acted as
    an uplifting force in our lives. I am speaking of
    music **which ennobles,** which grows, and blooms each
    time it is performed, in a faulty manner at first, then
    much improved until it has reached a state of per-
    fection; music which is approached in a spirit of
    piety and joy, broken down, worked on eight hours a
    day for no other reason but beauty.

    There was a period in my life when I learned
    the language of painting. For years now, however,
    I have lost contact with this art which I had so loved.

Q.  Do you feel that your notations in your texts substitute
    for the work of the director? Where does your work as
    author subside and that of the director begin? What
    is the *direct* relation between author and actor?

A.  At the outset, the director is enormously careful to
    maintain a good rapport with the author. He is, there-
    fore, sincerely pleasant. As the work proceeds,
    however, his dependency becomes more and more
    pronounced and hatred takes over. Finally, when the
    director becomes master of the play, the feeling of
    having once asked for help becomes intolerable. He
    considers any kind of direction, which he nevertheless

continues to solicit, an insult. Finally, ten or fifteen
days before the opening, when he thinks he can go
ahead alone — at the precise moment when the form-
less can be transformed, when the work, thanks to an
excess of rigorousness, surges forth — this man is
seized with a desire to find fault with the author and
any method is good to force him to expiate for having
written the text being enacted. This is an enormous
mistake: it is like refusing last minute training before
the march.

Now, in terms **of the musicality of my texts, my**
intimate contact with the piano — I used to play it —
left an indelible mark upon me. The pianist, like
all great musicians, repeats his part over and over
again, as frequently as necessary. At the end of his
life his technique has diminished; his repetitions,
therefore, become excessive. But his preoccupation
with beauty remains.

Actors must work terribly hard to portray a role —
at least in my plays — to satisfaction. I remember
an incident which occurred at a certain Festival. I
had to deal with a mediocre actor. After four weeks
of good and intense work we had reached that famous
period when the actor must work even harder in order
to give himself and the entire production class. And
so, he hardly worked at all and tasted the voluptuous
pleasure of enticing danger. Of the four hours set
aside for rehearsals, one hour was lost by his lateness
and the following two hours were spent chatting, like
a concierge with a neighbor. The usual topic of his
chats was the different ways of making love. His
eye scanned the theatre trying to search me out in
order to savor the moment when I would be ready to
burst. And when I reproached him he threatened to
work only fifteen minutes if I kept on insisting. And
when I finally did burst out, he left the theatre in a
dignified manner, thereby avoiding the fifteen minutes

which remained.

To return to your initial question. No, alas, my printed stage directions are not sufficient to guide the actor nor orient the director since both find reading distasteful, particularly texts printed in italics. I can assure you, however, that I shall be the winner. This is inevitable. I shall learn to write works which will require less effort, less precision and less rigorousness on the part of the interpreters. My roles will call for young actors, for how can one make a hardened actor pliable? Besides, the young actor has not yet gotten into the habit of living on a grand scale and is frequently still supported by his parents. He has not yet been mobilized by the movies, nor weighed down by television or recording for the radio. He has the time to devote to his work and does not consider a play a luxury, something which definitely guarantees his artistic standing vis-à-vis the diminished number of intellectuals. The young actor needs to reveal himself to the world before he can prostitute himself by reading his text at sight for the radio.

Q. Where does the work of the director begin?

A. Well, he waits for the author to finish inventing and then he hurries to begin his work right after that.

What is really unfortunate is that I have never considered myself anything but a servant, a "postulant," and that those who serve the Theatre want the word "creator" to be printed on their visiting card. There is not a being in the world who does not create if courage and faith exist.

Q. How important is the "subtext" (that is: action not expressed in words) in your work? Have you consciously worked for a theatre in which words are mere surfaces and actions are true essences?

A.  When I write my dialogues I am a prey to two contra-
    dictory states.   On the one hand I organize in a
    minute fashion both the ensemble and the details;
    all is premeditated and therefore requires an utmost
    amount of lucidity.  But, on the other hand, I let "my"
    destiny carry me along...because I believe in some
    crazy way in a type of infallibility.  This deference
    to intuition precedes the creation of the dialogue and
    develops along with it.  "To search for" means to
    view things consciously and this implies limiting
    oneself.  I must have the feeling of receiving and
    going out to meet.  Yes, all is constantly "subtext"
    but the words; the dialogue can be allusive as well
    as direct.  They prepare for the ensuing scenic
    climate and, of course, take into account the reper-
    cussions created upon the presumed finale.  All
    systems would render me sterile.

R.  Vauthier's theatre is obviously the theatre of a con-
    centric world: the word touches the surface and is
    then swallowed up, only to make way for the ensuing
    eddies and ripples.  The word is never anything else
    but a way of going beyond the word.  One can say
    that Vauthier's language is intimately linked to
    gesture — a type of dance which asks of words to
    remain with it and to determine the gestures which
    are to follow.  The visible and the audible are only
    means of going more deeply into the primal quality of
    things.  The same can be said for those created
    silences: they are filled with all exterior and interior
    noises and compete in finding the key to man and to
    the world in which he stands erect.

Q.  Certain themes recur throughout your work: the artist
    versus society, man versus woman, violence.  Have

you picked these themes because they seem to ex-
emplify something particularly important to us today?

A.   The themes in my plays are proof enough of the fact
that I am inhabited by these subjects — but I am almost unaware of this.

"The artist versus society" certainly plays a
part in *Captain Bada* and *The Dreamer*. For me, it
was a question of an uncontrollable impulse. After
reflection, however, I feel that the statement should
be reversed. It's society which is against the artist,
against what should be the best of itself.

"Man versus woman?" But no. I have seen so
many women in whom both grace and charity were
combined; and many others, less admirable, but sufficiently protected from harm so as to be in a position
to preserve the world's ferment. So that I do not feel
the slightest need of placing men and women in
enemy camps. I am only strict (frenetic, perhaps)
about one point — about those who make a caricature
out of their sex. One may perhaps say that my hopes
(and those of other men too) have been smashed, for
by considering woman as sacred, we make frenzied
demands upon them, whereas we readily admit masculine failings. Within the framework of my personal
experience, I have met with many obstacles on the
part of women. Yet, without them there is nothing.

"Violence?" Yes, but I was not thinking of this.
It seems to me that today the artist is aroused more
easily by violence than he was yesterday. Misfortune,
plus sudden outrageous attacks upon one render those
who are worthy of living violent. Even in small
matters: I become violent when I see someone only
pretending to listen; and if it is true that the contemporary era has become an obstacle to the creation
of beauty equal to that of the past, my suppressed
violence accumulates, and passes into what I write.

I must say that impulsive urges have something about them which elicits a smile. It would be dangerous for me to separate myself from my own, to the point of being able to look at them and judge them.

Q. If you had to describe your theatre in a few sentences, what would you say?

R. Vauthier's theatre is a "mystic" search, a search for the sacred and for the secret of man, and, at the same time, he possesses the dramatist's desire to organize the totality of the theatre's forces. Vauthier's plays are not a series of "short stories;" in his theatre stage and gesture play a predominant role.

Q. Your characters often seem to have a wooden, puppet-like quality, somewhat like the characters of *King Ubu* (Jarry). If you are not aiming for "naturalistic characterization," what are you aiming for?

R. Marionettes ... fetishes rather, or symbolic figures, stiff like statues or sacred marionettes. Such mario-nettes exist in certain magic or religious traditions. It is obvious that Vauthier, until now, has not been drawn to "naturalistic characterizations." It would, perhaps, be possible to perform his play, *The Dreamer,* within the same framework as the Boulevard plays.

A. I do not believe so because it does not have the same resources that a Boulevard play has.

R. At least if one tried to play it as a Boulevard comedy, its psychological and social aspects would still be there ... but this certainly would be a betrayal, yes, indeed, a profound betrayal. The play would be skin-ned, become an anecdote, a *passe-temps*; Vauthier's characters would be stripped of their inner patina,

the patina of the dream. If one removes the oneiro-
critical proliferations which reign in his work, what
would remain of this play could be described as "the
portrait of a dreamer," a young dreamer at grips with
a radio producer — but, at the same time, this would
make for a terribly banal evening in the theatre.
Whereas Vauthier, basing himself on **every-day** reality,
has **realized** an inner truth, that is, that reality has
been freed and becomes one with aesthetic truth.

Q. Can you tell us something about your mode of creation
   — that is, how you go about writing your plays?

A. I take notes on scraps of paper long before I begin
   writing a play. Then I group these pieces of paper
   according to the melodic lines which come to me
   before and during my work. The vision of the various
   attitudes guides me and constitutes an imaginary
   stage of corporeal symbols imbricated one upon the
   other which either provoke or accompany language.
   I let things come forth from a type of reservoir. Until
   now, exterior action in my plays has been reduced to
   a minimum.
   　　Because of sickness and various other commit-
   ments, *The Character Against Himself* took two and
   a half years to write. And yet, this text was conceived in a very short time. I remember I was on a
   road, on my motorcycle, in the Landes (Gironde). I
   was thinking of the disappointing production the
   **Théâtre** National Populaire had given of my last
   play ... and that I must write something else "immediately, in three months." I remembered a short
   story I had written formerly. I had to admit to the
   fact that this story could not be staged. Yet, before
   reaching the next turning point in the road, I thought
   it would be possible to "take it up again" and turn
   it into theatre. But how to go about this? If I re-

wrote the "short story" in order to be able to lean on something solid, would I be capable of preserving its freshness?  And while I was thinking that I couldn't — no — I looked at the next turn in the road with a sense of satisfaction, because the play which I wanted to create had suddenly come into being with the assumption "no".  It existed mid-way between its former state and the one to which I would now devote myself.  The theme of *The Character Against Himself* is the following: the drama of the artist who has acquired ability but who is terrified at the thought of not having been able to preserve his youthful ferment.

Two and a half years later it was finished.  One of my Parisian friends gave it to Jean-Louis Barrault to read.  He sent for me the following morning just as I was about to leave for the railroad station on my way back to Bordeaux.

**The subject for *The Prodigies* came to me in the train and was sustained by a classical musical** theme which I permitted to flow forth from me freely while softly tapping my foot **during** the entire trip.

Q.   Are your plays related or linked together in some way?  Is there a common denominator between them?

R.   Vauthier's plays are related to one another by characters caught in their own trap, weighted down by their organs as much as by their awareness of the exterior world.  They are tempted by the desire of incorruptibility and yet are held back by the flesh, by life, by a frequently exacerbated, indeed, vulgar daily existence.  They are obsessed by the imminence of a transfigured world; they are acted upon only through their martyrdom.  Vauthier's characters are living out the drama of those who have been unable to find a way of enlightening the world by their gaze.

They are awaiting confusedly the light and the instant of their death. At night these insomniacs are tragically haunted by day and, contradictorily, long for sleep as much as they do for dawn.

Q. You wrote a scenario, *The Abysses,* for the cinema. What can the film industry offer you that the stage cannot?

A. I was happy to write this film scenario because it gave me the opportunity to work in great detail on the *mise en scène.* The minute work involved led me to use several recording machines and not to write the scenario at first. I would make the improvements first on one machine then on the other. I was pleased when this text was no longer just a mass of words recorded on tape—when it was transformed into a typed manuscript. It took me five months — 280 hours on my machines — to create *The Abysses,* three hours reading time.

All the resources offered me by the cinema, its richness, the immense seductive nature of this art, are not, nevertheless, sufficient to lure me away from the theatre.

We wish to thank the editors of *First Stage* for permission to reprint in part the above interview (Vol. 4, no. 3).

## MARGUERITE DURAS

*Interviewer's Note:*

Marguerite Duras, whose parents were teachers, was born
in 1914 in Saigon (French **Indo-China**). She attended the
French Lycée there until the age of eighteen, then moved
to Paris where she took courses in mathematics, **political**
science and attended law school. After receiving her
"Licence in Law" she was employed as secretary in the
Colonial Ministry (1935-1941) and soon started writing.
Her first novel, *The Imprudents*, was written in 1942.
From this time on her fame and popularity have increased
steadily with such plays as *The Viaducts of the Seine
and Oise* (1960), *The Square* (1965), *The Musica* (1965),
*L'Amante anglaise* (1967); film **scenarios:** *The Sailor
from Gibraltar* (1952), *Hiroshima mon amour* (1959), *Destroy, She Said* (1969); novels such as *Moderato Cantabile*
(1958), *Ten Thirty on a Summer Night* (1960), *Abahn
Sabana David* (1970), etc. Marguerite Duras' unique talent
lies in her ability to capture a sensation, a thought, a
feeling in a dazzling poetic image. Man's dual aspect is
revealed in this manner: his surface tranquility, reflect-
ing the banality of his daily existence and his inner world,
turbulent, tremulous, seething with unchanneled instinctu-
ality. Marguerite Duras has assimilated the Oriental's
ability to remain detached from the subject under discus-

sion; to exercise extremely delicate sensibility in the appraisal of situations and relationships; to refine ever more discreetly that tenuous line between the illusory and the real.

Q.   Your childhood seems to have marked your works deeply.   Can you tell us about your early years?

A.   It's difficult for me to talk about that period in my life. My father died when I was very young.   My mother was extremely poor.   She was a teacher in a native Vietnamese school.   After my father's death she used up her meager savings to buy a large government concession — a kind of land development scheme. When it came time to plant the rice we realized only too late that nothing would grow in this area.   Each year, during high tides (which come with the equinox), the sea floods the entire land mass in this region. The rice we had planted died.   My mother had bought a kind of lagoon with her life savings. We had nothing left.

What my mother did not realize was that large sums of money had to be given to the white civil servant in order to be able to purchase fertile land. She was ruined.   I was twelve years old then.   Because of my mother's extreme poverty she became a kind of Vietnamese.   She was closer to the Vietnamese then she was to the whites.   We were never received by the whites, socially that is, since we were members of the last rung on the social ladder.

And this fantastic, fabulous injustice which had been done to my mother was probably the most traumatic experience in my life.   To have seen my mother weep, go mad with grief; to be disdained by everyone, hounded by creditors — to have to sell every last thing.   In fact, during our rest hour, my mother used to send me to the local Chinese jewlers to sell

whatever baubles we had left. With that money we
bought a little meat for our evening meal. It was the
first time I knew the meaning of injustice — and
equality at the same time. My mother, as I said
before, had become a sort of Vietnamese peasant
woman. We lived with the Vietnamese, completely.
I spoke Vietnamese almost better than I did French.
These are my *childhood riches*.

I left Vietnam after passing my Baccalaureate
examinations. I went to Paris and have never returned to Vietnam. I cannot go back. It I ever do
return it will be to write something on the war there.
But so many people are going to do just that these
days. I still have a kind of horror for this childhood
of mine.

As far as my writing is concerned, I am still
haunted or mesmerized by the type of mono-landscape
in Vietnam. The flatness and dullness of the plains
which I used to see as a child all over Indo-China
still live within me. Perhaps this is why I do not
like mountains even today .... Indo-China offers a
kind of hallucinatory landscape; long stretches of
rice fields, swamps ....

Q. Are your novels autobiographical?

A. The most autobiographical from the point of view of
events or facts is *A Dam Against the Pacific;* from
the point of view of an inner experience, it is *Moderato
Cantabile.* That is why I had to camouflage the events
and transform them into poetic form which *Moderato
Cantabile* really is. It is not written as a novel —
rather a poem.

Q. Are you an existentialist?

A. I don't really know. I wouldn't want to be. I don't

like Sartre. I don't mean as a thinker, but as a writer. It's very difficult for me to talk about Sartre. After all, he is, to a certain extent, the father of us all. Politically speaking, Sartre, Simone de Beauvoir and I, all think the same way. We always sign the same manifestoes – and together. We set aside our literary quarrels when it comes to politics.

Q. How do you create suspense in your novels, plays and film scenarios? Do you have a special technique?

A. I really don't know how I create suspense. I do not believe I do. Perhaps it's because I have no preconceived notions in terms of the story-line. I never make an outline of what I am going to write. I just start writing – sometimes even from the middle of a novel or play. In fact, the search for a theme or evolution of the protagonists becomes part of the book. I never know what is going to take place – never. The search itself provokes additional research and this research in turn is inscribed in the literary work. Actually, the play writes itself. What audiences are viewing on stage is really a piece of research work.

Q. Why do you portray only one part or aspect of a character rather than the human being as a whole?

A. To paint a character in his or her entirety, as Balzac did, no longer is of interest to any modern writer – or perhaps only to the conventional one. I feel that a *sign* or a *symbol*, or the description of one facet of a human being or of an event (and there is a profound affinity in this connection with abstract painting) is much more striking than a total description. In the play *The Viaducts of the Seine and Oise,* the protagonists are fluid or primastic beings; the atmosphere is a

blend of reality and phantasmagoria. Delineations
seem to vanish in terms of the protagonists and the
events recounted. You never know why the couple
committed the crime; as for the evidence, it is given
out in shreds, here and there.

Q.   Your characters are not only vulnerable, they are half
     mad or even really insane. Take the protagonists in
     *L'Amante anglaise*, guilty, or perhaps not, of having
     committed a murder.

A.   I only like vulnerable people. I think they are the
     only ones really alive. Sensitivity, as far as I am
     concerned, begins when one human being can suffer
     for another as much as he suffers for himself — even
     more so.

Q.   Why do most of your characters experience a progres-
     sive loss of identity? Your film scenario, *Destroy,
     She Said*, illustrates this point to perfection.

A.   A progressive loss of identity is the most desirable
     experience one can know. This type of corrosion or
     destruction of a personality is of great interest to me
     at this point. The faculty of being able to lose sight
     of one's identity, to witness the delusion or fragmen-
     tation of a personality.... That is why the question
     of insanity always tempts me in my **work**: in my novel
     *The Ravishing of Lol V. Stein*, for example, or *The
     Vice-Consul*. We all suffer from this loss of identity
     today — this splintering of a personality. It is the
     most widespread disease there is — but it's a good
     one.

Q.   Why are your plays — and I might add your novels and
     film scenarios — always so slowly paced?

A. I really don't choose such and such a pace or tempo for my work. The tempo is regulated by the conversations of the protagonists (which really follow a pattern of their own) and by the events taking place. This may or may not be true at the outset of the particular work, but as the play or novel unfolds, everything that happens takes on the rhythms of the conversations and events therein. Conversations cannot be curtailed or summarized.

Q. What were the circumstances which led you to write for the theatre?

A. People asked me to write for the theatre. I never thought of doing that on my own. Claude Martin helped me with my first adaptation of *The Square* (1960). The production, unfortunately, was rather weak. Since *The Square* consists of a series of dialogues without any action or plot, I thought that one hour and a half was long enough for the play. I was wrong. I rewrote the adaptation which was produced in Paris (1965) and this time the play lasted for two and a half hours. It was fuller and yet retained the fluid quality inherent in the very atmosphere of the drama. One should always try to face one's mistakes.

Q. Do you attend rehearsals? Do you participate in them or does the director handle everything himself?

A. I usually attend the first few rehearsals of my plays. Then I become terribly bored with them.

I directed the film version of *The Musica*. Since I did everything myself I must admit I was not the least bit bored. I was not witnessing something — or sitting back and observing. I participated in the work in progress. Besides, I got along very well with Delphine Seyrig, a little less well with Robert Hossein, a mysogonist who did not like being directed by a woman, I am afraid.

Q.  What is the function of dialogue in *The Square* and *The Musica*, works in which action is almost non-existent?

A.  *The Square* is a political discourse.  It is about a human being (a maid) who has reached the lowest rung of the social ladder, which corresponds, politically speaking, to the *lumpen proletariat*.  Because of her condition or position, she is the living example of what Marx meant when he outlined his theory of need.  This girl has actually created her own personal revolution and at the same time has become somewhat of a revolutionary doctrinaire.  But naturally in an empirical sense.  The dialogue in *The Square* is a very special one, highly ceremonious, totally anti-realistic.  And certain people have criticized me for this kind of dialogue and foolishly so.  Since the two characters in *The Square* (the traveling salesman and the maid) are in the lowest strata of society which never have the possibility of speaking out, of expressing their thoughts even in terms of generalities, I created a very special language for them; concise, almost theatrical, with a tempo or beat of its own.

  *The Musica* is different.  In this play the language I used was realistic.  The theme: the impossibility of love.  *The Musica* tells the story of a man and a woman who had sued for divorce three years before.  They see each other for the last time one evening in a hotel at Evreux in **Normandy,** the very night when the divorce decree is to be awarded.  They talk about their past, their story, the love they once had lived.  As they speak of these things, they realize that their love still exists; that it has been hidden by quarrels and by marriage. *The Musica* is a story about lovers — people who were never meant to be man and wife. Now, since their marriage has been dissolved, love again reappears.

What The Woman suggests in *The Musica* is the impossibility of living love, when she says to The Man: "If we ever meet again, it will be pure chance." Love then, which is never lived, unlivable and impossible—is true love.

Q. What did you think of Madeleine Renaud's interpretation of the role of the Mother in your play *Entire Afternoons Spent in the Trees?*

A. This play is so autobiographical that I hardly have the impression of having written it. I do not feel responsible for this work: it is so very close to the events I lived through with my own mother and brother.

I was accustomed to watching the actors rehearse in street clothes. When I saw Madeleine Renaud appear — shortly before the opening — in her costume, I was terribly shocked. I had the distinct impression that my mother was walking out on stage at the Odéon theatre to play out her life before me. It was a hallucinatory experience. I feel that Madeleine Renaud is an immense actress.

Q. Can you tell us something about the genesis of your cinematographic career? What attracted you to the film industry?

A. I took no steps whatsoever in that direction. Resnais came to see me and asked me to rework a film scenario for him. I tried to do it but failed. So I wrote a completely new scenario, *Hiroshima mon amour*. After that — since the movie was such a hit and

people the world over flocked to see it — I was asked
to write another script. I did just this.

Q.   Were you satisfied with the films based on your
     novels?

A.   I did not like *A Dam Against the Pacific. Moderato
     Cantabile* and *Ten Thirty on a Summer Night* were
     beautiful but they had nothing to do with my novel.
     I liked Jeanne Moreau in *The Sailor from Gibraltar,*
     but there were long sequences (certain comic scenes,
     conversations) which Tony Richardson cut.  I think
     the film is far too short.  Furthermore, I must say
     I did not like Orson Welles intruding into the picture
     as he did.

Q.   What about your plays *Yes, Peut-Etre* and *The Shaga?*

A.   They are comic works.  Since comedy is based almost
     **solely on language and, in this case,** on slang, they
     are really difficult to explain.  The theme is always
     the same: the strange encounter in the street of
     people who are half mad.  When I use the word mad
     I mean by this people who have lived sufficiently
     to have experienced life, but who are unable to stand
     this experience — or cannot cope with it.  These
     ''mad'' people are devoid of prejudices; they have no
     bad habits; they belong to no social class; they are
     totally free.

Reprinted, in translation, with permission of the *French
Review* (March, 1971).

## ROLAND DUBILLARD

*Interviewer's Note:*

For Roland Dubillard, author of *Naïve Swallows* (1962),
*The House of Bones* (1964), *The Beet Garden* (1969) and
other plays highly lauded by French critics, the theatre
is first and foremost a poetic realm. But poetry for
Dubillard — representative of "new theatre"— is language
which could be described as devoid of content or skirting
the banal. His dramas do not enact situations; his characters are not imbued with great passions. Indeed, his
protagonists differ from those we are accustomed to seeing
in conventional theatre. They are essences living in a
kind of anguished solitude. They express their turmoil
in the eternal present and speak with one another in a
language impregnated with dreams, silences and variegated
musical sonorities. Each word and phrase seems to usher
the spectator ever so tenderly and gently into an imaginary
world and hold him there intensely.

Q. You were influenced by such classical writers as
   Shakespeare, Molière, Racine and Corneille, as well
   as by the Surrealists. Were you also influenced by
   Artaud?

A. Yes. In the beginning, and I still am today to a certain extent. Many of us have experienced Artaud's
   tremendous personality. That was a long while back,

in 1948 — when we produced *Akara* by Romain Weingarten. That was a real "Theatre of **Cruelty**" play.
At that time I was fascinated by a strictly physical
rather than a literary theatre.

Today, however, my theatre is poetic. It is
designed to be played by actors on a real stage. It
tries to appeal and to arouse emotions — but mostly
through language. In this respect, of course, I have
strayed from Artaud's thesis. Yet, since I believe
that emotion is something quite physical and really
one of the most physical of phenomena — actually,
the most important element in a **play—I** adhere to
Artaud's theories. Unlike Artaud, however, I am
interested in literary expression: in the *word*. After
all, what one writes is usually classified as literature. He rejected verbally oriented theatre. Like
Artaud, on the other hand, I still feel that the theatrical spectacle is an *event,* rather than a representation. Something on stage must take place — something which surpasses and which is profounder than
the text itself — above and beyond it. Words are like
a passageway toward a profounder reality — amorphous, ambiguous, but ever alluring. I agree with
Artaud when he wrote that he was absolutely averse
to an intellectual theatre and to the thesis play. For
this reason, I cannot stand the theatrical works of
Sartre, Camus — and even more so of Montherlant.
Frankly, this kind of theatre bores me.

Q. What are your impressions of the so-called "communal" theatre as practiced by García, Savary and
   the Living Theatre?

A. I am totally detached from it. I have nothing to say
   about this kind of theatre. I don't have anything to
   do with these directors.

Q. Are you influenced by music?

A. Music has always played a primordial role in my work. Music is my favorite art. What I write is highly emotional as is music; it is built or structured to a certain extent as is a quartet or a symphony. Beethoven, I believe, has been the greatest musical influence in my life. I also like modern composers: Boulez, Cage and others...serial music. I play the the piano...not well, though.

Q. How do you go about writing your plays? Do you have a particular method?

A. I have no method; just a pattern, I guess. I write my plays both quickly and slowly. I mean by this that they require enormous preparation and frequently even before writing a word — I can spend a year on a play, that is, thinking about it. The work grows and organizes itself in my head. When everything has ripened, then I write the play rather rapidly.

As for the characters, that's another affair. I sometimes don't really think that I have created them. They emerge from me, to be sure, in the beginning, but then — rather strangely — they seem to live out their own lives. For example, as soon as my character is named — as I write his name down on paper — I see him before me. I feel him. I permit him to express himself...alone. He escapes me at this point. I, therefore, never construct a character nor do I build him. I let him roam freely. That's why I never know what my character is going to say or do before he actually does act. After he speaks his very first words — in the beginning — these fragments seem to situate him and determine his character and future course. He develops alone here on in. I listen to him talk and merely write down what he says.

Q. What was the theme of your last Parisian success, *The Beet Garden?*

A.  The opposition which exists between purely masculine
    **kinds of** activities and freedom *per se*. There are two
    male characters in my play who work together in a
    rather humorous disorder: that is, they enjoy great
    liberty and are interested in many things, all of a
    *material* nature. Love is introduced into the picture.
    It stands in opposition to this fascination. A young
    girl visits these two men. One of them will become
    deeply affected by her. This little society (now
    consisting of four people, two men and two women) is
    torn asunder slowly. *The Beet Garden* really centers
    on the difficulties involved in accepting love on
    rational terms.

Q.  **What** part did you play in this work since you are
    yourself an actor as well as a dramatist?

A.  I played the older of the two men, Guillaume. He was
    the first violinist of the quartet that keeps rehearsing
    during the entire course of the play. He is the one
    who is finally abandoned by his friend and who re-
    mains with the older woman.

Q.  Do you usually work with your director or don't you
    get involved in the production end of your plays?

A.  I try to give the director as much freedom as possible.
    Since I also act in my plays, however, I am obliged
    to discuss them with him — at least to a certain
    extent. I usually have great confidence in my direc-
    tor. In *The House of Bones,* however, many things
    went wrong. This drama was made up of a series of
    scenes which could be played in almost any order:
    one could alter, that is, the order of the scenes. The
    director, therefore, was permitted a great deal of
    liberty in the arrangement and disposition of these
    scenes. It happened, however, that he cut out cer-

tain scenes which I felt were of extreme importance.
Moreover, he changed the scenes around to such an
extent that the play ended at a moment when I thought
it should not have terminated. The entire concept of
the drama was alien to mine; the climate, the atmosphere was, in many ways, spoiled because of this
misunderstanding on the director's part.

I directed my last play, *The Beet Garden*, myself.
The only difficulties which arose were of a technical
order: that is, if you act in a play and direct it at
the same time you have to keep jumping on and off
the stage. You can imagine how difficult and trying
this can be. There were perhaps other difficulties,
of a psychological nature. Each time something
went wrong, I thought the play was at fault. I felt
anguished. I could not attribute it to some imper-
fection on the part of the actors...., Such a mental
state is depressing. Now, however, I think I've overcome this anguish.

Q.  Briefly, what are the themes implicit in *The Beet Gar-
    den?*

A.  There are several. It's the story of a quartet. Four
    people who settle way out in the country, in a kind
    of "culture" house. Certainly, the fact that these
    musicians have changed their environment − that they
    are really out of their element − is one of the themes.
    The other is suggested by the musicians themselves
    and their rapport with each other. The quartet does
    not play well. There are, therefore, professional
    difficulties which arise. The first violinist is to
    blame for some professional lacks or failures. The
    responsibility of such acts weighs so heavily upon
    him that he seeks refuge in a sort of semi-folly: he
    thinks he's Beethoven. A third theme centers around
    Beethoven's life. Everything about this play revolves

around a disguise, a travesty or a parody of several love episodes which Beethoven had experienced during his life, as well as his deafness and his death.

I must not omit the fact that *The Beet Garden* is structured directly upon Beethoven's last quartets which the musicians in the play keep rehearsing. In fact, I borrowed two of Beethoven's own methods: the repetition of themes and the variations on certain themes. These variations are frequently pushed to the extreme — so much so that one barely recognizes the original theme. This method influences the entire movement intrinsic to the drama and to each scene in particular. For example, the constant interruptions, the break in movement, the counterpuntal notions, the silences ... One can even cite precise examples of such rhythmic techniques in the text itself.

Q.   Do décors play an exceptional part in your plays?

A.   No. That really depends upon the play. In *Naïve Swallows*, the décor consisted of one shop — a closed area, to a certain extent. One could exit from it; but the store itself formed a unit, a place in which people were enclosed. In *The House of Bones*, décor played an enormous role because the house itself became the main protagonist. In *The Beet Garden*, the play's subject determined the décor which was constructed in the form of a giant violin case in which the characters were really enclosed. They were unable to open the door to leave. They could only open it in order to enter. This décor was very important and designed to create a feeling of claustrophobia.

Q.   Do sound effects play a role in your plays?

A.   **Sound effects are assuming a greater role in each play.**

They give life to everything which surrounds the play ... In my last drama I used a lot of sound effects which emanated from the outside: real noises such as the barking of dogs, the crying of babies, etc.

Q. How about lights?

A. I used a complicated interplay of lights in *The House of Bones*. The scene was constantly shifting. Moreover, it was abstract and included about forty characters.    Light isolated the various stage areas, magnifying or diminishing their importance as the case may be. In my other works, however, they did not assume such importance.

Q. Would you call your characters symbols, or real beings, or what?

A. No. They're not symbols *per se*. They do stand up, psychologically speaking. Each has his own personality. I forced myself to find a character capable of conflict; capable of actually contradicting himself completely. In fact, he is forever vacillating, changing his mood, his ideas, from one moment to the next. It is the actor who gives this character unity. It is complicated because he must, at the same time, reveal the dichotomy and the unity — simultaneously. It is through this arduous work — in which the fine actor is involved — that true poetry of the stage is born.

We wish to thank the editors of *Drama and Theatre* for permission to reprint the above interview (**Vol.** 8, no. 3).

## ROMAIN WEINGARTEN

*Interviewer's Note:*

"Weingarten's truth is the truth of the nightmare, a profound and living truth; the universe revealed in his work is authentic... naïve and complete... it is the universe of that rare... lucid being, the poet...'' So wrote one of Weingarten's most fervent admirers, Eugene Ionesco.

Weingarten's first play, *Akara* (1948), was performed by the Jeunes Compagnies in Paris and acclaimed by the avant-garde. It revealed a totally new theatrical language based on a series of concrete images woven about in fascinating patterns on stage. Its themes, which emanated directly from the unconscious, attempted to make a mockery of man's hypocritical relationships. *The Nurses* (1960) and *Summer* (1966) were equally well received. Here too audiences were immersed in a Surrealistic climate—a realm in which Men and Women Cats invaded the stage with their anguish, violence and acidulous humor. *Alice in the Luxembourg Gardens* was performed with great success in the winter of 1972 in Paris. Weingarten's linguistic virtuosity and the sensitivity of the acting techniques used in the production made for a delightfully absurd evening in the theatre.

There is nothing "realistic" in Weingarten's theatre.

It is composed of a medley of *"non-sens"* and takes its viewers or readers on a trip to that strange and fascinating land where imagination becomes an ever fructifying force.

Q.  What was your background?

A.  My father was Polish and my mother, French.  I studied philosophy at the Sorbonne...

Q.  How did you choose the theatre as a career?

A.  I composed only verse.  Then, suddenly, I wrote my first play, *Akara*.  I discovered the theatre through Roger Vitrac's *Victor, or Children Assume Power* and also through Antonin Artaud.  You recall that both Artaud and Vitrac were friends and had founded a theatre together.  In fact, Artaud produced *Victor*, a play in which the adult world was satirized and considered stupid, inane, hypocritical; whereas the childrens' world, thought to be fantastic at times, was astonishingly real and sincere.  I was profoundly impressed by this work.  Then I wrote *Akara*.

One enters the theatre as one does religion: completely and totally.  Some people have labeled my theatre "Surrealistic."  Yet, my plays are frequently in direct opposition to the "literary" and "scientific" aspects of Surrealism as explicated by both André Breton, the founder of Surrealism, and Antonin Artaud, one of its chief proponents.

Q.  Can you tell us something about *Akara?*  It's a play in which your world of fantasy or "madness" comes to life.  It features a Man-Cat and his guests.

A.   *Akara* was the first post-war **avant-garde** play. I don't
     believe that this first production — because of its
     timing perhaps — ever had any equivalent. *Akara* is
     a sort of nightmare — one which includes murder,
     bewitchment, a sort of "delayed" evocation of the
     horrors which I experienced unconsciously during
     World War II. When Ionesco first read this play, he
     spoke of it so frequently that people have associated
     me with the "theatre of the absurd" group. But the
     theatre of the absurd dramatizes the liquidation of
     dead people, not the murder of the living; the non-
     hope, not despair.
          I played the part of the Man-Cat (the lawyer) in
     *Akara.* Many of my colleagues — and I too — consider
     the *métier* of the dramatist to be a "global" affair;
     that is, that the author must take part in his pro-
     duction; he must make it possible to create a "finish-
     ed product." The theatrical object must be his work
     — from beginning to end.

Q.   You not only wrote and acted but you also directed
     your own play this winter, *Alice in the Luxembourg
     Gardens*. The play tells the story of Alice, a little
     girl, who is neither loved nor understood by her
     mother. She defends herself by becoming mute and
     by enunciating a series of **onomatopoeias**. Her un-
     conscious, revealed to the audiences, conjures up her
     mother in a variety of ruthless and monstrous crea-
     tures. Alice is finally liberated, crosses the Luxem-
     bourg Gardens only to revert once again to her former
     slave position. Could you tell us something about
     your concept of the *mise en scène* in general; then
     in terms of *Alice in the Luxembourg Gardens*.

A.   Essentially, there are three types of *mises en scène:*
     1.  spatial (which refers to the images)
     2.  time-concept (which revolves around rhythms)
     3.  action (directing the actors)

These are frequently referred to as the famous classical rules: unity of time, place and action.

My theatre, however, is an imaginary theatre. Alice is imaginary. I mean by imaginary a theatre which deals with an *inner reality*. It follows, therefore, that what is performed on stage is the world *within;* whereas the occult (the story of the lovers in **my 1966 play,** *Summer,* **for example) becomes the ex-**ternal, logical realm, the event or the psychological situation. It is very difficult to train actors to see the world in this manner: in reverse, so to speak. Paradoxically, it becomes a necessity to have them confront reality — their reality — constantly.

A scene, when analyzed by my actors, becomes a succession of elementary situations viewed in ultra-rapid sequences. These sequences must not be linked together logically, that is, rationally. Moreover, they must be endowed with greater or lesser intensity; they must be capable of arousing sensations not necessarily indicated or fostered by "what is said."

To create a *mise en scène* or to direct a play implies a permanent *process:* the reaching of a state of extreme and the breaking up of this state.

Extremes imply a systematic exaggeration of motivations; the breaking up of these extremes indicates a no less systematic contention of such an atmosphere. These are, briefly, the mechanics of the process and the means by which a "psychic" reality — not to be confused with its opposite, "a psychological" reality — may be attained.

Q.  Who are your ancestors in the theatre? Who were the dramatists who most influenced you?

A.  Artaud. Vitrac. I also admire Shakespeare, Kleist, Claudel. The poets of the theatre are those who fascinate me. Lewis Carroll.

Q.  Is your theatre politically oriented? philosophically?
Could you explain some themes or intriguing aspects
of your play *A kara?*

A.  My theatre is not politically oriented. It's poetry that
interests me: the thought which emerges from the
poetic flights . My theatre is realistic in that it
faithfully follows the explorations into the imaginary
world; it therefore becomes a quest for *reality*. I do
not mean the type of reality one confronts in the
**workaday world, but rather that inner reality about**
which we spoke before.

    *Akara* is the story of a **murder,** of black **magic**
written under the guise of a farce or a kind of short
story. The hero is a Man-Cat who is confronted by a
series of monstrous people: by a society of victims
and executioners, consumers and consumed. This
cat is a lawyer, and though he is **different,** morally
speaking, from the rest of society, though he is an
aesthete, he is, nonetheless "**alice,**" has a cat's
personality and is a cat. But this information must be
kept secret. It must not be spoken. During the course
of an evening reception at his home the Man-Cat's
mistress denounces him, or rather she "confesses"
that he is a cat. This takes place at a "card party" —
a perfectly absurd game, a kind of fantasy à la Lewis
Carroll. This interlude consists of a series of veiled
interrogations and secret questions asked of the
Man-Cat's mistress. Finally she can no longer parry
the questions. She gives in and tells the truth. The
cat escapes, but is caught and is killed at the end.

    Another aspect **of** this play (also symbolic) is
the role enacted by the woman. She is the *femme
fatale* **type,** a mediatrix of death, until she herself
becomes its victim.

Q. The domain of the dream is most important in your theatre. Can you explain the manner in which the dream insinuates itself in your plays?

A. Yes. My theatre emanates first from the domain of the dream: dream-images, that is, a revelation of a personal situation experienced collectively. When I spoke of imagination before I meant it as that organ of perception which paves the way for experiencing an inner reality. The dream is a kind of *screen* or *gate-way* through which a rapport between an inner and an external reality may be made known, so that *Reality* may be perceived.

It is absolutely not a question of a dialectically conceived theatre in the classical sense; that is, the imaginary of the real-dreamed or, in other words, the real-non-real.

Despite the eruption of Oriental doctrines or the revelation of psychological depths, the concept I have just outlined is difficult to understand and even more difficult to experience.

I first dream my plays, in the manner in which I have just outlined. I dream them most persistently when going through the writing process; the very medium stimulates my unconscious. I identify completely with my characters, my creations. These exist in that inner area where first, as amorphous and nebulous powers, they slowly begin to act and take form and appear later on in the theatrical arena — in another domain of *Reality*.

Q. Does the absurd, as far as you are concerned, possess its own type of logic?

A. No. The Absurd, in the theatrical sense of the word, has no logic; or rather it is *logic in flight*, or the acceptance of the absurdity of logic. On the other hand, the absurd at the "dream" level, possesses, of course, its own logic. Its logic, however, is entirely different: it is analogical, homological and symbolistic. It possesses its own language, its own language, its own images.

The very strangeness of this language stems from the fact that it possesses its own natural, innate language which is, at the same time, foreign to the one with which we usually come into contact in the **workaday world.**

It's evident that these two forms which the absurd has taken — the flight of from the logical (rational) and the logic of the dream *per se* — blend constantly in contemporary theatre.

Q.  Your language is not only **poetic,** it is hypnotic. It has a way of imposing itself upon the reader, of mesmerizing him. Do you have a special writing technique? What is your method? How do you go about creating a play?

A.  As soon as this strange or foreign language which I just mentioned is experienced affectively or on an emotional level — a personal level — it ceases to be absurd. In fact, once it has triggered off certain emotions, the question "what does this or that mean" is no longer posed. It is experienced. The emotion is the channel through which the answer is given: that is, it is the transforming agent. When writing I try to follow as closely as possible that secret curve which the emotion takes. It acts as a kind of **barom-** meter or method of punctuating "what is taking place" in silence.

Total theatre consists of an empty stage. I try to reduce everything to this state of silence, im- mobility, obscurity — linguistically speaking. Then if I succeed in this task — of living through the emotion or experiencing it as an entity unto itself, as a protagonist — then I am happy with what I have written. If I laugh, if I am moved, if I cry, then I have a feeling that what I have put down on paper is good. Generally, when I **do my writing,** my work consists in either adding to or deleting from that first spark of inspiration, which is really a kind of shaping of brute matter. I try to order, musically speaking, the movements on stage and the rhythms of the spoken words according to a variety of tempi: rapidly or slowly paced lines, those spoken in counterpoint, in unison, alone, etc.

It goes without saying that what I have just outlined for you is my *vision* of the theatre. I try, as best I can, to come as close to it as possible.

Q. What are your reactions to the theatre of Arrabal, Dubillard? To the work of such directors as Lavelli? Grotowski? Savary?

A. My career parallels Roland Dubillard's, so to speak. We are the same age; we have had the same difficulties, as we are both actors, dramatists, etc. I really appreciate his poetic theatre.

As for Fernando Arrabal, I do have some reservations concerning the facility of his theatre, in the domain of the dream — and this, despite his talent as a dramatist.

The directors you mentioned ... I must say that I do not trust directors in general. I find that Grotowski, without realizing it perhaps, and without wanting to, is working toward a type of expressionism which is completely foreign to me. I think that the only great *mise en scène* I have ever seen is Peter Brook's *A Midsummer's Night Dream*.

Q. You frequently use several theatrical techniques in

your plays at the same time: satire, irony, etc. Can
you tell us how you use these?

A.   I love to make people laugh.  I use satire and irony
     to this end.  Most so-called "normal" people appear
     in my plays in the form of animals, monsters or
     machines.   The amount of laughter which results
     depends upon the degree of fear audiences experi-
     ence . . .

Q.   Do you use sound effects and lights as **protagonists,**
     as had Artaud?

A.   Yes.  They should be *actors* in a play.

Q.   What role does the décor play in *Alice,* for example.

A.   In the Parisian production of *Alice,* the décor I had
     envisioned failed completely, but only for material
     reasons.
         I think that décor should be a kind of apparition;
     it should be capable of modifying the entire atmos-
     phere, not through mechanical means, but through a
     play of lights.  Décor is very nearly always a kind of
     death knell for scenic endeavor; it has a static quality
     about it.  It should be a drama in itself; project its
     dynamism into space, illuminate the heart of the play
     itself.

Q.   *Summer* had its first New York production in the spring
     of 1973.  Margaret Barker, director and co-translator
     of *Summer* wrote that Weingarten's play "evokes
     images found in our imagination and dreams wherein
     the powerful forces of the unconscious manifest them-
     selves.  It is these forces that people all over the
     world are becoming **aware of.**   The play includes
     four characters and one set.  **Two** cats who 'pretend

to be men' and who 'play the games men play.' In
their purely animal aspects they set the stage, change
the mood, cautious, independent, selective and play-
ful.     Simon and his sister, Lorette.     These young
people are orphans.     Their relationship to the Cats
and to a pair of Lovers (unseen, but who motivate the
play's action) develops from an Eden-like garden of
**'happy summer days'** to a nightmare that catapults
them into a new reality.'' How do you account for the
success of *Summer* in its original production?     Was it
due to a combination of the playwright, actors and
director in Paris at the little Poche-Montparnasse
theatre, working together during rehearsals until its
final form?

A.  Yes.

Q.  As a poet, words must be of great importance to you.
    Do you believe a play can ever be adequately trans-
    lated into another language?     Does not your *Dramatic
    Poem* depend a great deal on a play on words?

A.  As to the words or play on words — equivalents can be
    found.     But essentially, it is a matter of tempo; this
    is what should be respected.

Q.  Since you yourself played one of the Cats in *Summer*
    did you come to any conclusions as to why you have
    had this obsession with cats in your plays: one cat in
    *Akara* and now two in *Summer?*

A.  What I felt most keenly when playing the role of Lord
    Garlic in *Summer,* even more potently than when I
    wrote it, was a terrible lust.     This psychological
    problem which concerns the non-human and which the
    actor must confront, revolves around a cat's extreme
    covetousness (lust), a force which is apt to diminish

or change its focus with the least change in the air current, and without the slightest nuance of a transition. This trait, on the human level, is one of the rules of comedy.

Q.  You have said that cats do not allow themselves to be domesticated; you find in them a strange characteristic which creates a distance between them and other people. They have a great sense of independence. Do you equate them with your artistic view of life? That is, is the artist like a cat in that he must remain independent, aloof from the crowd?

A.  The cat gives the impression of being autonomous and this is essential. Yet, at the same time, the cat derides autonomy since it is domesticated. To be a domesticated animal without really being **one** also characterizes the artist.

Q.  Have you a certain phobia about commercial producers in that their ends may not be yours and that they may inadvertently misunderstand and destroy the intentions behind your work?

A.  It goes without saying that one does not write for the theatre in order to remain "distant," but rather to fill up the breach or the gap. The worries of a man of the theatre consist simply in finding ways and means of communication.

A director, in order to make the success of a play, should show confidence in his author, rather than always to think that he knows better than the author as to what was intended in the play. In any case, the author knows very well what he did not want to do.

Q.  Is part of what you are trying to say in *Summer* so

personal a view of mankind that you fear it cannot be
shared?   Or is it that you, like the Cats, look upon
the world as an introvert?   Are you aware of the
various characteristics in men and women of the Cat
archetype?   That of predator, hunter, destroyer, ma-
licious gossip, lovable pet, loyal companion, indifferent lover?  You say the unconscious is a misnomer.
We should say imagination. Whence the latter?

A.   This question is difficult to answer briefly.  What we
commonly allude' to as introspection concerns, in my
opinion, only the most superficial levels of the inner
man: what we refer to as "psychological" theatre.
The same can be said for "introversion."  A whole
repetory of images and situations emerge from a more
distant, more profound realm, from an area some place
ahead of me — expressed in a foreign and at the same
time universal language.  I think it is important to
understand this language, because I am persuaded that
it is through this special language that we communicate with each other and with the world and that
it is through the *inner* that one finds "the way." Animal figures are, among others, words which come from
this special language.  And I must say that the cat
expresses something very much akin to what the
psychoanalysts call the pleasure principle.

Q.   The cats embody many human characteristics.  Yet
*Summer* is not about cats acting out their idea of men.
Rather it seems to be a story of the destruction of
innocence, a Paradise Lost to two young teenage
orphans, by the intrusion into the world of two Lovers
whose love affair takes place over six days and six
nights.  It ends in disruption and heartbreak.  Is it
to counter the tragedy of these young people that you
counterpose the independence and self-reliance of
the cats, and possibly of the artist?

A.   The cats are there, really as guardians of Paradise—
     that is to say, of pleasure. And this pleasure is that
     of the lovers, at the heart of which children and cats
     are placed — just as they are in the garden. But there
     is no paradise that does not contain within itself the
     seed of its own destruction. Already, at summer's
     solstice, the days begin to grow shorter, and the
     lovers separate. But is this "stuff" from which a
     play is made?

Q.   You feel the nature of your play to be more allusive
     than expressive. You feel the value of silence, be-
     cause that which a person says in real life is not
     actually what is going on. And so do you feel that it
     is not in the words that the fortune of the play lies,
     but in the over-all theatrical conception the actors and
     director must seek to find together? Has this an
     oriental background?

A.   My idea was to let an arrow fly through the air, let
     its trajectory be described not on the stage, but in the
     spectators' mind; but to describe this trajectory is to
     deprive it of its effect. Certainly you can relate this
     idea to Oriental concepts, but it can be found just as
     easily in the effects of the constant breaks which
     characterize all good American films, both comic and
     serious. It is one of the essential rules of drama.

Q.   In speaking of the importance of casting you say that
     too many actors need to rid themselves utterly of their
     "tricks of the trade" and seek within themselves a
     response to art, to beauty and the ability to dream.
     It sounds to me as though you will need to find actors
     who can rely on their intuition and yet harness it to
     the practical demands of this most unusual play. Do
     you think you can transmit your thoughts to American
     actors without a speaking knowledge of English?

A. It is really a question of basing oneself on the emotions that the movement of the play implies, not on the words which, as in real life, often have only a remote relationship with "what's going on." Perhaps it will be easier for American actors than for the French who are always so drawn to some semblance of "logic."

Q. In this time of violence and bloodshed, of man's loss of traditional values by which hitherto he has been too willing to lead his life, do you feel, along with Miss Margaret Barker, that *Summer* might prove to be an oasis? There are those of us parched for poetic theatre not only to seek entertainment in it, but also to escape from the paucity of language and puerile conception based on forced accounts of violence. Do you not believe that the word of the poet and the insight of the artist might illuminate some of the dark recesses of the soul?

A. I have no illusions concerning the influence of art in general. Everywhere people are trying to live, and this in itself takes considerable effort; for many, art is looked upon as a distraction, an evasion or even — madness. So?

Reprinted in part with the permission of the editors from *Arts in Society,* "The Social Uses of Art," vol.9, no. 3.

## NATHALIE SARRAUTE

*Interviewer's Note:*

Nathalie Sarraute, born in 1902 in Ovanovo-Voznessensk, Russia, went to France at the age of two. She was an excellent student, developed into a fine linguist, and excelled in the domain of the intellectual. She earned degrees at the Lycée Fenelon, the Sorbonne (where she prepared a "licence" in English), Oxford, the Faculty of Letters in Berlin, and the Faculty of Law in Paris. In 1932 Nathalie Sarraute wrote her first work, *Tropisms,* a highly original volume which set the pace and style for all of her future creations. The drama inherent in Mme Sarraute's novels and plays stems directly from the interplay of tropisms, the hidden forces within each individual which are at the "root of our gestures, of our words, of the feelings we manifest...." Tropisms are usually expressed in imagery; they are the amorphous quantities which come into being, expand, and vanish at a rapid and quixotic rate, generating impressions and sensations during the course of their peregrinations. In all of Mme Sarraute's novels, *The Portrait of a Man Unknown* (1948), *Martereau* (1953), *The Planetarium* (1959), *The Golden Fruits* (1963), *Between Life and Death* (1968), *Do You Hear Them* (1972) and her plays, *The Silence* (1963), *The Lie* (1966) and *Isma* (1970), she has tried to bewitch her readers by bombarding them with sensations which have arisen as a result of these mysterious and hidden tropisms which the sensitive can perceive behind the most banal of conversations and the most rudimentary of gestures.

Q. Can you tell me about the discovery, the genesis and the evolution of those "inner movements" which you call *tropisms*, that is, the course they take from their concretization in the work of art?

A. It's very difficult for me to answer this question because I am absolutely unaware of the genesis or the evolution of these inner movements. I wrote my first few short texts which I entitled *Tropisms* spontaneously, without even knowing what tropisms really were nor what they represented. My impressions guided me. I experienced them very strongly and I wanted to translate the rhythms I felt, the images I saw — always in a natural manner. I was hardly conscious of what I was doing.

Q. Did the form, the meaning or the manner in which you used these "tropisms" evolve in the course of your work?

A. An evolution certainly did take place. When I was writing *Tropisms*, I was convinced that novels could never be written in this manner. What I wanted to bring out and dramatize in my work were inner movements, a sort of disintegrated matter, an amoeba-like substance, as it changed form-wise. But it was only when I began writing *Tropisms* that I became aware of the fact that certain types of sensations — and always the same ones — kept returning in the course of my research work and in the short pieces I was writing.

I did not feel the necessity of constructing characters and of relating plots. To show the movement

itself was sufficient as it unfolded in anonymous
characters.  But I realized that if I continued to show
these movements separately and without linking them
together in one way or another, I was in effect limiting
them.  These tropisms could never really develop.
I thought, therefore, that it might be more interesting
to take two people rather than one and so permit these
movements to amplify and develop.  This is why I
thought of writing *The Portrait of a Man Unknown*,
which has been called by some an anti-novel since the
whole romanesque side of this work, the traditional
novel form, shows up in *trompe l'oeil:* the character of a
miser and his relationship with his daughter.  That
was all appearance; reality could be found only in the
inner movements, these tropisms which develop within
themselves and which have little to do with what we
call avarice.

Q.   Did you have a reason for diminishing, imperceptibly
     of course, the number of images in your work (from
     *The Planetarium* to *The Golden Fruits*, for example);
     while at the same time increasing the scenic play
     and dialogue to such an extent that you wrote, in fact,
     three plays?  Was this step toward the oral form in-
     tentional?  Or did it come naturally?  Can you explain
     this evolution in form?

A.   I did not notice any diminution of images in my work
     until now and I am not in agreement with this opinion.
     I have the impression that there are as many images
     in *The Golden Fruits* as there are in *The Portrait of a
     Man Unknown*.  There are, in fact, only images in these
     works; but they are not introduced by means of com-
     parisons.  I do not say, for example, "he was like a
     man who had known military degradation."  I *show*
     military degradation.  I do so by means of images.  In
     the course of one conversation in my work concerning

a book, one has the distinct impression that one of the interlocutors is undergoing the actual pain of military degradation. That is certainly an image. There are many such images in the novel, *The Golden Fruits*.

I am forever looking for images as I write. Yes, it is quite true — there is more dialogue in *The Planetarium*, in *Martereau*, in *The Golden Fruits* than there is in *The Portrait of a Man Unknown*. This is the case because in the latter work, the featured character was never present at the crucial scenes. There was, therefore, less dialogue.

I wrote *The Silence* because I was asked to write a radio play. First, I refused. Then, one day I tried, and I wrote *The Silence*. But I am never spurred on by preconceived ideas. Nor am I aware at any particular moment of the reasons I write in one way or another. I really cannot tell you why or how my books evolve. I believe there is far less dialogue in *Between Life and Death* than in my other works, simply because it does not seem to fit into this work. There are, however, more tropisms in this novel than there is dialogue. I do not believe this to be the result of any so called evolution in my writing; it is simply that I am pushed in one direction or another during the course of my work.

Q. How did you succeed in transforming a banal conversation (or event) into something fascinating?

A. People have said that I am forever trying to depict banalities and platitudes. I believe I have done just the opposite. In my work, platitudes — as Sartre very well explained — are simply "common **places**," that is, "common places" where people meet. Tropisms manifest themselves only on the outside — by means of these "common places" which emanate from conversations and dialogues. Tropisms both reveal

and camouflage themselves under the apparent guise
of a banal dialogue. Dialogues — and many people
are unaware of this — have not been included in my
works in order merely to underline banal utterances.
They have been placed in my work, on the contrary,
to bring forth these tropisms. It is not, therefore, a
question of listing or of revealing banalities as such,
as Ionesco has done, for example, but rather to show
just how these banal statements shield and at the
same time reveal tropisms.

Q. Can you tell us the differences which exist between
your conception of the novel and that of the "new
novelists" or the "new realists" as they are called:
Alain Robbe-Grillet, Michel Butor, Robert Pinget, etc.

A. I certainly have some points in common with these
writers. They too wanted to extract the novel from
what we all felt had become a **meaningless form: the**
depicting of characters, the relating of **plots, etc, which**
detract **the reader** from what we consider to be essential. Each of us writes in his own personal way,
and very differently. Robbe-Grillet, for example,
describes the exterior world: things, objects as seen
from the outside. I, on the other hand, describe inner
movements. His universe is more or less immobile
whereas mine is in perpetual motion — in a state of
constant transformation. One could in fact say that
our **ways** of writing **are** diametrically opposed both
in terms of temperament and vision.

Q. Is your vision of man pessimistic? You depict most
frequently weak and obsessed beings: Alain in *The
Planetarium,* the uncle in *Martereau,* the father and
daughter in *The Portrait of a Man Unknown,* **personalities in *The Golden Fruits,* etc.**

A.   I am really quite surprised whenever I am told that my
     vision of man is pessimistic and that my characters
     are obsessed and weak. I did not want to depict such
     beings. I merely set out to paint tropisms. I sup-
     pose, however, that one must be a bit obsessed in
     order to focus one's attention on these inner move-
     ments. One must be highly sensitive to even notice
     them. Active people — extroverts — are usually well
     balanced and do not dwell upon their inner world.
     They feel tropisms, but repress them unconsciously.
     Yet, despite this repression these inner movements
     exist in all of us and when I choose to show them, I
     am forced to depict sensitive people, preoccupied
     with themselves and the inner movements within their
     beings. They therefore might give the impression of
     being obsessed. These beings I portray are actually
     "movement detectors," not characters *per se.* For
     this reason, it is not really a question of depicting
     weak or obsessed characters, but rather of seizing
     these movements by means of an ultra-sensitive de-
     tector.

Q.   Has there always been a struggle between the active
     and the passive individual in your work; the one who
     lets himself be dominated and the one who seeks to
     dominate?

A.   I would not call it a struggle between the active and
     passive beings, but rather between various types of
     tropisms and appearances. There is always the kind
     of individual who seeks to delve deeply into himself
     so as to perceive those tropisms I have mentioned and
     others who prefer not to see them, but take great
     pains to mask them. A state of flux always exists,
     therefore; constant play between the exterior and in-
     terior worlds, visible and invisible reality.

Q.  What are the autobiographical elements in your works?
    Do you have an Aunt Bertha, a Martereau, etc. in your
    family or among your friends?  Do you see yourself
    in these beings?

A.  Autobiographical elements exist everywhere in my
    works just as they do in everybody else's.  In my case
    I never write anything that I have not truly experienced
    or have not known anyone else to have experienced.
    This does not mean that I extract situations from my
    own life.  I have never known a more generous person
    than my own father; yet I have described an avaricious
    father.  I have never really used autobiographical
    elements or situations but simply sensations, impres-
    sions scattered here and there.

Q.  Have you ever studied music?  Your sentences fre-
    quently resemble waves, echoes; they have a particular
    tone and varied rhythms of their own.

A.  I did study the piano as every young lady did in my
    day: from the age of eight to twenty-three.  But I did
    not have a very good ear.

Q.  Are you a painter?  Your verbal designs are exquisite.

A.  I love painting.

Q.  You have said that Joyce, Proust and Dostoyevsky
    have transformed reality for you.  Can you elaborate
    upon this statement?

A.  Dostoyevsky was one of the first writers to break up
    the classical character type featured in the novel up
    until his time.  Balzac's beings, for example, are
    whole; either a miser, a social climber, etc.  Dos-
    toyevsky's creatures have conflicting character traits;

each facet of a personality within the same being is forever at odds with another.

As for Proust: his work was a revelation to me; a vision as seen through a microscope. Yet, Proust's microscopic vision was in some way fixed — in a souvenir. The substance of his vision was not in the process of being formed.

The Joycian interior monologue is made up of words which flow through one's conscious mind. What I depict is rather what one does not have the time to express and which I am forced to show through images; that is, what takes place even before the interior monologues come into being. There are very few interior monologues in my work.

Q. You are not interested in psychology in the traditional sense of the word. Yet, you are fascinated by a new type of psychology which permits you to penetrate into each being's collective and anonymous side. Can you tell us something about this new world? Place it for us?

A. I do not believe that I have made any discoveries in the psychological or scientific fields. I am not trying to compete with scientists. I merely want to translate certain impressions which are actually poetic. But it is very difficult to define in words exactly what one "feels" — what poetry *per se* tries to express. When the reader begins to "feel" what I have been trying to say, when the sensations have been transmitted to him, I believe I have succeeded at this particular moment in my endeavor. I try to depict a way of feeling and of seeing things which is my own, but which many other people feel in a similar manner.

Q. You talk about the "common substance," "common patrimony," "the common mass." Were you in any way influenced by C. G. Jung and what he terms the "collective unconscious."

A.  I cannot really define the statements you just mentioned because I am not a philosopher. When I speak of "common **substance**," etc., I believe that tropisms exist in each one of us, in both the introvert and the extrovert. Tropisms create certain rapports between people; form certain friendships and antipathies; even determine our conduct towards others.

Q.  **Is the** fluid exuded by your characters intended to touch the reader? Do you try to bewitch the reader by invoking visual and auditive sensations, by repeating with minimal variations the same vicissitudes, the same ideas and remarks?

A.  Yes. I do believe that the fluid which emanates from each of my beings should flow forth and affect the reader. I believe that the novel, like poetry, must transmit **certain types of sensations;** these can be generated by language, rhythm, images.

I am forced to choose simple images so that my readers will not have to think too hard about what he is reading, so that the sensations which arise from the image itself will effect him directly. It I tell the reader, for example, that someone felt like a bird before a serpent, this image is so simple and banal that the reader will feel its impact immediately. This same image, nevertheless, must translate something highly complex, mysterious and irrational. The reader, therefore, must be able to seize the complexity of the emotions through the image itself; in other words, the banal is the vehicle by which things not capable of being expressed can be felt and understood. Tropisms cannot be expressed by means of the written word, but only through images capable of generating sensations.

Q. What is your reaction to Simone de Beauvoir's statement: "...man has become fixed when described by the writers of the school of the Look (*l'Ecole du regard*); if he is referred to, it is as an object...he will be eliminated in favor of objects; in any event, he is deprived of his historical dimension."

A. I really do not understand the meaning of Mme de Beauvoir's statement. She speaks of the *Ecole du regard*... I don't believe that beings are described as objects by members of this so-called school. Furthermore, I do not belong to this school. This group probably earned this name — and incorrectly — because Robbe-Grillet, as I have already stated, describes the exterior world. His characters all suffer from one passion or another; they are truly obsessed beings. Nothing is seen in an objective manner. And man has certainly not been eliminated in favor of the object. In my case, the human being plays a predominant role, the object being the instrument which a man uses in order to express or to hide his anguish. The object is nothing without man who looks at it and uses it.

Q. How were you able to develop your sensations, your antennae, to the point of being able to concretize the amorphous? Do you have a special technique?

A. No. I have never tried to develop these sensations. I do not feel them any more keenly in my daily life than others do. When I work, however, since this is really what interests me, I am obliged to concentrate in order to be able to describe what I feel. These tropisms or inner movements never appear at first glance. To discover them requires tremendous effort, concentration, attention, preparation, work. People always think that when I am with them, I am able to feel the sensations I describe in my books. I don't

feel them any more deeply than anyone else at those
moments. It is only afterward, when I try to recon-
stitute them, search them out, that I discover them
and they in turn play an important part in my reality.

Q. You say that each novelist "must abstract himself from
the exterior world in order to perceive the **essential**."
Could you explain this statement? Does this mean
that the novelist must be detached?

A. I believe that the novelist, the painter, the musician —
all artists must abstract themselves during their working periods from reality as they know it — that is,
categorized reality. When creating, the writer is
exploring new inroads and he must, therefore, wander
away from everything which he has already known and
which others have discovered. He can leave the
beaten path rather easily because it begins to bore him.
When writing, for example, one realizes suddenly that
a transitional paragraph must be placed here for purposes of clarity. But to do so begins to bore you.
You grow tired of conventions. In this case, you have
to eliminate everything that bores you; give up that
transitional paragraph even if you risk a great deal
in so doing — to include it would mean that you are
really not yourself, that you are not alive, not creating something truly original and personal. A creative
artist must bring forth only what is of interest to him,
what fascinates him. To find yourself alone in a small
domain, though more or less circumscribed, is exciting
because it is yours alone.

Q. Can you really see yourself as you are? your friends
and your family as they are with that "inner eye" you
mention?

A. My children have said to me: "It is unbelievable how

wrong you can be at times about people.'' When I am with people I always have a tendency to give them a good deal of credit. I am not the least bit suspicious about people. My daughters tell me: ''People take advantage of you.'' As long as I am not too disappointed in them, I have faith in them. I do not feel that I know myself any better than I know anyone else. I believe that my work has really nothing to do with my daily life; they are two separate entities.

Q. Did you attend the rehearsals for your plays *The Silence* and *The Lie* at the Petit Odéon?

A. I was very happy each time I went to the rehearsals. The atmosphere created by Jean-Louis Barrault, Madeleine Renaud and the entire troupe was absolutely admirable. I felt myself to be part of a big family and I was sorry when the rehearsals came to an end.

I played no part whatsoever in the creation of the *mise en scene*. It was Barrault who decided he wanted to direct the plays — which had already been performed on radio. I had never thought of it in terms of a theatrical production. All the senic inventiveness stems from Barrault. I only gave advice concerning the actors' intentions and my intentions as far as the dialogue was concerned. I found Madeleine Renaud's interpretation admirable.

Though she played a relatively minor role, she just radiated. She has extraordinary stage presence and even those who did not like the play itself felt her magnetism most keenly. The lead role could only have been played by a man — it had to be a neuter character. If a woman had portrayed the part, one would have immediately detected the feminine traits and attitudes. I must also confess that the entire cast: Dominique Paturel, Gabriel Cattand, Jean-Pierre Granval, Nelly Benedetti, were absolutely remarkable.

They all played with a kind of passion. The text was terribly difficult to learn, they told me, because the sentences were choppy, unfinished; some sentences are repeated and one has a tendency to become confused. But I think they certainly performed brilliantly.

Q.  The plot of *The Lie* is relatively simply. Simone and her friends are playing a parlor game. They decide during the course of their conversation that one person is going to tell a lie. The others are to ferret out the guilty party. Simone casually tells her friends that she spent the war years in Switzerland. Pierre believes she spent them in France. He discerns her lie. Or does he? Simone denies having lied. Pierre is tortured by the uncertainty of it all. He declares he will no longer believe anything she says. Tensions reach a nerve-wracking pitch. **The little lie, then, by** its very nature, even when uttered in the spirit of fun, provokes tropisms and as a result assumes tremendous proportions, which in turn, constitute the play's action. The critic Jacques Lemarchand wrote of this play: "Nathalie Sarraute leads the play with precision, a stealthy cruelty which is pleasing to the heart...." In *The Silence* the same type of rippling action occurs. Audiences are introduced to another mundane group. One man has just finished telling his friends about a trip he has taken. Everyone is delighted with his narration. One person, however, voices no reaction. He remains silent. No one can fathom his silence. Is it a timid, angry, jealous, insulting silence? The drama revolves around each person's growing desire to penetrate this one man's silence: to discover why he chose to break contact with the rest of the group and seal himself off in his own world. About *The Silence*, Jacques Lemarchand said: "A cruelty which finds its accomplice in the rather snobbish naïveté of those who suffer...." What does Jacques Lemarchand mean by cruelty? What do you understand by this word?

A. I cannot see any cruelty in my works. My only concern is to express in a totally natural way those inner movements which I call tropisms. I would not have used the word cruelty in this connection. People are much more cruel in daily life. I have always felt that my characters possess great tenderness, much more so than those beings one sees about.

Q. Do you want spectators to feel a certain *malaise* when viewing your plays?

A. Yes. If the spectator does not share in the *malaise* emanating directly from my plays, if he does not decend to those insalubrious zones where tropisms are formed and arise, then my efforts have been in vain. The goal of my plays is to transport each individual at least for two hours into those regions we ourselves do not seek to penetrate.

Q. What kind of absolute do your characters search for in your plays?

A. If absolutes exist, my characters try desperately to communicate with others. They feel a necessity to fuse, to contact others. Somebody's silence, for example, breaks the contact. Even a lie breaks it. It is always a question of repairing a break. There is always one character who cannot stand the solitude and isolation of a break and begs the others to mend it and not provoke another.

Q. Was the step you took from the novel to the radio play difficult?

A.  No.  When Werner Spies came to see me — sent by
Radio Stuttgart — to ask me to write some radio plays,
I told him frankly that I thought I would be unable to
do so.  Those tropisms could not be described solely
by means of dialogue.  Then one day as I was thinking
about such a possibility, I realized that dialogue could
express the inexpressible.  I wrote *The Silence*.

Q.  Do you think you will write film scenarios?

A.  No.  I do not think that those inner movements can be
transformed into something tangible on the screen.
I think they can be concretized through dialogue: an
unreal dialogue, the type I have used in my plays.
I say unreal because people do not speak in real life
as they do in *The Silence*, for example.  Their dialogue
is made up of what seems to be banal conversations,
but what they say is not banal at all.

   When you are facing a person who is silent, you
usually make believe you are unaware of his silence;
you try to make him talk a bit every now and then,
to cheer him up; but you never say the things my characters say — and the way they say them.

   I am convinced that the cinematographic image
could not possibly render these tropisms of mine.
Furthermore, my plays have no **décors**.  They could
take place anywhere.

## JEAN-CLAUDE CARRIERE

*Interviewer's Note:*

Jean-Claude Carrière, born in the south of France, began writing when he was studying at the Ecole Normale Supérieure at Saint-Cloud. He has quite a few successes to his name: two novels, *Lézard* and *The Alliance* (1962), *A Dictionary of Nonsense* (written in collaboration with Guy Bechtel) (1964). In the film industry he has written scenarios and dialogues in collaboration with Etaix (*The Suitor, Yoyo*), Louis Malle (*Viva Maria, The Thief*), and Luis Buñuel (*The Diary of a Chamber Maid, Belle de Jour, The Monk, The Milky Way*). In the theatre, *The Memory-Aid* was enthusiastically received by the Parisian critics in 1969.

Q. Can you tell me how you met Buñuel?

A. I met him by chance eight years ago. He was looking for someone who could work with him on French film scenarios. We first worked together on *The Diary of a Chamber Maid,* based on Octave Mirbeau's novel. After that he wrote *The Monk,* drawn from Lewis' novel but not as yet produced for financial reasons. I wanted to mention *The Monk* to you because of Antonin Artaud's French adaptation of this Gothic novel which you

described in your **book,** ***Antonin Artaud, Man*** *of Vision.*
You recall that he too had wanted to make a film
version of the novel. We even have photos of Artaud
in the role of the Monk.

Q.   I imagine that working with such an imaginative, dy-
     namic and creative a person as Buñuel might present
     some difficulties. How do you go about collaborating
     with him? What are your techniques?

A.   I work with him as any two people work together:
     five, six and seven hours at a stretch sometimes.
     First we discuss the scenario in question: try to ex-
     plicate its themes, even in their detail, etc. Each of
     us takes notes. At night — alone — I try to write a
     scenario and dialogue based upon our discussions.
     The following morning we read what I have just writ-
     ten and most of the time we discard the entire scene.
     Then we begin all over again. You must realize that
     when working with Buñuel one is never on an equal
     footing with him. I am actually more of a super-
     secretary than a collaborator. My job really consists
     in guiding him, in trying to pursue one of many of his
     ideas. Indeed, ideas and themes gush forth from his
     mind as does oil from a giant well. Sometimes I look
     upon myself as his first spectator. I think what he
     really wants from me are my impressions, my reactions
     to what he has to say. This is my real work.

Q.   Can you go into detail concerning your **latest film,**
     *The Milky Way?* Why does it differ from other films
     Buñuel has created?

A.   First of all the other films were adaptations. We,
     therefore, had a structure and a theme before we even
     began. *The Milky Way* is completely original. We had
     to spend a great deal of time documenting ourselves

in the field of theology since the picture revolves
around the notion of heresy. What is heresy? How can
one be a heretic? The film is a kind of romanticized
documentary based upon various heresies within the
Catholic Church; it tells the story of two people, in
today's world, who have decided to walk from Paris
to the shrine of **Saint-Jacques-de-Compostelle** on a
pilgrimage, and of all those they meet on the way.
They meet people from different areas and various
walks of life. Neither time nor space — as we conceive of them logically — exist any longer.

As the people discuss their points of view, their
religious outlook and finally arrive at their destination,
the shrine of **Saint-Jacques-de-Compostelle**, they have
developed a personal mental outlook.

Q. Can you elaborate upon this mental outlook?

A. It cannot really be defined. It depends solely upon
the spectator, the way in which each one reacts to
the film and the various points of view touched upon.
The question of notion of heresy is a very complicated
one: heresy can be something quite novel and free
as well as highly dogmatic. Such heretical attitudes
are not merely limited to religion as you well know,
but appear in literary, political and artistic attitudes.
For example, the Czechs are heretical and the Rus-
sians dogmatic, intransigeant. Heresy is nothing
more than "truth without hope." Actually it is a
search for a very personal reality: one which is par-
celed out of the original vision. I mean by this that
certain heretics accept dogma in toto except for one
detail. They are willing to kill others and to die themselves in order to preserve this one small detail.
Heresy is frequently part and **parcel of fanaticism.**
It all depends upon how you look upon it.

Q.  Is Buñuel a religious man?

A.  No. He's an atheist. But one must realize that Bunuel
    was deeply marked by the religious education he re-
    ceived at the hands of the Jesuits. He has always
    been interested in the Catholic universe. Yet, he is
    completely and profoundly atheistic much in the same
    manner as is Fernando Arrabal. In this connection,
    we might add that Arrabal has been greatly influenced
    by Buñuel. He adores him.

Q.  Can you tell us something about your own career. You
    were certainly influenced by the Surrealists since the
    dream world plays such an important role in both your
    novels and your plays.

A.  I really cannot say. I am incapable of assessing any
    such influence. It has been said, however, that my
    play, *The Memory Aid,* was a classical type — well-
    knit — comedy and that you really have to examine it
    very closely to realize how illogical it is. Some con-
    sider it highly conventional theatre; others, Sur-
    realistic.

Q.  Did you work with the actors when they were preparing
    *The Memory Aid?*

A.  Yes. Very closely. I was present at all the readings
    and rehearsals. We worked together trying to bring
    forth the very special tone needed for this drama. I
    also worked with the director, André Barsacq. He
    gave me very useful advise on certain points. I be-
    lieve his *mise en scène* was just right.

Q.  *The Memory Aid* does not have a plot. On what does
    the tension or suspense rest?

A.  I believe that we have been delivered — and its been
    a long while now — of that absurd notion of ''plot''
    or ''story.'' In terms of these vehicles *The Memory
    Aid* has nothing new to offer. And even the opening
    situation — a woman who enters a man's apartment
    and does not want to leave it — is probably not new.
    We know from the very outset of the drama that she
    will remain, that she will impose herself upon him.
    Suspense, therefore, if there is suspense, is intrinsic
    to the details, to the manoeuvers she uses, to her
    strategy and especially, it seems to me, to the changes
    which operate or which come about within the two
    characters and which surprise them greatly. In ad-
    dition to this, a great uncertainty — absolutely con-
    certed — reigns upon the whole love story and in this
    connection each spectator can, if he so chooses, in-
    terpret the events as he sees fit; project upon them
    painful and pleasurable points of view. I believe that
    ideally, this would be true ''suspense;'' that each
    spectator would be perpetually surprised in what the
    play would teach them about themselves. This, how-
    ever, is an ideal.

Q.  Are your characters flesh and blood beings or symbolic
    apparitions?

A.  One of the two — the man — seems to me to be a char-
    acter. I am less certain about the woman's role. For
    certain spectators, she is a woman imagined by a
    man ... who would be the ideal feminine or at least
    a reflection of it. I try to avoid discussing the char-
    acters. After all, I'm nothing but the author.

Q.  Are you in the process of writing another play now?

A.  Yes. I began it yesterday. But I really cannot speak
    about it since I have just started it. I did write an-

other one-act play which lasted twenty-five minutes:
*La Giroise.* This word does not exist in French and it
is around this ambiguous problem that the theme of the
play centers: the non-existence of the word *giroise.*
This work is really like a game played between two
people. It centers around language and no one knows
the rules; in fact, each of the participants might be
inventing these rules as they go along.

Q. You like words, don't you?

A. Yes. In this play the word *giroise* is mysterious and
increases the drama intrinsic to the work. The word
is first found in a book which the characters are reading. The word occurs and re-occurs: each time the
meaning is a little different. The characters ask each
other to define it as they meet up with it. It does not
take too long before we realize that actually two
imaginations are pitted one against the other, that
each is struggling valiantly to win. If one character
does not succeed in redefining the word, he might be
losing something quite important — something very
important — something very grave is at stake.

Q. Yours is a theatre in which dialogue is primordial,
isn't that so?

A. Yes. At least for the time being. This does not mean
that it will always be so. Sets and sound effects
play a normal secondary role in my theatre — in fact,
I would really like to do away with décors completely.
You certainly know what Alfred Jarry said about them:
there are certain things which are particularly horrible
in the theatre: sets and actors. It is, however, very
difficult to get along without actors in the theatre.
As for sets, that's another question. Alfred Jarry
wanted his actors in masks and would have them
play without moving their faces at all. In this way,

the actor would no longer be the sterotyped and fixed accoutrement he is in ordinary theatre. As for sets, we are still dependent upon these to a certain extent.

Q. Does the unconscious play a role in your theatre?

A. Yes. I hope so at least. Inspiration — the genesis of the play — comes to me through my dreams. For weeks and even months I can think out certain situations and characters — dream them out so to speak. Then, I sit down and write my play very quickly — or my novel— and everything comes to me at this stage of the game quite rapidly, simply through an association of ideas. Perhaps because the unconscious does play such an important role in my theatre, my writing technique might resemble in certain respects what the Surrealists indulged in, "authentic writing." This would really be an ideal state: let all ideas and notions emanate freely from the unconscious. Yet, one must have a certain control over what one includes in a play: dramatic elements, theatrical conventions....

Q. What are your impressions of contemporary theatre? Of Arrabal, Ionesco, Beckett, Genet?

A. I don't consider myself very close to Arrabal. As for the three pillars—Genet, Beckett, Ionesco — they are infinitely fascinating. Unfortunately these playwrights have not really found audiences worthy of them in France. Here the theatre-going public is rather bourgeois, snobbish even. Those who would really appreciate this kind of theatre cannot afford the price of a ticket.

Q. What is your favorite contemporary play?

A. *Endgame* by Beckett. I consider it a masterpiece. I

have seen it several times. I really cannot explicate my feelings concerning this play. All I can say is that I feel myself transported into another universe each time I see it or read it. It has such tremendous force and vitality, such depth and vision — that it leaves me limp. It's theatricality alone is remarkable.

Q.   You also seem to be impressed with Artaud's works. Could you elaborate upon this question?

A.   I have been a fan of Artaud's for a long time. I've read everything he has written. I cannot really tell you why he enthralls me — perhaps it's because of his powers of *clairvoyance*, his prodigious sense of language. I have never known of any writer capable of endowing a word with such extreme power and force. I can spot Artaud's language any place and any time. The rhythms he infuses into language, his actual mutilation of words **are unique.** Each time he writes, it is as though he were giving birth to — expelling — totally new words. One has the impression that one has never seen them before. Let anyone read Artaud's adaptation of *The Monk* and he will be struck by the vigor of his language and his totally original flow of words. His *Heliogabalus* is absolutely admirable. It seems to come straight from Plato — particularly his discussions concerning unity and multiplicity. He treats these questions in a prodi-giously enlighten-ing manner. One would have liked to discuss Plato with him. I'm sure he had a very particular way of discussing such principles. After all, Artaud was a metaphysician also.

Q.   Are you a mystic?

A.   No. But I'm concerned and curious about these things. I'm not a rational type of person, but rather emotional.

Q.  You mentioned Jarry before.  I believe you admire him
    very greatly also?

A.  Jarry does impress me.  Everything he did during his
    brief life — thirty-three years — was extraordinary.
    He was actually the founder of a completely new
    theatre.  There is, as you know, a close tie between
    Jarry and Artaud since the latter founded the Théâtre
    Alfred Jarry.

Q.  You have written two **novels,** *Lézard* and *The Alliance.*
    Could you tell us something about them?

A.  Neither of them pleased the critics.  The title of the
    first novel, *Lézard* is actually a pun.  When speaking
    the word in **French,** it means the animal "lizard;"
    it can also be confused with "les arts," meaning
    "the arts."  The second **novel,** *The Alliance,* also has
    two meanings: "the ring" and an alliance between
    two people.  This second novel is being adapted for
    the movies.  It has been slightly altered.

    The novel relates the story of a marriage between
    a **veterinarian** and a lady who owned an apartment.
    They are constantly and mutually suspicious of one
    another.  Actually, the novel corroborates the state-
    ment which has been made: that doubt is the most
    powerful aphrodisiac.  This couple could neither live
    with nor love each other unless they suspected the
    worst things about each other.  The film, however,
    introduces another idea: the animals surrounding the
    veterinarian will play an important role in the film,
    adding, thereby a truly fantastic dimension.

Q.  In what direction is the theatre headed today?

A.  I don't know.  I don't think it's enjoying a very healthy
    state, however.  I have confidence in the theatre and

I realize it must try everything — including the antics of the Living Theatre. I am always wary of those people who set out to do something ultra-modern; who want to become avant-gardists. Yet, the Living Theatre, the theatre of derision, the theatre of the ridiculous, of nudity are all important — indispensable. It is they who shake up the torpor and the drowsiness which forever plagues this art.

Q.  Have you seen *Hair?*

A.  Yes. I was most impressed with it. I saw it first in London, then in New York with a different cast. I don't consider it scandalous at all. Nor am I against nudity in the theatre or in the movies for that matter. We have to experience all these techniques in order to evolve. We cannot stagnate. When I went to New York — I've been there three times — I lived in East Village. There, I met real *hippies*. We must distinguish the real from the pseudo-hippies. They were very much annoyed with *Hair*. They felt that it was a commercial exploitation or everything they are doing. The play itself is a very clever utilisation of themes which are very much in style today.

Q.  What are your impressions of Grotowski's way of viewing the theatrical ritual.

A.  I have mixed feelings about his work. I saw *The Akropolis*. I really don't like it. It does not touch me. In all fairness, however, I must admit that it is very interesting. Yet, I wonder whether his quest isn't a little passé today; a little too expressionistic, perhaps too similar to the rigidity of a theatre which flourished ten years ago. Form has become so important for Grotowski that all spontaneity has been abolished. Furthermore, his extremely possessive attitude

vis-à-vis the actors he directs seems far too rigid a
point of view. It seems to surpress everything which
comes forth freely and unhampered. His actors re-
mind me of automatons at times, playing out something
which has been taught to them in the most perfect of
manners.

Q.   Do you think that the stress laid today on form in the
theatre is comparable to this same trend in the novel?

A.   Yes. Perhaps. I have frequently asked myself why
the so-called "new novelists" are so obsessed with
form. I could be a little mean and answer my own
question by saying that they have no real ideas,
nothing to say and that's why they stress form to such
an extent — the exterior. Yet, such an answer would
not really be exact. Actually, this interest in form
first became apparent in painting and in music. The
movies have not yet succombed to its wiles, but they
will. The question of form is extremely important and
so vast a subject that it cannot be treated in a few
sentences. I used to attend all the art exhibits. Now,
I don't go to any. Have I changed? Has painting
changed? Is it my fault that I am no longer moved by
what I see in the pictorial arts? I have read very few
modern novels lately and if by chance I should begin
one ... I doze off very shortly and the book drops
from my hands. The "new novelists" are really
writing exercises and not novels. The same cannot
be said about the theatre. A play is dependent upon
the spectators; their participation is indispensable.

Georges-Luis Borges, an Argentinian writer, has
made some admirable statements concerning writing
in general. One of his ideas is the following: a text
does not exist unless there is a reader to enjoy it.
The same can be said of painting. If no one looks at
a painting, it has not yet taken on life. Borges has

also said that Cervantes influenced Kafka and that it is equally correct to say that Kafka influenced Cervantes. If you read Cervantes today after having read Kafka, you are really not reading the same author as you would have had you never laid eyes upon the latter's stories and novels. One reads Cervantes in a new light, having experienced Kafka's turbulent universe first. The result: Cervantes has been influenced by Kafka since your vision of his work has now been altered.

To return to Borges' first statement — this work of art which exists only from the moment a viewer experiences its aura — one might say that the modern trend in art may die out shortly or become transformed into something else since it does not attract a real audience. There are exceptions, notably in the musical field. John Cage's music, for example, moves me. He too is preoccupied with form, objects, new instruments and original sonorities — all types of new materials. Yet, there is something deeply fascinating which emerges from his vibrant and original tonalities.

We wish to thank the editors of *Drama and Theatre* for permission to reprint the above interview (Vol. 7, no. 3).

## *FRANÇOIS BILLETDOUX*

*Interviewer's Note:*

*François* Billetdoux was born in Paris on September 7, 1927. In 1944 he studied at Charles Dullin's Ecole d'Art Dramatique. One year later he became a student at the Institut des Hautes Etudes Cinématographiques. He became program director of the Radio-Télévision Française in Martinique in 1949. A novelist, a producer of radio and television skits and a song writer, Billetdoux' success in the theatre has gained rapidly with, among others, *Tchin-Tchin* (1959); *The Behavior of the Bredburry Couple* (1960); *Then Go to Törpe's* (1961); *You've Got to Go Through Clouds* (1966), *How Goes the World, Mister? It Turns Mister!, The Widows* (1972), etc.

Q. What drew you to the theatre?

A. I was drawn to the theatre little by little. I was very young — around seven or eight years old — when I began my theatrical career. At the lycée I was part of a **troupe** of amateurs. As soon as it became possible I began studying with Charles Dullin. When I was fifteen years old I began working on the radio — as an actor and in various other capacities. All this experience served me well later on as an actor in the theatre.

Q. What was the name of your first play?

A. My first play "for the theatre" was entitled *To the Night
the Night* (1955). I specify "for the theatre" because
before *To the Night the Night* I had written many
(around thirty) plays for radio and television. This
work prepared me to write plays for the stage — which
is what I really wanted to do.

Q. How long does it take you to write a play?

A. It varies. It really does not depend upon me. Many
factors which are difficult to analyze play a part in
this whole story. I believe I wrote *To the Night the
Night* in two nights. I wrote *Then Go to Törpe's* in
two stages. I dictated the first two acts in four days
and then I waited a while. I dictated the last two
acts in eight days. On the other hand, the last play
I **wrote,** *You've Got To Go Through Clouds* (produced
by Jean-Louis Barrault and Madeleine **Renaud), took**
me six months to write. I believe that it takes me
much more time to think my play through — that is,
constructing it and assembling **the various elements—**
than it does to write it. The time it takes to write a
play varies and depends upon the difficulties of form
and expression — that is, the difficulties of finding
the right **manner** of expressing one's ideas and intentions. But you must not think that I have any fixed
rules. When I begin a play I never know how long it
will take me to finish it. I write quickly or slowly
and I think that with age things come much more
slowly.

Q. Were you influenced by American westerns? Antoine
Bourseiller calls your play *How Goes the World,
Mister? It Turns, Mister!* a "western métaphysique."
Is this true?

A. Westerns in the sense of their being a "type" of dramatic entertainment have not really influenced me. But it is a western in the sense that works of this type are like accounts or narrations of westward movements or marches toward the west: it is the westward march of the whole Occident. And this is true geographically speaking, too. We know that land masses advance westward and drink up the sea: almost all conquests or exoduses are westward movements. Perhaps this is due to the rotation of the earth; I do not know. I take "western" to mean a westward movement: it is an Occidental problem and as for the word "métaphysique" one must be careful when using it. It's a "big" word and misunderstood most of the time. Everyone talks of "métaphysique" these days without knowing what it means.

Q. Could you tell us something about the themes of *How Goes the World, Mister? It Turns, Mister!*—that is, the relationship between individuals, the theme of liberty, fatality, and man's condition in the universe?

A. Yes. I could, but I would need a lot of time. This play at the beginning was in a way a meditation upon the different aspects of liberty. "Liberty" is a difficult word to use because it has many meanings. It can be used with various intents: social, biological, etc. My play is a series of tableaux or a series of queries on various questions one might very well ask oneself: In what respect are we really men? What are our obligations toward others? To what degree must one participate in a collective event? To what extent must one accept one's destiny?

I situated this play in 1945 because, in my opinion, the last war marked a turning point in history. After this war the planet, the world, began existing as an entity and let us say that at that moment nation-

alism no longer existed — though it really did deep
down. But now each one of us concerns himself with
things that are taking place on earth and it is from
this time on that we can really ask ourselves what
**"true liberty"** really means vis-à-vis ourselves and
others. What is our relationship with the world? It is
multiple. All these things interested me, plus the
desire to write a **good play,** and this is normal for a
man of the theatre.

I don't believe there are plays in which the
question of fatality doesn't arise. In former times
fatality was imposed by the gods; today, and more and
more so, fatality stems from the hands of man because
man has become more and more aware and more responsible. Man has become his own god. It really is
from this point of view that one should talk in terms
of liberty and that is why I chose this period for my
play — from 1945 on, our problems are going to arise
and have been arising in different **ways;** questions are
also asked in a different light now.

Q. What part **does "the dream" play** in *Then Go to Törpe's?*

A. The part played by the dream? I would say rather the
part played by psychoanalysis, and this role is multiple and complicated. If one could give a résumé of
the unconscious elements which compel us to write
such plays one would find rich source material indeed.
But such a **résumé** is impossible, and to analyze
Mlle Törpe's inner motivations would necessitate
many hours of discussion.

Q. What does Mlle Törpe represent symbolically speaking?

A. She **represents** many things but I would not say symbolically. My main source of worry when writing a
**play—outside** of the fact that I want it to be **"round,"**

that is, to have it live its own life — is that this play
be capable of resisting or capable of holding its own
when analyzed from all the different points of view,
that is, Marxist, dramatic, stylistic, etc. A play must
live a life of its own and as far as I am concerned if
a character were only symbolic I would be very much
disturbed. Mlle Törpe is more interesting as a real
character than as a symbolic one. I believe that after
having read the play one is aware of the type of inner
adventure which was hers.

*Then Go to Törpe's* takes place after a certain
political revolution, and from the dialogue, one can
understand the characters and how Mlle Törpe's political and religious relationships came about. One
can analyze her exterior and inner movements. I
believe she possesses all the characteristics of someone who has been able to attain a certain esoteric
realm. I would say that in the play she has reached
the moment of "crisis." She was wrong and her mistake was her desire to become a personal doctor without belonging to any profession. Had she been a
priestess or a psychiatrist, she could have avoided
the suicide of her boarders in her hotel. She should
have sent them to specialists to help them get over
their ills. But she wanted to act on her own and use
her own intuition as her guide. It is a known fact
that when one is emotionally involved one should not
base one's method of caring for others on one's intuition alone.

Q. How has music influenced your theatre?

A. Music has influenced it enormously. I really would
have wanted to be a musician and I am one — I become
one when I compose my plays. I try to avoid all the
logical principles one learns because after all logic
is merely a way of expressing oneself. It does not

really permit one to penetrate the inner corners of
our being.  Those profound areas in man do not obey
the logical rules set up by man.  In my opinion it is
through the musical structure of a play that one can
begin to understand certain things.  I shall give you
an example of the musical composition of my plays.
I say to myself: I have a main theme and I have motifs
and from this nucleus certain elements must develop
melodically and others like percussion instruments.
In this respect, my work is like that of a musician.
In addition to and also through these various melodic
**sounds, I try to create "real" characters.**

Q.  How were you trained to become an actor?

A.  I do not believe that my training was very good.  I did
not practice acting sufficiently.  My training stemmed
mostly from my radio work: analysis, **rhythms. All this**
theatrical work helped me prepare myself for the acting profession.  But there was something else which
helped me enormously: my training in the cabarets
and music halls of Paris.  I directed a great many
skits and shows.  I also performed in these same
cabarets.  This work is arduous and gives you additional training.  Of course, I took Charles Dullin's
courses and those of Jean le Goff of the Comédie-
Française.  An actor must play every day on stage so
that, after a certain number of performances, he can
discover what holding the stage really means.  One
can talk a great deal concerning the trade of an actor.
For me, however, acting is a sport with therapeutic
value.  It's a trade I would suggest everyone take up.
It is better than psychoanalysis because it forces
everyone to answer, to obey Montaigne's famous saying, "Connais-toi toi-même" (Know thyself).  After
all, when one is fat like me one must neither deceive
oneself or others and so one must say: be happy you

have a belly, and this sort of satisfaction, namely, the ability to face the truth and enjoy it, is a kind of therapy.

Q. Were you influenced by Antonin Artaud? If not, then by whom?

A. It is always difficult to answer such a question. I was and am a great reader and I did not choose such and such a master. I regret not having had direct masters. I can perhaps talk of many influences: Dullin, le Goff... but I was not really anyone's **pupil.** By **reading a lot,** by being confronted daily with the many problems which beset radio, I could do a lot of experimenting as far as dramatic conception is concerned. I felt and was stimulated by all these things. So, I am as much taken by Artaud's ideas as I am by Gordon Craig, **Stanislawski,** Dullin, etc. Working with Dullin was a great experience. His peasant side attracted me. Perhaps he was most influential in my formation? I cannot really say! I am open to all influences whether they be those of the **Peking Opera** or of African culture... All this experience does and will serve me.

Q. How do you see **the play,** *You've Got To Go Through Clouds?* Its themes, etc.

A. It's an **enormous** play. It has a cast of forty-five characters. It tells a whole life and in some ways you could call it a type of analysis or "balance-sheet" of the **Occidental** bourgeoisie. The **bourgeoisie,** after having been attacked in certain **areas,** should try to reassess itself and give itself a good **working-over.** It seems to me that even the proletarian movement aims at a certain bourgeois state. We must again analyze this "bourgeois state" which has been the subject of so many novels for so many years. After all, Balzac described the bourgeoisie more than he did any other class. I think we have reached the point where the bourgeoisie is about to disappear as a social class. There is such a mixture of classes, and this mixture is more important than one imagines. This is one of the reasons why political problems are so difficult to settle in France today. If France is ahead of other countries as far as political unrest is concerned, it's because of its **"chaos,"** and its ''chaos'' is in fact a **positive—let** us **say, exemplary—** force.

Q.   Is there a conflict between your role as actor and dramatist since you practice both trades?

A.   I really do not think a conflict exists. I think that because I create **characters, the** fact that I know the acting profession helps me to describe male and female characters, or those of animals, and in the latter case I could become an animal in order to better describe it.

One thing I try to avoid **is writing parts for my-** self. That is always an error. It's this that Sacha Guitry did. Molière and Shakespeare avoided this **defect.**

My problem arises when I have to interpret a character in one of my plays. This requires particular study. I must forget, especially during rehearsals, that all the other characters are just as close to me as the one I am portraying. I must succeed in bringing out the aggressive side of the character I am portray- ing. It is this character which must fully enter into the game, producing the clash of wills with the other protagonists. And so I must virtually rid myself, so to speak, of all the other characters. They will be- **come my enemies of sorts.** To get rid of all the char- acters one has created and to portray just one — as an actor, of course — is most difficult.

There is also an advantage: since I am the creator of all the beings peopling the stage, I know them better and I can go further than the other actors in ridiculing the character I am interpreting. Also I think I can demand more from myself than from the other actors.

So acting has its satisfactions as well as its difficulties.

Q. Can you tell me something about "humor" in your plays?

A. This is very difficult because when you begin analyzing humor, you kill it. I practice humor and satire. Humor and comedy have become a necessity for me, and perhaps a kind of liberty with respect to people; a kind of tenderness and perhaps a way of avoiding abusive and limiting mental attitudes which are so stylish today. Today one must obey rules and regulations: be conventional, a rightist or leftist, a devout Catholic, an atheist. One must fit into categories. These systems are ridiculous. That's why I indulge in humor.

Q. How did the plot of *The Behavior of the Bredburry Couple* come to you?

A. One evening as I was reading the newspaper, *France-Soir,* I came upon the following notice: An American wife has put her husband up for sale for $30,000. I bought the newspaper for several days thereafter and there was no further mention of this American woman. I questioned myself because when one reads a newspaper one has the impression that the reader is the butt of a joke. I asked myself how she could sell her husband in a land where laws such as alimony exist. I came to the conclusion that she did not sell him for the money; she sold him for love. The fact that she put him up for sale stems from an old tradition. It is a modern version of the "dowry." The exchange of one individual for money is a fundamental rule of society.

Q.  Can you talk to us about *Night Shirts,* which you wrote in collaboration with Eugene Ionesco and Jean Vauthier?

A.  It really was not a collaboration. The three of us were asked to write a play on the same theme, using the same décor of one bed and three doors. The first play by Ionesco was called *The Nights,* the second, by Vauthier, was entitled *Badadesques,* a sequel to *Captain Bada,* and my play *For Finalie.*

   I admire Vauthier and Ionesco. I like Ionesco personally and think that he has had an extraordinary career. The discovery of the theatre late in life and his conscientiousness as a dramatist fascinate me.

   Vauthier is different — much more egocentric. But I am not judging him as a playwright because of this. Vauthier is more of a poet in that "he tells himself" more willingly in a poetic frenzy or delirium, which has become a necessity for him. There is something very astonishing about his work in the extreme precision of his dream. I know that he used several recording machines when he writes and he writes practically as a musician plays. He wants to point out and describe to the actor all the intonations and gestures necessary to portray the role. Vauthier's plays cannot be interpreted from several points of view. There is only one interpretation which he, the dramatist, wants to see realized: a perfect exteriorization of his inner dream.

We wish to thank the editors of *First Stage* for permission to print the above interview (Spring, 1965).

## LILIANE ATLAN

*Interviewer's Note:*

Liliane Atlan was born in Montpellier, France, in 1932.
She was a student of philosophy, literature, and the great
Hebrew texts: the Bible, the Midrash, the Kabbala. Liliane
Atlan is both a poet and a playwright. Her first published
drama, *Monsieur Fugue*, was performed in 1967 by the
Comédie de St-Etienne, and in the fall of that same year
by the Théâtre National Populaire in Paris. It was acclaimed by audiences. *The Messiahs*, her second play,
(1968) introduces audiences into cosmic realms where
Messiahs of all types observe the chaotic condition on
Earth: man a prey to violence and horror. These Messiahs
dream of saving the planet. Some of them have actually
descended upon it, but have failed in their mission. As
man's lamentations rise to them, these same Messiahs cannot help but be moved by such desperate calls. and once
again prepare for another journey downward. In *The Little
Carriage of Flames and Voices* (1971) we move into the
double world of a soul divided. A woman split in two attempts to find a panacea that will end her torments: eroticism, drugs, knowledge, revolt. Nothing heals her fragmented
self. Still she searches for "the little carriage of flames
and voices, the one that will give her peace of soul."
*Lapsus* (1971) is a collection of brief texts that take the

reader into a dream world which is at odds with reality.
Filled with the most poignant Hebraic symbolisms — images
both colourful and stark — the entire volume exudes a
nostalgia for "the sacred" and a longing for tranquillity.

Liliane Atlan's theatre sweeps audiences into their
very depths, inspires them to prod, challenge and search
for some inner discipline or a faith which will permit
them to hope, and to survive past and future holocausts.

Q.  You were first captivated by the theatre when you were
    twelve years old.  Can you tell us something about
    this experience?

A.  Yes.  During the Second World War my sister and I
    were kept hidden most of the time.  We almost never
    went out.  We had to entertain ourselves.  My sister
    would dress up, would disguise herself.  She was the
    audience.  I was the stage: the actors, the author ....
    Everything lived within me: I screamed, gesticulated,
    died.  I would speak out my lamentations, my dirges,
    my psalms.  After the war nothing seemed possible.
    There was no way out for us.  Man and his gods had
    died in the concentration camps.  I emerged from my
    sorrow perhaps by reflex action.  One has to live, to
    bear the torture of life.  We began to view the world
    with lucidity, realizing that all paths until now had
    led to an impasse.  I decided, along with some of my
    Jewish friends, to search for an answer among the
    Hebrew **texts—the** Bible, the Midrash, the Kabbala — to
    discover a way of life and a **non-Christian** way of
    thinking.  My roots exist in these texts, whatever
    their limitations may be.

Q.  Did you ever write novels?

A.  Yes.  I used to begin writing one every three months.
    I never finished any of them.  One day, I realized

that what I had been writing was theatre.

Q.  Your plays, *Monsieur Fugue*, *The Messiahs*, *The Little Carriage of Flames and Voices*, were all successfully produced. Do you attend rehearsals?

A.  I attended all the rehearsals of *Monsieur Fugue* performed in France in 1967, and this winter in Hebrew in Tel Aviv.

I had never had any stage experience before. I therefore changed and modified my text in terms of the difficulties, frequently of a rhythmic nature, encountered by the actors. I did not, however, participate, technically speaking, in the creation of the *mise en scene*. We each had our task cut out for us: each worked alone and as a unit, in complicity with the collectivity. We had the feeling of creating something as a group, functioning and exteriorizing our ideas and feelings with the help of the others, reaching depths which we might not have experienced alone.

I thought that these marvelous working conditions and the elation I felt at the time were usual in the theatre. I realized my error when *The Little Carriage of Flames and Voices* was created at the Avignon Festival in 1971. I was the "author." The question of "serving my text, my subjectivity" never arose. The director replaced my point of view with his, which does not imply any lessening of interest.

A text never has *one point of view*. It is relative. In this case, real group work is required. Each individual participant plays out his own well-defined role, bringing his own vision to the ensemble. He surpasses or goes beyond himself, since he is part of the living corpus. He is not solely involved with the text, nor with the *mise en scène*, nor the play of the actors, but with all these, and with something else besides — the spectacle. No other goal — with all of the difficulties and gropings involved — is possible. Such an objective cannot be reached unless each one ( author, director, actor) *serves* something besides himself, outside of himself, unless he devotes himself to the theatre as a whole.

The real crisis in the theatre, as elsewhere, arises from the fact that people serve themselves first. The sterility of many avant-garde groups is an example of such a situation, as are the hatreds which arise among the actors themselves. We may even have the impression that the theatre is nothing at all to-day — that it's dead. On the other hand, there are groups of actors who may be truly *disinterested,* particularly when a play concerns them directly. It is at this point that a bond is suddenly created between the stage and the audience — true theatre is then established. Even if the acting remains rudimentary. When *Monsieur Fugue* was performed in Tel Aviv (the play ran for five months) we had one objective during rehearsals: to be worthy of the subjects treated (ghettoes and concentration camps). While finding our way, a kind of communion or friendship was born between us.

Q. What authors influenced you most forcefully?

A.   O'Neill, Lorca (I learned from them that poetry was possible in the theatre), Artaud, Beckett, Genet, Césaire, Kateb, and Gatti.

Q. What were these influences?

A.   They are very difficult to define. After having read **Artaud's** *The Theatre and Its Double,* I wrote *The Doors.* For the first time, and despite all sorts of defects, I experienced a kind of freedom in writing. Gatti proved to me that such a state of freedom is possible if scenic time and space are used in such a way as to bring a new sense of *relativity* to the theatre. I also feel close to Kateb and Césaire because their search is similar to mine. They belong to two different cultures — as I do; foreigners to both of them, unable to renounce one or the other. Frequently, they do express a concept or a sensibility which is not basically theirs. And then everything enters into a kind of perpetual contradiction. Plays or poems emerge from this chaos. We cannot henceforth escape the relativity of these cultural and linguistic levels.

Q.   What would your ideal theatre be?   A theatre in the round? An arena? A garage? One out of doors?

A.   There is no ideal theatre. The acting area should be suitable to the play — an outgrowth of it. I had thought that a planetarium would be most suitable for *The Messiahs*, a play which is lost in the immensity of the cosmos; or a theatre fashioned in such a way that the actors would be performing in a type of "celestial vault;" other dimensions occurred to me. But to represent the galaxies in all of their complexity would make for a static condition. Perhaps it would be better to make *movement* visible, to show the relationships existing among beings, planets and worlds, in a very simple way or on any kind of stage. Instead of building theatres — the very form itself becoming a hindrance, a type of ossification — I believe that one should renew one's concepts, the text, the actors' play and the *mise en scène* periodically. These incessant mutations must play, grow and incorporate themselves into what we call the universe. Perhaps in time a new poetry may be discovered.

Q.   How do you react to so-called modern theatre?   To the plays of Arrabal? Weingarten? Dubillard? And the *mise en scène* of Grotowski?

A.  Real theatre — modern theatre — is one which should
work against the times, against the fads. It should re-
discover meaning, savor something which would render life *real*. Arrabal's theatre does not interest me.
I really don't know Weingarten's work at all. The
plays that I've seen by Dubillard please me but don't
leave a deep impression upon me.

   I saw Grotowski's *The Akropolis*. I felt both
admiration and repulsion for his work. Everything
which participates in horror without combatting it
becomes its accomplice. I do not think one can found
a viable *aesthetic* on violence alone. Or rather it
just does not concern me. Perhaps it is because I
identify with the victim. The manner in which Grotowski referred to Auschwitz in *The Akropolis* seemed
false and insulting. But perhaps I'm just allergic and
unjust. I think we have lost the feeling for art. And
the most famous directors today — those who pride
themselves on the fact that they have *nothing* to say —
are the very ones who are producing a consumer-
aesthetic! This has nothing to do with real poetry.
Real poetry lives in Beckett's *Happy Days*. He says
the most terrible things in a pitiless way. Yet, one
leaves the theatre after seeing this play in a state of
*wonderment*, enthusiasm. I think that the theatre's
function is to awaken *enthusiasm*.

Q.  Can you tell us something about *The Little Carriage
of Flames and Voices?*

A.  I really can't talk about this play. I tried to carry out
my ideas, those I've just discussed. I tried to go
through hell (in the real sense of the word) and still
maintain my enthusiasm. I don't know whether I succeeded.

Q. Were you influenced by Artaud?

A. YES. In such a profound manner as to make it terribly
   difficult − even impossible to articulate. It's really
   ridiculous to talk about Artaud now. Everyone today
   claims to have been influenced by him.

   When I was reading *The Theatre and Its Double*,
   I had the impression of seeing in writing what I was
   thinking, in an obscure way. His words sometimes
   frightened me because I was living them. I understood
   them in the deepest of ways... of levels... too painfully.

Q. Your new work, *Lapsus*, is made up of a series of inter-
   related images, deeply rooted one in the other, as
   though emerging from your very depths. What inspired these images?

A. Most of the texts which make up *Lapsus* were originally
   dreams which I transcribed. Even the title comes
   from a dream I had in a half-waking and half-sleeping
   state. I had the impression of being able to intercept
   and to channel a type of logic which belongs to another realm, one which can be reached only through
   the dream. Night possesses its own logic. I wanted
   to describe this state. My only criteria was that of
   exactitude. Frequently when awakening I thought I
   had lost the key to that other world. At other moments
   the very act of writing permitted me to rediscover it.

Q. What effect does the Kabbala have upon you?

A. I'm not inspired by it in a systematic way. Rather I'm
   impregnated by it. It becomes visible in everything
   I write, notably *The Little Carriage of Flames and
   Voices*. To refer to a tradition − whatever it may
   be − permits one to maintain a stand, counter to or

at cross-currents with the times in which we live.
But our epoch has so overwhelmed us, affected us so
deeply that eventually we become aware of the fact
that we are also basically at odds with it. We need
irritants, counter-forces. We need an absolute! Cre-
ativity is born or captured by means of a series of
contradictions. Real theatre must busy itself with
this struggle.

Q. What are your plans for the future?

A.  I've almost finished *The Dream of the Rodents* in
which I struggle with this very problem of opposites.
I must go further in terms of the theatre and try to
solve the problems I mentioned above. I don't as yet
know where my search will lead.

## ARMAND GATTI

*Interviewer's Note:*

Armand Gatti, born in Monaco on January 24, 1924, is of Italian and Russian extraction. In 1940 he left Monaco to join the French Resistance in the Corrèze. There he was arrested and deported to a work camp. After a dramatic escape, he went to London and enlisted as a parachutist in the Special Air Service. Gatti began his career as a journalist in 1946 and eight years later was awarded the Albert-London prize, the highest honor given to a journalist. In 1954 he co-authored *The Life of Churchill*. In the same year he also went to Guatemala during the height of its revolution, traveled through South and Central America and the United States, and, later, went to China and Siberia. In 1955 he published the first of twenty-six plays, *Black Fish*. It won the Fénelon prize. In 1950 Jean Vilar produced Gatti's *The Buffalo Frog* at the Théâtre National Populaire. Now well-known as a playwright in France and abroad, Gatti is the author of such successful plays as *Child-Rat* (1960), *The Voyage of the Great Tchou, Chronicles of a Provisional Planet, The Imaginary Life of the Street Cleaner Auguste G . . .* (1962), *Public Song Before Two Electric Chairs* (1966), *V for Vietnam* (1967), *The Thirteen Suns on Rue Saint-Blaise* (1968), *The Passion Of General Franco* (1968), etc. He has also written and directed films, among them *The Enclosure*, made in Yugo-

slavia, and *The Other Christopher,* photographed in Cuba.
   Armand Gatti's theatrical search consists in creating
a non-linenear theatre, and in giving stage life to characters living in several **parallel** worlds at the same time.

Q.  Why were you drawn to the theatre?

A.  I really don't know.  Circumstances willed it that way.
    I think I could have done most anything.  I don't be-
    lieve in predestination.

Q.  Can you tell us something about your first play?

A.  *Black Fish.*  It was based on an old Chinese tale
    which dates back to 200 B.C. and has been told and
    re-told ever since . . .. The story deals with the found-
    ing of China and the problems which arose with the
    establishment of the ensuing liberal dictatorship.
    When writing this play, I asked myself whether there
    was such a thing as a liberal dictatorship.  *Black
    Fish* is topical because it treats a subject which re-
    peats itself in each century and with each generation.
    The characters in my play know **inside-out** the events
    leading up to their revolution.  Yet, they still persist
    in believing they can escape the course of history—
    perhaps in the same way Roland was convinced he
    could win the battle against the Saracens.
       The historical incidents in *Black Fish* unfold
    as they occurred in history, with one difference: we
    are in the theatre.  The spectators, therefore, will
    confront each historical event in turn and in front of
    *three screens.* These screens have a two-fold purpose:
    they are constricting in that they force the spectator —
    and the protagonists too — to face the event squarely
    whenever he might be tempted to escape into a world
    of fantasy and change the course of history; they are
    liberators in that each viewer thinks he can crush

these walls of destiny. The screens are also a vehicle whereby the suspense and drama of each individual event can be built up.

Q.  How long does it take you to write a play?

A.  I wrote *The Imaginary Life of the Street Cleaner Auguste G...* in two weeks and *The Second Existence of the Tatenberg Camp* in three years. It depends on how I feel.

Q.  How much of yourself do you put into your work?

A.  Unfortunately, a great deal. Perhaps too much. I know I can write a play only if I have lived it. Such an approach, I think, adds to the play's living quality. An intellectual approach is not sufficient. I could not have written *Public Song Before Two Electric Chairs*, a dramatic rendition of the Sacco-Vanzetti trial, had I not been to the United States.

Q.  Do you have any special writing techniques or methods?

A.  No. I have no methods whatsoever. I mean by this that I have no rigid conceptions about writing just as I have no preconceived ideas concerning life in general. Everything depends upon my mood at the time. There are what writers call privileged moments, when one experiences what is commonly called *inspiration*. During these periods I can work for five days and five nights without stopping. But there are other moments when I am flooded with despair, when nothing comes of my labor. At this period I usually take one character at a time and leave my apartment with him or her. Then I walk all over Paris — for hours on end. I remain alone with my character until I begin to understand the personality of the being with whom I am dealing. Once I am able to communicate with my character, the battle has been won. Then — and only then — can I continue to write. At that time, I am able to give the character body, substance, flesh and blood. After the personality and the destiny of one character has been firmly established in my mind I go about understanding the other characters in the same way. Once all of them have been realized, I force them to confront each other. Sometimes these confrontations are disastrous for them, and for me. But it is from this confrontation that the action and interaction of the drama emerges.

Q.   Does the dream play a part in *The Imaginary Life of the Street Cleaner* **Auguste G...**?

A.   No. The dream in itself, as far as I am concerned, does not exist. Reality — every day reality, that is, the *concrete*— is a hundred times more interesting. It is this concrete reality which stirs my imagination, more forcefully than any dream could ever hope to. In other words, the object, the **thing, the workaday** world, acts as a stimulant for me. I believe in poetry, but not the dream.

Q.   Do, you encounter any particular difficulties when writing a play?

A.   Yes. One in particular. I try to create *theatrical simultaneity* on stage. My plays frequently take place on different continents (China, the United States, and Cuba, for example); that is, they are not only spatially varied, but time differentiations are also achieved by a blending of past, present and future events. To **penetrate such spatial and time differentials** and to render them dramatic and viable is difficult to say the least. My theatrical search consists, however, in trying to live in several *parallel worlds at the same time:* to create theatrical simultaneity.

Q.  Can you give us an example of how you have made use of your spatial and time concepts to **produce** theatrical simultaneity?

A.  Yes. My play *The Imaginary Life of the Street Cleaner Auguste G . . .* illustrates my idea. The play resulted from a personal experience, really a segment of my life, since my father was a street cleaner. It is, in fact, the recapitulation that a simple man makes of his life just as he is about to die.

The curtain goes up and Auguste G. is forty-six years old. He is lying in his hospital bed. Nothing has really happened to him during his life and so he tries to *invent* events. That is why I called it *The Imaginary . . . .* He tries to invent his life and give it meaning. He tries to understand the myths and symbols of the world about him: the war of 1914, for example, the police, unions, love, bosses — all these aspects of life which had escaped him when he was actually living through them. Auguste G. tries to make sense out of this array of absurd events, which he does, as his end approaches.

To add drama and depth to his life, I use *theatrical simultaneity.* The stage then becomes a series of phases in Auguste G.'s life. We see him at nine years of age, at twenty, at thirty — people emerge from his past and his present. These people, constantly transformed age-wise, fade in and out and into one another on stage. Time and place are forever shifting throughout the drama.

Q.  Were you pleased with the staging of *The Imaginary Life of the Street Cleaner Auguste . . .?*

A.    Yes. Roger Planchon's company played it just the
      way I thought it should be performed. Jacques Ros-
      ner did an enormous job directing it. It's the type of
      play which requires an entirely new concept of the
      *mise en scène*. René Allio created the décors—simul-
      taneous decors: a dance hall, offices, trenches, and
      more were all visible on stage at the same time.

Q.    What do you mean by a new concept of the *mise en
      scene?*

A.    I say *new* because scenic or stage time is non-existent
      in my play. The usual theatrical time, that is, clock-
      time, has been completely abolished. The only time
      which exists in my play is *flash time*. In other words,
      what audiences see are concrete images: a series of
      flashes which last perhaps sometimes but twelve
      seconds: Auguste G. at forty-six years of age, at ten,
      at twenty, etc. This flash or simultaneous time re-
      quires a new structural theatrical organization which
      differs from the one we know. We call this type of
      theatrical conception *non-linear* theatre. The director
      of *The Imaginary Life*... tried to make the various
      structures presented on stage as concrete and as
      meaningful as possible to both the protagonist and
      the audience. That is why he constructed sets featur-
      ing trenches, offices, etc. Naturally, this play re-
      quired an enormous amount of machinery. In the
      movies, such feats can be accomplished by staging a
      set and then filming it, and so on. In the theatre,
      however, these events and scenes as I have conceived
      of them must flow in rapid succession so that the
      rhythmic effects created by them are not lost and
      excitement is added to the spectacle as a whole. This
      theatrical technique permits us to go beyond what we
      can achieve in motion pictures, which do not permit
      this kind of simultaneity.

In *The Imaginary Life...* three different events go on at the same time on stage. Since the hero is living at three different ages, three different temporalities are rendered concrete before the audience. It is impossible to achieve such an effect in the movies unless you cut your picture into several different compartments as Kandinsky did, for example, with certain of his canvases. But even if you cut your film, each motif, placed in a different area, lives a separate life. There is no point, I feel, in adopting such a technique in the movies. In the theatre, however, this kind of simultaneity is fascinating because it adds a new dimension to the play and to the spectators' ability to identify with what is going on on stage. For example, when Auguste G., who is lying on his hospital bed, finds himself confronting all the women he had known during the course of his life, it means that he is practically making love simultaneously to Pauline, his great passion at twenty; to his wife at thirty; to Angelina, an older woman he met late in life. All of these stages and periods in his life converge one upon another without the hero ever seeing or being aware of any other presence but the one he is experiencing at that very moment. There is, then, a type of "melting" or "blending" of time — a fusion within the same image and at the same moment. From a technical point of view, such converging or blending of time and space permits the author and director to go further ahead in theatrical innovations.

Q.  How did the audience react to your theatrical innovations?

A.  *The Imaginary Life...* was very successful. As a matter of fact, on one evening I invited three hundred street cleaners to a special performance. Two hundred and ninety eight had never entered a theatre before. Five days later, they asked to see me. They presented me with several minature brooms and pails. These street cleaners had understood everything because they had brought their own experience with them. The imaginary is really part and parcel of daily life.

Q.   You are not only a playwright and a journalist, but a movie and theatrical director as well. Do you see any conflict between your role as director and dramatist?

A.   No. There are no conflicts. I have no real conflicts with myself. If I don't like a part of my play or picture I just change it.

Q.   **René Saurel,** writing in *Modern Times,* stated that you ''rebelled against all classical rules, all constraint....'' Can you explain this statement?

A.   Yes. Classical rules do not fit in with our times. Much of our modern theatre is as old as the monks who used to go on pilgrimages. It is infected with ''linear'' conceptions. A whole new way of thinking has arisen out of our scientific discoveries: that is, thinking in terms of time and space. There is a whole new adventure to be lived in the domain of the theatre. An artistic, scientific, aesthetic adventure is being lived in the novel, in music, in the pictorial arts — but really not yet in the theatre. There is, perhaps, a reason for this. Non-linear theatre needs a new type of audience: a non-intellectual one. Intellectuals usually live in strict accordance with their acquired knowledge and with everything that remains ''behind'' them. Everything they see and hear is referred back to and compared with that certain point in their past which acts as their landmark. The tendency of living in the past, of remaining behind, was frowned upon — as you must recall — in Biblical times. Those who looked back were transformed into a pillar of salt. Salt is very tasty, I admit it, but pillars of salt are static and unregenerate — and, finally, they crumble.

Q. What kind of audiences are you referring to?

A. At the Théâtre de la Cité in Lyons which is directed by Roger Planchon, we have a new way of going about things. Before putting on a play the actors, the directors, the scenic designer, all those connected with the enterprise, visit whatever aspect of society our play deals with: factories, homes, schools, etc. We then sit down and discuss what we have learned from the experience. Once the play has been staged, the actors, directors, etc. discuss it once again. A whole new series of impressions has now arisen from the work that has been done on the play and the experiences that have emerged because of it. What I have just said to you sounds very easy. It is not, in fact. It is very complex. The director's goal at the Théâtre de la Cité is to produce as many modern plays as possible.

Q. Could you go into more detail about your non-linear theatre?

A. Yes. A linear play means one in which one or several characters come into focus during a single period of time. This type of theatre "disdains" man because it does not give him any "possibilities." In the theatre which I am searching for, I have replaced clock-time with another world which possesses its own logic, its own way of seeing things. I call the time I have found — "time possibility". I mean by this that when

a man is born, he is not born alone, but one hundred
or two hundred characters are born at the same time
within him; that is, he is born with all sorts of "possibilities." He could be this or that. But he finds
himself imprisoned within a framework — first his
parents, his environment, his education, his village
or city, his experiences, etc. And so he slowly begins
to limit or kill some of the many "possibilities" life
has offered him. Little by little there comes a time
in his life when only two or three possibilities remain.
When he looses all "possibilities" this person, so
far as I am concerned, is dead. Sometimes a man is
born long before his birth is actually recorded and
dies long before his actual death.

Q.    Have you written a play in which you make use of
these "possibilities"?

A.    Yes. *Public Song Before Two Electric Chairs.* This
play, an intellectual drama, deals with the case of
Sacco and Vanzetti, the two anarchists who were
accused of murder and executed in 1927 in Charles-
town, Mass. The play takes place simultaneously in
five parts of the globe: Los Angeles, Turin, Boston,
Lyon, Hambourg. In each of these cities the play is
performed before different spectators. The play's
interest does not reside in the spectators' being pro
or con the plaintiffs. The question is to discover and
dramatise their reactions to the victims. How and for
what personal reasons do these modern spectators
identify with the two unfortunates? The Professor in
the audience, for example, identifies with the anarchists; the business man, with the attorney, since he
stands for social order and justice. These reactions
on the part of the theatrical audience are so dramatised
as to almost forcibly involve the actual audiences
watching this play in a Parisian theatre. The drama

really lies in the violence and depth of the onlookers'
reactions — and this makes for a pretty round of emotional involvement on all sides.

   You see, then, that the Sacco-Vanzetti trial is
not the real theme of *Public Song* ... but rather the
audience-play relationship within the theatre. I am
not, therefore, reworking Pirandellian time nor the
play within the play, but rather I am having audiences
face themselves. So, actually, the death sentence
meted out to **Nicola Sacco** and Bartolomeo Vanzetti
has been decided upon by the spectators themselves
in this "participation play."

Q. Is there any similarity between what you call "possibility" and Gide's "disponibilité"?

A. No. I conceive of life as a combat and not as a meditation. Life is a joy, a misfortune, a fight with its
   ups and downs. And so, when I talk of linear theatre,
   and I say it disdains men, I mean it presents man
   without "possibilities" because he sees himself in
   only one way. These "possibilities" make for man's
   greatness, his power, and his heroism. We are actually
   living many lives simultaneously but we are conscious
   of only living one. Why? Because we are enchained
   to one point of view. We look at the world in only
   one way. Man becomes liberated only when he lives
   his adventure as an individual — forcefully and dynam-
   ically — and this adventure is his life.

Q. Does the unconscious enter into your theatre?

A. I don't know. I never ask myself philosophical questions. I never went to school. My only education
   was and is life. When I returned from prison camp, I
   realized that one must live all experiences on all
   levels.

Q.   You once said that theatrical dialogue must be direct
      and not ambiguous.    Could you explain this point?

A.   Yes.   The theatre is something direct.   It is like a
      blow received by the spectators.   They do not have
      the time to look up systems and logics.   Once the
      blow has been thrust the dramatist must move swiftly
      on to the next act.

Q.   Is your theatre social as well as lyrical?

A.   Historical elements are necessary in order to place a
      play.   For example, if the story is about a king, then
      he lives in Africa, in Crete, etc.   He is conditioned
      by his country and his environment.   The situation
      of the Jew who lived in Germany under Hitler and the
      Jew who lives in Germany now or before the war is
      totally different.   If a play is situated in an imaginary
      country,   the audience will feel that such events
      *cannot* take place in *our* country.   But they can and
      they do!   When you do not situate a play its impact
      and power are lost.
             I do not write political theatre.   It is too con-
      stricting.

Q.   Can you tell us something about your **play, Chronicles
      of a Provisional Planet,** which deals with a subject
      similar to *The Deputy?*

A.   The story deals with earth men: Americans, French-
      men, and others, who, as astronauts, leave in search
      of a new planet.   And what do they discover on this
      planet?   A crime!   The Jews are being exterminated.
      They discover historical characters on this provisional
      planet who are like **Himmler, Hitler,** Eichmann, etc.
      but are called by other names.   The situation is
      actually a reversal of world-life.   The astronauts in

this play are really looking at their crimes from the outside. The guilty party, the criminal, though he was not fully responsible for the murders since his cronies were to blame, is not killed as was Eichmann. His crime was far too monstrous. His punishment will be to be sent to another planet. Death is too good for him. At the end of the play all the characters really responsible for the blood bath say ''Be careful when a play ends: a new one always begins.''

What is of importance in this play is not its historical **situation,** which can be repeated over and over again, but rather the blindness of certain individuals. The murderers should have been guilt-ridden. Yet, they were not. They all spoke with clear consciences. They refused to see their crimes.

After the Liberation of Paris someone said to me: "There are people who were put in prison unjustly — who did nothing." I say, *those are the people who should go to jail* — those who did nothing to remedy the situation. The person who tried to please both hangman and victim is the biggest coward of all. Worse than the SS men were those who became fat and wealthy from all the suffering about them and, to top it all, did so with a clear conscience. You can destroy a whole ideology with a clear conscience, especially if it stems from a principle as insane as Hitler's.

Q.  How did you train your actors to play in your plays? A new technique must be required to express ''simultaneity of time'' as well as man's ''possibilities''?

A.  Yes. Let's take the play *Chronicles of a Provisional Planet* for example. I asked the actor who was to play a Rabbi in a ghetto to forget his portrayal, to look upon himself as a singer at the Metropolitan Opera. After he spoke his lines as a singer, I asked

him to forget what I had just said and think of himself as a German worker, etc.   A few days before
opening night I said to the actor-Rabbi: "Consider
yourself a Rabbi now — and nothing else."   The actor
realized at this point that he had been confronted
with all sorts of possibilities when portraying his role.
His creation, therefore, achieved richness and complexity.   He enlarged his **vision,** adding other personality traits to his character: the pride of an opera
singer, the realism of a German worker, etc.   The
Rabbi became a multi-faceted character which made
him far more human.   I approach all my actors in this
manner.

Q.   How do you feel about Brecht?

A.   He tried to create a political theatre.   One really can
see Piscator in his work.   But one of the great con-
tributions to modern theatre was the form born with
Piscator and which found its true expression with
Brecht.   Brecht begins with the event.   His language
stems from the event, from a given period.   It is a
"living" language.   His theatre answered the need
of a whole generation.   Now, we have different problems.

Q.   I heard you once spent a few weeks in New York?

A.   Yes.   I traveled from Guatemala to New York, to Moscow, to Peking.   I was in New York in August during
a heat wave.   I realized I was arriving in a new world.
After a while I found myself in a hotel on Broadway.
Then, my desperate search began.   A whole series of
events took place and I felt myself floating about.
I met drunkards and I followed them into their dives,
became part of their **group,** etc.   I sank lower and
lower into **degradation.**   But I wanted to find out, to

experience this new world in all of its vigor and force and in its seething violence. Days later, I returned to my hotel. I was fascinated by your city and could find no other way of penetrating it except by discovery and search. It was like searching for the Holy Grail and I was that knight making my way in a forest of cement.

Reprinted in part from the *Kentucky Romance Quarterly* (Vol. XIV, 1969).

## GEORGES MICHEL

*Interviewer's Note:*

The Parisian born Georges Michel was orphaned at an early age: his father was deported by the Nazis and his mother died shortly afterward. He was brought up by his grandparents who not only taught him the watch-making trade, but instilled in him a love for work. At fifteen, when his grandparents died, Georges Michel found himself alone in the world. Financially unable to continue his academic studies, living in Belleville, a section of Paris crawling with delinquents, he could have gone the way of the destructive neighborhood gang. Instead, he opted for the creative road, pursuing the clock-making trade and later turning to writing. "I react by writing ... others react by breaking windows."

Georges Michel is well known in Paris thanks to the support given him by Jean-Paul Sartre, who published his **play, *The Toys,*** in the existentialist review *Modern Times* (1962) and prefaced his theatrical **piece, *Sunday's Walk,*** (1967). Unlike Sartre, Michel does not draw up metaphysical systems in his plays, nor does he "denounce the absurdity" in the world. He says he "merely" wants to "change the world and its people," presumably through the effect of his plays. A victim himself of injustice, of solitude and poverty, he feels compelled to dramatize on stage the wrongs he experienced and saw others endure during his young life. He does just this in both his novels and his dramas: *Aggression* (1967), *Bravos* (1969), *Crossbow and Rapiers* (1970), *A Love Nest, The Benches* (1970), *I am Twenty And Want to Die* (1971), etc.

Q. When did you first begin writing for the theatre?

A. Late in life. At the age of twenty-five. I was not well-read at the time. In fact, I had read practically nothing. I began writing because I felt overwhelmed by a sense of powerlessness. You see, I lived and still live in a very poor working class neighborhood in Paris — Belleville. I used to witness street scenes quite frequently which just revolted me. Since I could not step in directly and stop what I saw I just began writing. I thought in this way that I would be able to counteract my extreme sense of powerlessness.

Just as soon as I placed the words "the end" on my first novel, I began my second. After the first few pages, I realized that the subject lent itself far more readily to the theatre than to the novel. And so my first novel became a play, which I called *Staircase C*.

Q. How was your first produced play, *The Toys*, received by the critics? The audience?

A. The critics received it very well. As for the audience, they did not know me at all and so were more reticent. *The Toys* was performed thirty times and played to a half empty house nearly each time. This semi-failure, however, had a positive effect upon me. It gave me the right to ask the directors who wanted to stage my play to let me help direct it — and others as well.

Q. What about the sets?

A.  I always draw my own. I have been painting ever since
    the age of two. I know you are going to ask me who
    influenced me.    I'll anticipate your question...
    Abstract artists especially... Bissière, Mondrian...

Q.  In *The Toys* you satirized the degrading effect modern
    civilization has had upon man.  Does this mean you
    are opposed to our **present-day** civilization?

A.  Yes.  I am opposed to a civilization which does not
    search for ways to make man happy, but rather keeps
    finding means and ways of degrading him.  I am op-
    posed to a civilization which transforms man into a
    robot; a society of consumers totally conditioned to
    buy more and more goods.  Such a civilization not
    only alienates man, but cuts him off from any possible
    contact he could have with his fellow men.  It culti-
    vates a narrow kind of individual — totally false — and
    which paves the way for intense solitude.

Q.  Do you really feel that man has lost his individuality?
    His identity?   What do you believe the man of the
    future will be like?

A.  In a society based on excessive consumption man can
    be nothing more than a number, a puppet, shaped from
    the outside and turned into an obedient consumer.
    Moulded in this fashion, man searches *only* for sym-
    bols of power, wealth, virility.   Science today no
    longer serves man, but works against him.   In our
    society, the object has become an excuse for think-
    ing, a goal in itself.   Man has been plunged into a
    type of immaturity which bodes ill.  If man does not
    question himself now and re-examine all the forces
    about him — the very ones which are trying to crush
    him — he will become a robot surrounded by other
    robots.   Undifferentiated robots.   The machine and

man will become one and the same thing. The desire
and dream of certain people of being transformed into
stone so as to be unable to think anymore will have
been realized.

Q.   You filled the young couple's apartment in *The Toys*
     with more and more "perfectly useless objects" in
     order to show the extreme ferocity of your feelings
     against the "invasion of matter into the people's
     minds." Were you influenced by Ionesco, who also
     loaded the stage in *The Chairs* with chairs?

A.   No. I was not influenced by Ionesco. You have to
     like and admire a playwright in order to be influenced
     by him. I do not like Ionesco's theatre — outside of
     *The Chairs*.
          My theatre is neither "absurd", nor metaphysical,
     nor symbolic. It stems from reality, without being
     realistic.
          The objects which I have accumulated in *The
     Toys* are not symbolic. They are very real objects.
     They are the product of excessive consumption. What
     is of import to me is to show how objects in general
     transform man; and also why they are attracted by
     these objects.

Q.   What literary influences have you undergone?

A.   I think I owe a lot to Sartre. One cannot read all of
     Sartre's works without being influenced by him. If
     I wanted to go back still further, I would say that
     Jean-Jacques Rousseau and Gustave Flaubert in-
     fluenced me.

Q.   In the play *Sunday's Walk*, you satirized the "family
     cell": the family which takes its weekly Sunday walk
     on the Grands Boulevards; the family anchored in their

habits, indifferent to the troubles of others, indifferent
to the world, blind to all that is new and imaginative.
Would you say that these people act in ''bad faith''
in the Sartrian sense; that they have never lived? that
they resemble the ''bourgeois of Bouville,'' a group
of callous and innocuous individuals Sartre described
so brilliantly in his novel, *Nausea?*

A.   The family I depicted in *Sunday's Walk* is like a million others—the type of family you meet in the street
every day. There is no difference between this family
and any other.

         If you want to talk about ''bad faith'' you have to
speak of it in depth: in terms of the ''bad faith'' described by Sartre in *Being and Nothingness*, where the
young girl in question is perfectly aware of what she
is doing with her hand.

         The ''bad faith'' of my family is far more serious.
This family has adopted a way of life and a set of
patterns .... They let themselves be trapped by the
force of their own words and end up, or very nearly so,
by believing what they have said. They act in ''bad
faith'' and the bases for their activities are laziness
and cowardliness. Rather than taking the trouble to
question themselves at all, they merely enunciate a
series of platitudes. They apply outdated ideas to
events which require new conceptions. These people
flee whatever is difficult. The less personality they
have, the more convinced they are of having one.
Perhaps they did have one — a long time back when
they were young. But they have become *thingified*
as adults. They have donned the attire of respecta-
bility, so as to protect themselves from any responsibilities whatsoever. They are the respectable
people. The rest of humanity is nothing — just a
group of labels. Each image on stage evokes auto-
matically certain platitudes enunciated for such and

such an event or the garbled talk or chatter which must be said to a person or a group of people. No one tries to understand relationships or even himself.

Q. Are you an existentialist?

A. Yes. I agree with the basis of existentialism which is that "existence precedes essence." This formula, which is harmless in **appearance,** opens up an entirely new conception of the world. If one adds to this that "man is not what one makes of him, but what he does with what one has made of him," we have the basis for a way of life whereby man becomes responsible not only for all of his actions, but for everything which surrounds him. At a time when man seeks to shirk all responsibilities, when he has become indifferent and apathetic, Sartre plunges him into the world and forces him to open his eyes. This attempt, in my opinion, is most important; it forces man to accept his share of responsibility. When you think of where an attitude of resignation can lead, Sartre's way of conceiving life takes on even additional force.

Q. Sartre wrote the preface to your play, *Sunday's Walk.* Can you tell us something about the genesis of this preface? How did you meet Sartre?

A. I wanted to write and to keep on writing for ten years before showing my work to anyone. After eight years, however, some of my friends who knew what I was writing about spoke to other friends.... Sartre heard about my endeavors. A watchmaker had been writing for the past eight years without showing his work to anyone! Sartre's curiosity must have been aroused by this. He sent me a short note asking me to bring him what I had written. I brought him my first play. He read it. We saw each other again and spoke about

it. I brought him another, the second, which was *The
Toys*. He published it in his magazine *Modern Times*.
We spoke about every play and novel that I had ever
written. And we became friends.

Q. What are your feelings concerning theatrical innovators
such as Alfred Jarry, the author of *King Ubu*, or Antonin
Artaud, the father of the "Theatre of Cruelty"?

A. Jarry's works are interesting. He enlarges and distorts
reality, which makes the impact of the stage happening
that much more forceful. The grotesque and the burlesque frequently have a greater effect upon audiences
than does a serious work, making them more aware of
their human condition. Jarry paved the way for a
freer theatre. He went beyond the psychological
theatre; he succeeded in grappling with important
themes which I call "great human tendencies:" in
*King Ubu*, cowardliness, meaness, stupidity.
    As for Artaud, he interests us because his work
bears the markings of a man who experienced the
weakness of the theatre of his day very deeply, and
he reacted violently, passionately against it. He
wanted to crush tradition's constricting framework.
He also rejected psychological theatre. What I believe to be of primordial importance in Artaud's work
is his desire to create or bring forth in the theatre,
as he said, "a certain number of indestructible, un-
deniable images which will speak directly to the
mind." Such an idea is even more valid today than
it was in his time, and this, because of the incessant
bombardments audiences undergo − of an audio-visual
nature − in the theatre. They are so saturated with
exterior operations that spectators reach a point where
they are unable to react normally to any given event
on stage.
    I believe that one of the goals of the theatre

should be to create these indestructible images which would continue to live even after the spectator has left the theatre, and grow in importance in his mind — finally forcing him to begin questioning himself, his life, his entourage.

What makes for Artaud's richness? Each person sees in his philosophy and takes from it what he feels he needs. And in so doing, he achieves some strange results, diametrically opposed to what Artaud had originally intended. Let's take the **Polish director, Jerzy Grotowski**, as an example of what I mean. He has analyzed, and thoroughly so, all of Artaud's innovations and conceptions on the acting level. He agrees with Artaud's statement "that gestures and movements are as important as the text." The trouble with Grotowski is that he has carried this idea a little too far. His theatre, therefore, is a "poor theatre." He wants to suppress make-up, lights, costumes, décor, and all background noises. But when doing this, he runs the great risk of also doing away with an audience. As it is, he invites only a certain number of spectators to attend each performance. And there is a reason for this. The theatrical magic which is conjured forth by the theatrical happening operates only if the spectator is seated right next to the stage. If the play were to be performed on the usual stage, and the audience seated about twenty meters from the stage, the spectators would laugh rather than be deeply moved. Grotowski forgets that television and the film industry are his competitors. He wants to do away with the very elements which make the theatre an art unto itself and perfectly distinct from the other two. Just as gynmastics is good for an athlete, to be trained by Grotowski is an enriching experience for **an actor. Not** so, however, for a dramatist.

Q.  Can you elaborate on your **play,** *Aggression,* which has
now been translated into English (Avon Books)? How
do you interpret the concept of aggression? It can be
a very positive force in society, preventing stagnation
and the perpetuating of the *status quo.* Aggression
may also be helpful in paving the way for the emergence of new elements which can then be integrated
into society.

A.  My play deals with aggression in the form of confrontation: that of two worlds, society versus groups of
young people, the latter always bound by constraints,
restrictions, various hypocritical credoes, and feelings
**of alienation.** *Aggression* also **dramatizes the manner**
in which one group manipulates another: that is, using
film, publicity, television, **billboards,** etc. as a means
of reaching its goal.

Aggression also gives audiences a picture of
young people as they face an adult society, so self-
satisfied, self-contented in its ways. These staid
people offer youth what seems to them to be an ideal
in life and a superb code of ethics, but which is in
reality an empty philosophy based on the possession
of costly objects. Artificial needs are created in this
type of society with its large window displays just
gorging with all kinds of merchandise. The young
**people, seeing all these objects, but not having**
the means to purchase them, feel the cruelty of frus-
tration. We know, scientifically speaking, that such
feelings engender violence.

A charm exists — in terms of language — between
these two groups as they confront each other. The
adults in the play express **themselves** in rather phleg-
matic, detached terms, **and,** frequently, in a rather
affected manner, **underlining** in this way the vast differences existing between them and the others. Be-
**neath their serene and innocuous verbiage lie other**

sentiments that come to the fore: a lack of understanding for others and a kind of aroused anger when they face people who do not resemble them and whose ideas are alien to their way of thinking. The harshness of the language as spoken by the young is, in reality, a kind of defense mechanism. They are well aware of the effect their words have on the listener and they indulge in such crudities when adults are listening. Their intention is to shock them.

*Aggression* is not a play concerning the conflict of generations. There are old people who are only seventeen years old and young people who may be sixty. The goal of my drama is to compel people to question and to sound out their feelings in terms of our present-day global situation.

Q.  You seem to be very much absorbed by this question of manipulation, on both the individual as well as on the collective, the national as well as the international levels. To manipulate people and nations has become a science today; courses are offered in colleges to those militantly committed to changing the world or to those attempting to gain control over others. People should perhaps learn how to overcome the onslaught of studied ways and the acceptance of facile answers to complex questions. In this manner, perhaps, some semblance of balance and individuality might be retained.

A.  It would be difficult but worth the effort. To try to convince others by manipulating individuals and nations is far from bringing about a new state of being. In my play, *Crossbow and Rapiers,* I dramatize the manner in which one nation encourages another to make war. This kind of technique is Manicheism in its most elementary form.

The need or the desire to arouse a sense of hostility or anger in others has always existed. That's why I used such words as "crossbow" and "rapier" in the title of my play — to give it a medieval sounding name. The only change to have taken place throughout the ages is the manner in which governments or the masses have prodded others into action. **Today it's through audio-visual means.** It is far easier than it ʼwas before to think of one's neighbor as a bastard or to kill an enemy once a radio or a television has been brought into the home. The word and the image have become weapons in the service of the lie. Outside of this mechanical means, society still uses the age-old ancestral reflexes of arousing both the individual and the collective to seek the revival **of obsolete values from a dead past. It is really rather comical to see all these puppets in a modern state manipulating the head or heads of other nations.** It is due to this kind of activity that man's stupidity is revealed and that hatred blossoms forth.

Q.   In *Stampede toward Order* you also deal with the problem of manipulation.

A.   Yes. This time the way the bourgeoisie was manipulated after the great fight: the riots raging in France in 1968. A return to order was announced in accordance with the classical procedures and by the authorities in power. They all wanted a return to that sacrosanct tranquillity which seems to be an ideal. The "business" of returning to order seems vital; it entails a renewal of fascism. Such a goal is first accomplished by what one may allude to as "the electoral farce," which is really a means of burying or of hiding the real problems facing the state. Once the farce has been accomplished, a gradual suppression of liberty — little by little — takes place. Means and ways of repression come into being. Free speech is curtailed; in fact, to speak is tantamount to a criminal act in this society which is based on the lie, hypocrisy and scandal. Even the person who remains silent feels restricted by the very powers implicit in this new order. One day he could go too far and talk...

Q.  What is the function of the theatre? Should it be political and a militant force, as Sartre had thought of it? Or should it indulge in a kind of aesthetic hedonism?

A.  Certainly the theatre should not merely offer entertainment. It must attack, modify and alter the mental outlook or views of the spectators. It must make the individual want to think for himself, to become aware. A play should unleash a whole new world which will prod the viewer, compel him to question his acts and those of his fellow men. The theatre should shock him into assessing his role in society and vice versa.

Q.  What are the means at the dramatist's or at the director's disposal to effect such a change in point of view? Audio-visual procedures could certainly be used to condition such a change.

A.  The theatre must become a kind of **counter-information** service, a **counter-advertising** agency. It must show audiences that what television, radio and the press say is just simply *not* so. It must teach people to evaluate things for themselves, to maintain some kind of perspective in terms of material things.

   **The news media today seem to** give great importance to those things which are of little **significance**, and to silence what is truly vital. The theatre's function, as I see it, is to **rearrange** or to bring some semblance of order into this chaotic situation. People today are really interested in aesthetics; in masking real problems. They must reject the pretty speeches and denounce the huge enterprises offered by our society as it seeks to manipulate all in sight.

**We are so inured to this kind of manipulation** that we have lost track of our own strength, our own individuality and creativeness. We have become submerged. The individual is blinded by the mass of objects which have entered into his life and by the mass of panaceas being bombarded his way. He has not developed a point of view nor has he created an identity for himself. His life is devoid of purpose and meaning — save for the acquisition of more and more objects! Profit is society's supreme goal. Man, therefore, figures as a number in this consumer society: a puppet, created, moulded and formed from the outside. Society — the product of a collection of pseudo-individuals — merely wants to hold on to the symbols he has known—symbols of power, wealth, virility. The object or the material entity helps him fill a void in man's existence. The theatre's task today is to force people to become aware of the feeling of alienation which has permeated our civilization.

Q.  The theatre — as with all artistic and creative efforts — must either renew itself or die. How would you go about renewing the theatre?

A.  The play is not the only means of renewing theatre: what is even more important is the inter-action between the play and the spectator. It is on this level — this contact between the spectator and the play — that work must be done and that our search must be oriented. It is not a question of soliciting participation on the part of the spectator, *en passant,* during the course of a play. This is a naïve way of approaching the problem. The actor in this case remains actor and the spectator, spectator. Paradoxically, the closer the actor is to the spectator during the course of the performance, the further away he really is.

It is possible to construct a play which would transform the actor-play into a single unit. In this case, the actor would become a spectator like anyone else, but a spectator acting in the midst of others and recognized as such. No subterfuge would be involved. The notion of a "finished product" would be abolished. "Open plays" would have to be written or "suggestions of plays" with a rather definite frame of reference upon which the actors and spectators would have the freedom to create and to improvise.

This kind of "trap theatre" would be effective in terms of moving the spectator, making him capable of understanding the basic contradictions and conflicts in the world in which he lives.

This new theatrical structure, or approach to the theatre, would be more effective in confronting the problems which beset man today. Since the individual would be the center or focal point of all conflicts (actor-spectator) and not relegated to the privileged or protected area in a theatre where he would sit by passively, observing the events unfolding before him, he would be an active participant in the drama, and, therefore, fully aware of the problems corroding him and his nation.

It is not merely on the technical level alone that renewal in the theatre can and must take place. The theatre — as a vehicle — must intrude, and assert itself upon reality and daily life. Only when it becomes part of our workaday world will the problems facing man today be objectively and openly worked out.

The theatre can and must participate in the *real* world, and when it does it will succeed — in a modest

way — in effecting a change in society which is so
*blocked* in so many ways.

A section of this interview was reprinted from *Drama and Theatre* (Volume 7, no. I), 1968.

## GABRIEL COUSIN

*Interviewer's Note:*

Gabriel Cousin was born in the working-class district in Perche, France. He is self-taught. During World War II he was taken prisoner and sent to Austria. After being repatriated, he struggled to earn a living in German-occupied France. Interested in sports, he took a Master's degree in Physical Education. In 1949, his first volume of verse, *A Worker's Life*, was published; six years later, his first play, *The Drama of Fukuryu-Maru* was printed. Other theatrical works followed: *Black Opera* (1960), *The Barker and the Automaton* (1961), *Journey to the Mountain Beyond* (1964), *The Crab Cycle* (1969), *Descent onto the Reef* (1971), etc.

Cousin's theatrical universe is socially oriented. His wry humor, incisive style and aesthetic bent make his dramas potent forces. He believes the theatre should be based on actual events and present-day situations, and should attempt to alter man's vision of life and his role in society.

Q. How did you become interested in the theatre?

A. I came to the theatre rather late in life. I spent my youth among workers. I never went to the theatre.

I think that sports was the decisive factor in my life. Sports brought me to the theatre. Stadiums — even before I became aware of the role they played in my life — led me directly to playwrighting. I first studied the techniques involved in the theatre: diction, mime, dance, singing, improvisation, etc. Then I joined a theatrical troupe: The Companions of Saint John. We produced a lot of giant spectacles — all of which were out of doors.

The first real catalyst in my life was Jean Vilar. His production of T. S. Eliot's *Murder in the Cathedral* is indelibly fixed in my mind. There was something magical about this production — something which really "possessed" me.

There were other reasons, perhaps even more important, which drew me to the theatre.

1. The theatre is something alive; poetry is incarnated in the characters portrayed, in the situations dramatized. A book, on the other hand, is more or less dead — it sleeps on a shelf.

2. The theatre is a collective work: an ensemble of poetry with a director, a scenic and costume designer, actors, author, etc. Nothing is more exciting nor more beautiful. Nothing makes me happier than a work which brings people together. In a collective enterprise each individual brings aspects of himself which he then uses for the common good. Solitude no longer exists since each person belongs to an undertaking. This is real team work.

I felt great satisfaction when the **Théâtre Quotidien of Marseilles performed my play,** *The Barker and the Automaton*. I realize that the joy one experiences when working with others may in some way be artificial — and is certainly fleeting. Nevertheless, it gives one a sense of belonging. This idea of working together, in a team, may be a type of transposition of the excitement one experiences during a football or baseball game.

Q. What, in your opinion, would be the ideal theatrical area? A proscenium stage? A circular one?

A. A stadium would be my choice. The seats are all on different levels and the stage, at bottom, is circular. If the climate is favorable, I would have all plays performed out of doors. Spectators come into contact with nature itself at such moments: with night, day, every phase of the physical universe, which then interpenetrates the play itself. One could say that under such conditions there is a fusion of dramaturgy and the elements.

The kind of area I prefer would, then, resemble a gynmasium — a kind of circus of Greek amphitheatre. A stage, conceived on various levels in circles and half circles — in other words, multiple scenic levels — would give the playwright extreme freedom of expression. Spectators, at the same time, would feel a certain degree of simultaneity, of synchronization. The scenic space would be malleable in all senses of the word. One could readily pass from one acting area to another by means of foot-bridges. Audience and actor would be one. No separation, no artificial barrier would be used.

In any case, the Italian proscenium stage seems to me to be condemned for good, in spirit as well as in a technical sense. This kind of stage was perfectly suited to classical theatre, and even romantic theatre, where the playwright and actors wanted to foster a sense of illusion, where they wanted the spectator to remain in a kind of limbo. Today (as Brecht has pointed out) dreams and illusions are no longer goals in themselves. Audiences are no longer foreign to the actor. Audiences must use their cri-

tical sense, sharpen their thoughts, remain alert
throughout a performance, and in this way participate
in the drama unfolding in front of and around them.

Q. Were you influenced by Antonin Artaud?

A. Yes. The theatre in the beginning — and this is true
of all civilizations — was a form of religious expression. Today, psychoanalysts have attempted to replace religious sentiment, which has become degraded
and anemic . . . Artaud's vision (and that of the Greeks)
of a theatre of *catharsis*—one which seeks to dramatize
the "genesis of creation" — is really a new form of
religious theatre.

To restore to language the power of disorienting
man physically, to restore to it its incantatory power,
would enable language once again to tear apart and
create something solid. I tried to inject this new
vitality into language in my play, *The Barker and
the Automaton*, with barking and screams throughout
the drama. I attempted to do the same thing with *The
Black Opera*, with Millie's final cry to Prez.

Artaud asked for "a poetry in space." He searched for a language based on "animated signs." He
wanted spectators to sit around the acting area, or
have several acting areas since he suggested doing
away with the stage. I was influenced by Artaud in
terms of my play's construction, the scenic device I
used, and the fluidity or movement within the drama
itself.

Artaud influenced me insofar as the theatre and
the invidivual were concerned; Jacques Copeau was
important to me in terms of the theatre's role in society; I was also most impressed with Brecht's and
Piscator's political views.

Q. In *The Barker and the Automaton* you show the progres-

sive degradation of two human beings who are prac-
tising a trade of which they are ashamed, and which
they keep secret from one another. Is this to say
that modern man in general is ashamed of what he is
doing? That he can neither see the world about him
lucidly or within his own soul?

A.  This is a complex question. I would say yes. Today
people are frequently ashamed (without really knowing
it) or even fearful of the jobs they hold. And this
kind of shame and fright is related to their notion (or
lack of belief) in God. The greater is our loneliness,
the more responsibility is ours. We are *responsible*
for our actions. An extreme example of what I mean
was felt by Einstein at the end of his life, after he
had become aware of his terrible act — the creation
of the atomic bomb. The "freer" we are to explore
our own soul, the less clearly we see into it and the
less meaning our lives seem to have.

   In the theatre today there is, in my opinion, a
return — in a renewed form — to the sources of tragedy.
If man looks at his society in a lucid manner and
sees it as his attempt to find happiness by creating a
consumer society whose sole goal is to acquire more
and more objects, he may realize that he is lost.
Our vision, our notions of good or evil, our anguishes,
are far more painful than they used to be when man
could find a reassuring answer in some divine force.

Q.  You attacked atomic fallout in *The Drama of Fukuryu-
Maru*. Do you always have a *cause célèbre* in your
plays? Do you write thesis plays?

A.  I do not choose a play's theme. It is the theme which
imposes itself upon me. It so happens that some
ideological, social or simply human fact or bit of new
strikes me in some way. It penetrates me to the point

of becoming an obsession. The only way I can get
rid of this gnawing *thing,* is by writing about it. I
either write a poem or I build a play around it.

I would like to contribute to the destruction of
man's alienation today and to denounce man's tragic
form of existence. These ideas must be expressed in
the theatre today. To try to discover the heroes of
our time; to express life today; to organize certain
themes or topics which emerge directly from certain
historical events; to dramatize the struggle going on
between old and new forms of social life and morality,
etc. — all these can be told and retold in the theatre
today.

I should like to mention Einstein's name again
in this context. It was he — about seventeen years
ago — who enabled me to understand the role of the
theatre in modern life. I assembled some documenta-
tion on the atomic bomb and wrote *The Drama of
Fukuryu-Maru.* It was at that time that I read his
famous sentence: "A new way of thinking is essential
if humanity is to survive." This is how I treated the
working class situation in *Officina,* a pantomime-
oratorio which was performed in Italy, with music
by Honegger. The danger of atomic fallout was the
topic of *The Drama of Fukuryu-Maru,* which opened at
the Marais Festival and was directed by Jean Dasté.
The alienation in contemporary life of the robot-man,
who has become the slave of his mechanical and
publicity-filled society, inspired me to write *The
Barker and the Automaton.* The problem of hunger
in the world prompted me to write *Journey to the
Mountain Beyond.* Today, the phenomenon of fear
has conditioned our way of thinking; it invades us
without our realizing it...

I do not, however, attempt to solve our problems
today via the theatre. I simply try to reveal them and
to inform the public. I have confidence in the spec-

tators' critical approach.    I want simply to inject
some kind of disquieting attitude, to try to arouse
their conscience and to disturb their placidity in
some way.    It is up to man himself to change his
life style.  Let him face this fact.

Q.    **People** have compared your theatre with Brecht's.
      Could you tell us why?

A.    They have also compared it to Claudel's.    Brecht's
      plays have had an important effect on my development
      as a dramatist.    He enabled me to *see* — in a few
      years — what it might have taken me decades to find
      out by myself.    He showed me how contemporary
      theatre should be renewed — not only in terms of
      structure, but of depth and meaning.  He gave me con-
      fidence.    He showed me that dreams are possible —
      that is, that it is possible to carry them out.
          I discovered Brecht rather late in life.  I saw his
      *Caucasian Chalk Circle*.  At that time, my play, *The
      Drama of Fukuryu-Maru*, had already been outlined.
      Brecht helped me find a form which in terms of tone,
      rhythm, language and scenic elements, would express
      my personality, my sensibility and, most of all, my
      preoccupations at that time.    One could certainly
      not be expected to use traditional or classical theat-
      rical concepts to express ideas in our age of audio-
      visual expression and high speed.  We — particularly
      the French who are so blocked in this respect —
      needed to free ourselves from our customary ways.

Q.    In your play, *Black Opera*, you handle the problem of
      segregation.  What led you to consider such a subject?

A.    As usual, the topic imposed itself upon me.  I had to
      do something, therefore, about the subject of racism.

Q.   Did Sartre's play, *The Respectful Prostitute*, which
     also treated the problem of racism, influence you
     when writing *Black Opera?*

A.   No.   Only inasmuch as writers of the post-war gener-
     ation are frequently influenced by Sartre.   The great
     difference between Sartre and myself — more important
     than any other — is the fact that he did not attempt to
     renew the theatre from a technical point of view, in
     terms of form.   It is not the theme or the dramatic
     situation which is of sole interest to me, it is the way
     these emerge on stage.   Moreover, language for Sartre
     is primordial.   It is the vehicle for his thought.   All
     of Sartre's plays could be produced, if necessary,
     with the characters sitting around a table and talking.
     It is the human body — the physical and visceral
     aspect of this form in space — which fascinates me.
     It is the body in terms of its muscles, its motility,
     the physical situations of the characters themselves
     as they become involved in their drama, which is the
     basis of my theatre.   The theatre — at least mine —
     should express physically man's inner drama.

Reprinted, in translation, with the permission of the *French
Review* (March, 1971).

### *JEANINE WORMS*

*Interviewer's Note:*

Jeanine Worms was born in Buenos Aires, Argentina. Eclectic in her taste, she is the author of novels (*One Must Never Say Fountain*), of essays (*An Apology for Lying,* and of plays *(The Store* 1971). The theatre for her is a means of attacking all that is stereotyped, hackneyed, narrow and decadent in society. Her weapons are grammar and syntax. She juggles her words, indulges in puns and in a medley of verbal acrobatics. Mrs. Worms moved to Paris in 1951 when the theatre of the absurd was just coming into its own. From the masters of this theatrical genre — Beckett and Genet — she learned how to satirize superficial love, banal relationships, perverse political situations. Very much of an individualist, her plays are original and personal. Her domain is laughter: tender, bitter, corrosive. It is no wonder that her plays *Afternoon Snack* (1972) and *A Cat Is A Cat* (1968) — among others — received accolades from the critics.

Q.  Why and how did you come to write for the theatre?

A.  I began writing one-act plays for the theatre as soon as I moved to Paris. *A Cat Is A Cat* and *Later* are of the period.   Because of the enormous difficulties involved in finding producers and directors for non-commerical theatrical ventures — plays by unknown dramatists — I gladly accepted the offer made to me by the publisher Fasquelle-Grasset to write a novel. I also wrote and still write essays.

One of the most exciting experiences occurred in 1953 when the well-known director Jean Vilar asked **me to adapt a Spanish play.** I suggested Valle-Inclan's *Lights of Bohemia,* which had never been staged before — not even in Spanish. Its first production, therefore, took place at the Théâtre National Populaire in Paris — and in my version. Ever since this time I have devoted my energies to the theatre.

I don't believe I shall ever write any more novels. The novel form just does not seem to suit my temperament. It's also perhaps a question of language. The essay form, on the other hand, is much more my style. In fact, I am planning to write an essay entitled "Against Happiness," at least against individual happiness which seems to me to be destructive insofar as it creates and encourages **illusion. It is the** harbinger of "misfortune." Such a point of view in no way implies a withdrawal on my part — that is, the giving up of the fight for establishing better social conditions for everyone. I am a fighter for human rights.

The French language lends itself admirably to **the theatre: elliptic by nature, it has a cadence, really impossible to describe,** all its own, and sonorities which seem to stimulate emotion. I consider *rhythm* basic to my theatre — an element of creation itself. It expresses *truth,* that is to say, it possesses its own power of conviction which permits the play to take on form and depth. It is a living organism which grows *organically.*

Life in the theatre is intense. As far as my plays are concerned, it is the inter action of characters themselves which fascinates me and not the specific anecdote in each play.

Q. Can you tell us something about your first play?

A. *The Stuffed Ones (Les Empaillés)* was performed on French television in 1951 and in the theatre with the Frères Jacques in 1970. The idea for this play came to me when my husband and I had just moved to Paris and were looking for an apartment. We went to many real estate agencies and discovered that they also filled another function as matrimonial agencies. Some of their ads ran like the following: "Monsieur of fifty years of age, charming in all ways, is looking for a woman in her thirties...." I found this kind of advertisement infinitely pitiful. To get married! To depend upon an agency for this! Only terribly solitary persons would resort to such a device. I tried to imagine the kind of life these persons would lead: the utter loneliness of such an existence, the empty chairs which faced them daily. These individuals are dried up, hollow inside, and because of this void they are always trying to *stuff* themselves with anyone − in order to fill the terrible abyss which is their life.

My play opens in a matrimonial agency but instead of advertising the plight of a single man searching for the right kind of woman on colorful bits of paper, my play features window displays filled with "stuffed men." A nice class of women − just as "stuffed" as the men − come along and choose from among them.

I was very irritated, mostly with what one commonly refers to as the "dignified" bourgeoisie, when I wrote this play. I knew this class of people at the time only in terms of the French colony living in South America. *The Stuffed Ones* gave me the perfect opportunity to laugh at them, their formalities, and

their egoism, which is certainly an important factor
contributing to their distress and solitude.

Today I probably would not write this kind of play
based on an "exterior" event. Yet, the action *per se*,
insofar as there is action, exists in terms of the characters themselves: the inter-action between them, the
emergence of this kind of human being and the ensuing
*malaise*. I try to create a condition of *malaise* in some
of my plays — a kind of painful, claustrophobic atmosphere. Such feelings are born from my observations,
as I look around me and see the many people who live
*inauthentically*, that is, who are not true to themselves
but whose lives are patterned on those of others.

Q. Are you present at the rehearsals?

A. I try to attend rehearsals if the director permits me to.
The ideal situation would be to get together with the
director, the actors, and the scenic designer at the
very outset; to discuss the play, clear up any possible
ambiguities; then to remove oneself completely from
the picture. After a while, to return to the theatre
with a fresh outlook and point of view.

Such situations do occur. In fact, from the initial
get-together, there arises a real sense of friendship,
a warmth which grows among all those participating
in the theatrical event, and this is a compensation for
the aridity of the dramatist who works *alone*, in solitude. The pleasure of working with others, of living
their joys, of sharing the same adventure in the creation of the dramatic spectacle, is immeasurable.

Q. What is your relationship with actors and directors?

A. I have always been on very good terms with them. The
actors are chosen after discussion with the director.
It's really a question of discovering the kind of actor

suitable to my type of play. He must know how to handle words, make the most of them, bring them out. He must not be the type of actor who seeks a flashy kind of role, who wants to be a star, have his name in lights on a theatre marquee. My theatre requires an actor to love his art, to be willing to sacrifice his personal vanity for the play, and to have a conscience and integrity. Despite all these precautions, the dramatist always feels "betrayed." But it's best to feel betrayed by those with "talent."

Q. What authors or philosophers influenced you most profoundly? What were some of these influences?

A. Plato — because of the comic rigidity of his logic and his clownish dialogues. There is always a knowledgeable fellow (a Socrates) and a clown (a questioner) — the one who knows everything and flaunts his wisdom, and the imbecile, in a continuous state of amazement and wonder. Flaubert also influenced me. After I read his novel, *Bouvard and Pécuchet,* I wrote *Pardon Monsieur.* I also like Lorca a great deal.

The authors I most admire are not always those who influenced me most incisively. Racine is at the top of my list. His restraint, and the tragedy which emerges from his every line, are extraordinary. I don't aspire to write as he does, of course. Yet if he is considered — as he is — to be one of the sources of our modern metaphysical theatre, I suscribe to his views and ways. But Ionesco, Beckett, Dubillard are also his descendants. Kafka is another writer I admire. His works illustrate the theme of the fall. Yet, my plays in no way resemble his work.

Probably the person who influenced me most directly was the scholar-poet-writer Roger Caillois. I studied with him at the French Institute in Buenos Aires after completing graduate studies in philosophy and sociology. Roger Caillois was my "master." Not because of the themes or forms in which he wrote (he does not like the theatre and frequently asks me rather spitefully, "Well, are you still writing those *histrionades?*"), but for the rigorousness and lucidity of his thought processes.

Q.   Can you tell us something about your conception of comedy? Is it cruel? Scathing? Does it resemble Molière's humor? Ionesco's?

A.   It's very difficult to talk to you about my type of comedy. I always attempt to be humorous in my one-act plays. I'm never really sure of having succeeded until after the performance. Comedy, of course, is frequently *a mask*. It avoids the pathetic or circumvents it.

Comedy lives all around me. All I have to do is listen to the people chatter away. A sentence heard in the street or in a cafe exposes a world with all of its ridiculous innuendoes. But I never use the sentences I hear — that is, exactly how I hear them. To do so would be to betray my characters, to distort their personalities. They must find their own humor and usually do.

My plays bathe in a type of comic *climate* which stems from life itself: man's state of conformity, his intellectual narrowmindedness, and his mediocrity — all products of our consumer society.

Laughter is the best way of denouncing our errors and our illusions. There is a kind of laughter from which one does not recover.

I don't know whether my type of comedy resembles that of Molière or Ionesco. There are many others who know and practice the art of provoking laughter: Labiche, Chaplin, Buster Keaton, Harry Langdon, the Marx Brothers, Jarry, Beckett, Swift... All of these

people and so many others possess the genius of
being able to create comedy.

Q. According to the critic, Guy Dumur, you take "grammar
and syntax seriously."

A. Yes, that's correct. I am very much interested in grammar and syntax. They help clarify and pinpoint thoughts.
In the theatre, however, I look for *short cuts*, ways
of provoking ideas, and of exploding sensations. I
invent words like *intuitioyinner* or *intuitiotinstion*,
etc., just to amuse myself, because they are funny.
They expose certain fads and tics of which my characters are victims. I also use epithets: for a baby
I'll write "that little consumer" or "that little audio-
visual".... My characters are frequently victimized
by words rather than being masters of them (banalities,
stock phrases....). Just as in life, they are carried
along by slogans, and they believe the words and
prognostications of publicity mongers and political
dictators. My language, I must admit, is frequently
cutting. But it's the best way I know of denouncing
the dangers that may result when masses of people
begin believing stock formulas, accepted without
thought or reflection — which opens the doors to dic-
tatorship.

Q. Is your theatre psychological?

A. I believe I already told you that my theatre is *objective*.
This does not, of course, mean realistic. Realism is
like amateur photography: the photography of someone
who cannot *see*.
    I couldn't care less about "psychological" the-
atre in the conventional sense of the word. A gallery
of portraits does not interest me, nor do individual
cases.

In another sense, one could say that Beckett is
one of the great "psychological" authors. He reveals
man nude before his destiny; Brecht is another, but in
a different way, because he is conscious of reality.
Psychology should be situated above and beyond a
"character." It is on this level that I would like my
theatre to be "psychological."

Q.   Do you enjoy modern theatre?  The plays of Arrabal?
Weingarten?    Dubillard?     The *mises en scène* of
Grotowski?

A.   I experience real joy when watching a good play by
contemporaries...    Dubillard,    Georges    Michel...
But I am rather distrustful when it comes to accepting
a theatre which flatters a certain fad or which coin-
cides with a momentary style (Arrabal).   Styles and
fads are powerful weapons which the artist places in
the hands of a consumer society.  They are by nature
superficial.  Styles change. Only the work of art remains.

Though directors — perhaps even more than dramatists — seem to yield to the public's taste and to seek
popularity, their work, nevertheless, interests me.
Grotowski seems to me to work in a neo-declamatory
style.  The "nudity" of the soul of the actors does
not interest me any more than did the gallery of portraits I mentioned before.  Theatre is not therapy.  It
is not designed to help solve world and personal
problems;  on the contrary, it is a "waker-upper."

Nevertheless, Ronconi's theatre — his production
of *Orlando Furioso* — is sheer joy; Bob Wilson's
theatre of silence is successful.

Theatre is always a collective work.  Each participant contributes to the spectacle's health, according to his competence.  Let one element of the *ensemble* falter (author, director, actor, technician...)

and the entire production collapses.  The director's
job is to think out a text and to imagine how it can
be transformed into a play.  Bob Wilson uses silence
as a dramatic tool.  Silence with him is significant.

Q.   Can you tell us about the themes of *A Cat Is A Cat*
and *Afternoon Snack?*

A.   When I first started writing *A Cat Is A Cat*, I thought
of writing a mystery play.  The themes are love and
friendship.  One always dies a victim of those one
loves or of those who love you.  The play's context
is the world of gossip, of prodigious slander.  The
entire play takes place in a particularly grotesque
climate.  *Afternoon Snack* was written last summer.
Its theme is capitalism and petty bourgeois turpitudes,
revealed most innocently by two women as they gorge
themselves on cakes during an afternoon snack — just
like their respectful husbands who devote their efforts
to making money . . . all for profit.

Q.   What are your plans for the future?

A.   I've just finished a two-act play called *Sandwich*.
Though it might not have political or social import,
it deals with the repressive aspects of society (a
minor employee attempts and succeeds in going on
vacation . . . but . . . .) I'm also going to adapt one of
my novels, *A Magnolia*, for the stage, and write a one-
act play for the German Broadcasting System.
     I would really like to say a few words about one-
act plays.  They are, generally, considered minor
endeavors.  Why, when some of our best playwrights
have written superb one-actors: Albee, Pinter, Genet,
Ionesco?  When Beckett writes a two-act play, the
second is a replica of the first on another level.  I
think that one-act plays suit our modern dramaturgy.

One-act plays respond to modern audiences' limited
span of attention. They require, however, extreme
**discipline on the part of the author,** because one-act
plays are compressed, intense — not one extra word
should be present in the dialogue. Their impact is
all the more powerful.... To denigrate one-act plays
is to be prejudiced. After all, does this mean we
should consider Webern's short works minor?

I would also like to mention the sinister state of
affairs existing in French theatre today. Many French
dramatists are actually starving; others cannot find
producers for their work. Such an unfortunate situation
arises from a fundamental misunderstanding — voluntarily maintained — and basic to our society. We
claim to believe in the beautiful virtues of liberty
and "Kultur" — but these obey only one law: that of
**profit and gain.** Why should private theatres produce
plays unless they are commercially profitable? But
this kind of play usually appeals to a staid public.
It's difficult for producers to take financial risks.
It's probably different in the United **States,** where
capitalism is more powerful and therefore indulges
at times in financially risky productions.

Theatre today — in many countries — is merchandise. The director's job in this case is to whet the
consumer-audience's appetite — to sell him a play.
Theatrical research today consists in feeding audiences a series of pictures or images. It has become strictly representational theatre.

Usually, the creator of the play is most rebellious in accepting something which is not *authentic.*
Today, however, in our consumer society where the
object holds sway — often referred to as *thingifi-
cation* — any image, thought or emotion which is
saleable will be offered to audiences. Man has already fallen from the category of *being* to that of
*having.* Today he dwells in that of *appearance* (giving

the appearance of power, the appearance of liberty, etc.). To be truly creative in the eternal sense of the word is to add to life, to add to *being*, but not, of course, in terms of appearance. Pirandello has demonstrated this aspect of the theatre most forcefully. I am for a written theatre, a theatre which talks to an audience's deepest part — not merely to an ectoplasm.

## RENÉ DE OBALDIA

*Interviewer's Note:*

René de Obaldia, the son of a Panamanian Consul and a French mother, was born in Hong Kong in 1918. He came to Paris shortly after his birth. His talents for the theatre manifested themselves rather early in life, at first, simply as *"divertissements"*, as "impromptus", or as joyful interludes from his novel writing and other intellectual pursuits. In his first full length play, *Genousi*, directed by Jean Vilar, René de Obaldia sought to "reveal the notion of the absurd in a logical construction." He succeeded in his attempt, and other dramas followed in quick succession: *The Grand Vizir, The Satyr of La Villette, The Unknown General, The Agricultural Cosmonaut*, etc.

René de Obaldia's most startling contribution to the theatre is his unusual sense of humor. Indeed, he was awarded the prize for "Black Humor." He is able to transform his thoughts, feelings, anguishes — frequently rather macabre in content — into the most side-splitting theatrical dialogue. It is no wonder that his plays have been performed in the finest theatres in the world. It is certainly a relief these days to be able to go to the theatre to laugh heartily and, at the same time, be titillated intellectually.

Q.   What was your background in the theatre or, as one
would say in French, what was your "formation"?

A.   Do you mean my "formation"? or my "deformation"?
I think that life itself deforms us in many ways. We
would probably have to define the words "formation"
and "deformation."

Q.   Then how did you choose the theatre as your vocation?

A.   In a rather strange manner. Actually it was not my
first love. What first interested me and still fascinates
me is poetry. I started my writing career as a poet.
I wrote poems and then prose, short stories and finally
novels. There came a time in my life when I found
myself associated with the "International Cultural
Center" at Royaumont. The director asked me to
participate in cultural exchanges. We met many
students, professors, writers of all types and from a
variety of countries. There were lectures that we
had to prepare, meetings we had to attend, etc. It
was during one of these meetings that I thought of
writing a two-or-three character play so as to liven
up the work we were doing. What interested me most
at this point was to show that culture *per se* is really
not something deadly; that it is something very much
alive, exciting and productive. So I wrote *The Grand
Vizir*, my first impromptu, to liven up those literary
gatherings. And it did.

Q.   I saw the play in New York last year. It was a mar-
velously humorous satire. Did you look upon yourself as a professional dramatist after this first theatrical venture?

A.   No.... It was just a simple *divertissement*. I looked
upon myself as an amateur. Then I wrote *The Sacrifice
of the Hangman,* another impromptu. The play was put on

by non-professionals.    A  Professor  of  philosophy
acted the part of the Hangman; a Jesuit portrayed the
Innocent  man;  and  I  incarnated  the  part  of  the  Widow.
I  never  considered  myself  a  professional  and  really
did  not  think  of  becoming  one.    I  was  a  thousand
miles  away  from  realizing  or  believing  that  my  impromptus  would  be  published,  translated  and  then
performed  in  many  different  languages  and  nations.

Q.    Can  you    tell  us  something  about  your  first  play,
        *Genousi?*

A.    If I were to go into detail, this interview would last for
        days.    Suffice  it  to  say  that  it  was  Jean  Vilar,  former
        director of the Théâtre National Populaire and founder
        of  the  Avignon  Summer  Theatre  Festivals,  who  asked
        for  my  play.    Vilar's  death  was  a  terrible  loss  to  the
        French  and  to  international  theatre.

                Jean  Vilar  had  become  quite  interested  in  my
        novels.    He  asked  me  whether  I  had  ever  written  a
        play.    I  remembered  that  I  had  written  one  about  ten
        years  before.    It  was  *Genousi*.    He  read  it  and  ac-
        cepted  it.    The  cast  was  extraordinary:  Maria  Casarès,
        Georges  Wilson,  etc.  Vilar  produced  *Genousi*  at  the
        Théâtre  Recamier  in  1960.    At  that  time  this  theatre
        was  a  sort  of  trial  theatre  for  plays  which  were  to  be
        produced  later  on  at  the  **government-subsidized** Théâtre
        National  Populaire.

                It  was  after  *Genousi*  was  performed  that  directors
        ''consecrated''  me  a  dramatist.

Q.    What  was  the  theme  of  *Genousi?*

A.    Love.    But  with  a  rather  unusual  background.    The
        play  takes  place  in  the  kind  of  cultural  environment
        which  I  knew  well.    The  **language, or rather** the  kind
        of  phraseology  interjected  in  the  play,  was  a  brand

of "ridiculous **preciosity**." What I mean is that the characters spoke an unbelievable jargon: outdated, outmoded and almost incomprehensible. To express the simplest of ideas, the most abstruse philosophical jargon would be used. I interwove a love story into this atmosphere with terribly comic results. The comedy, however, rests on a linguistic level. The heroine, for example, a Genousian (an imaginary place), speaks only Genousian, a language which is of my invention. Since the play is a love story, the spectators realize soon after that that the only two people who really understand each other are the lovers. In fact, they don't really need language at all — love suffices in their case. In *Genousi*, then, there is a kind of relationship between language and human emotions. Language is decorticated, peeled down to basic elements, to raw feelings, translated or transformed through the medium of the word.

Q.   Do you attend rehearsals? What is your relationship with the director?

A.   Yes. I generally attend rehearsals. First of all I almost always get together with the director before rehearsals even begin. We discuss the various problems: décors, casting, etc. I must say that I have been very fortunate as far as directors are concerned. Jorge Lavelli directed *The Grand Vizir*, Jacques Rosner, *The Unknown General*, etc. When the director understands the play and the dramatist's intentions, there is no real recessity for the dramatist to be present at rehearsals. If the director is a mediocre one — then, of course, I feel obliged to be present at as many rehearsals as possible.

When *Some Wind in the Sassafras Branches* was performed at Prague, the Czechoslovakian director had come to see me before he began rehearsing the

play. He wanted to ask some questions. We talked
about the play. He invited me to the opening. I was
absolutely thrilled with the production. His directing
was remarkable.

Q. Who was this director?

A. Dudek.

Q. Do you choose your actors?

A. Yes. But one must be careful, discerning — practically intuitive in this domain. Some actors are absolutely
marvelous. Yet, these very same actors may not be
able to "penetrate" what has been called my "unusual" theatre. They might be unable to relate to
that humorous or even corrosive side of my theatre.
So it's very important to establish this fact in the
beginning. So far, my relationship with the actor
has been a good one. Both of us look upon theatre
with a passion . . . . It is a passion!

Q. Who influenced you most in the literary domain?

A. I would say that Elizabethan drama has had the greatest impact upon my work. All Elizabethan theatre —
not just Shakespeare or Ben Jonson. Elizabethan
theatre is total theatre — comedy, tragedy, drama,
farce — not merely a fraction of theatre. **Rather, the**
Elizabethan had a way of looking at the play — at
life — which permitted the events to emerge from life
itself, in all of their nobility, grandeur and horror.
Worlds would swarm, confront each other, collide and
merge.
    As for modern theatre, I would say that Pirandello
had the most important influence upon me. There is
no distinction made in his theatre between the world

of fiction and that of reality. Where does one end and
the other begin? Are we dreaming or are such bizarre
things really happening? It is rather disorienting to
say the **least** — like quicksand.

Q. Would you say that your ideal theatre would be one in
the round, open, or do you still enjoy using the Italian
stage with its proscenium, etc.

A. **There** is no set theatre as far as I am concerned.
There are no rules for the theatre. Everything depends
upon the play. Recently I wrote *And At the End There
Was a Bang* – for a cast of twenty-two people. This
play was performed at the Celestins Theatre in Lyons,
an Italian type theatre; then in Brussels at the Royal
Parc Theatre in the same seventeenth-century type
stage. Last year it was performed in an open theatre
at the Drama Festival at Vaison-la-Romaine. I would
say, then, that this play could be performed in any
kind of theatre. Other plays do not have such elas-
ticity. It always depends upon the style of the drama,
its depth, and its relationship to and impact upon
audiences and actors.

Q. What are your reactions to the plays of Arrabal, Weingarten and Dubillard?

A. It is very difficult to answer such a question. I know
them all well. It is not up to me to pass judgment or
express whatever reservations I may have concerning
my contemporaries.
   You have asked me a very delicate question and
**placed me in a rather embarrassing position.** What I
can say is that there is certainly an affinity between
**Weingarten's works, Dubillard's and mine.** We are
all searching for something. Secondly, we are poets,
first and foremost. I like what they are doing in the

theatre. It's enjoyable, beautiful even. We're of the same family. We have a spiritual rapport.

Q.   What about directors such as Grotowski?   Savary? García?

A.   I don't know Savary's work at all.  As for García's — I really don't know it either.   I saw *The Constant Prince* directed in Poland by Grotowski and found it highly interesting.   I go to Poland quite frequently. I must admit that there is not one Grotowski in Poland, but twenty — and far more modest ones.   What I mean by this is that there are many directors in Poland who discipline their troupes as does Grotowski, on a physical, spiritual and emotional level.   But this is not an end in itself and what these directors have been producing in terms of theatre is truly remarkable.   The actors are masters of their gestures, their manner, their body, the text, the entire atmosphere.   There is, however, one big difference between Grotowski and the other Grotowskis: the others do not inspire terror in their court.   Grotowski seems himself to be a kind of Guru — a Demiurge.   He has created a way of life for himself and his following.

Q.   What were you trying to satirize or to reveal in your ultra-modern play, *The Agricultural Cosmonaut?*

A.   Well, it's about going to the moon; the experiencing of that fabulous adventure.   But there is another side of the story.   I wanted to show that "*Science*" acts at times "without *conscience.*"   This does not mean that I do not consider the Cosmonauts as supermen types.   They are in certain ways.   But this is really not the question in this drama.   Man should try to discover what is best for him, and how he can become truly fulfilled and lead a relatively happy existence.

Perhaps going to the moon is not the answer.

In *The Agricultural Cosmonaut* we find a Cosmonaut who has been going around the earth at unbelievable speeds: 240,000 kilometers an hour. Suddenly, he sees something from his heights which attracts his attention. He lands and investigates. It's a small, isolated farm in the Beauce region of France. There are many peasants living in the Beauce region as you undoubtedly know. It is called the "granary" of France. When the Cosmonaut finds himself on *terra firma* he discovers that the pace on land is quite different: everything seems to move very slowly on the farm, including the cycle of the seasons, etc. He begins to re-discover nature and enjoy the leisurely pace of this type of civilization which he and his scientific cohorts had been fighting against.

It is difficult to explain this comedy because the humor, the satire and the very pith of the play reside in the language and in certain situations. I might add that *The Agricultural Cosmonaut* also verges on the tragic and pathetic.

In the Beauce region, then, the Cosmonaut meets two peasants. They are absolutely backward in all ways. It is as though they had come out of the Middle Ages, that they had lived a walled-in existence and that they know nothing of what has been going on. Later, we discover that this Cosmonaut is the long lost son of these peasants; that he had walked out years before. The situations which arise from the return of the prodigal son-Cosmonaut are absolutely farcical — and hair-raising also.

The play's fundamental theme would be: return to one's sources, to the earth, to a slower pace, to nature. In fact, you don't have to be a Cosmonaut to feel this way. Many city dwellers today feel this same need.

Q.   Your plays are droll.  Can you tell us something about
     your brand of humor?   your techniques for creating
     such humorous dialogue?

A.   I think that if I begin to talk about humor — I myself
     will be devoid of it.   Humor cannot be defined or
     rather if it is analyzed — in the manner of a Bergson,
     let us say — it becomes an analytical, intellectual
     search.   Humor is something spontaneous as far as
     I am concerned.   "Humor" has been called "the
     courtesy of despair."   That's a nice definition.   It's
     like asking for a knife without a handle — with a
     missing blade also.   There is something humorous in
     this statement.   The same thing could be said about
     what people have called "Obaldia humor:" it's some-
     thing natural tinged with the corrosive.   Humor is
     worth so much more than intellectual exercises.   In
     fact, humor, I feel, is an armanent, a weapon for me.

Q.   Can you tell us about *The Unknown General,* one of
     your plays which was recently performed at the
     Comédie-Française?

A.   It's a tragic farce also dealing with a contemporary
     subject.   It concerns a General who was overburdened
     with enormous responsibilities on an intellectual level.
     His job is to defend the Occident.   He is faced with
     crisis upon crisis: depressions, refugee problems,
     rebellions, etc.   He tries to regulate each situation,
     frenetically, frenziedly, madly.   The world, he is
     convinced, will destroy itself at any moment.   This
     feeling is expressed in a scene between himself and
     his wife.   They live in an atomic-proof kitchen.   As
     the play opens, his wife is peeling potatoes.   Cer-
     tainly, as the wife of the General she should not be
     peeling potatoes....   Yet, she does so because no
     maid can be trusted in this household where so many

important secrets must be kept.

The wife complains because her husband does not want to have children. He says: "I do not want to be the father of my orphans." There is an absolutely terrible **presentment** of some impending **catastrophe** throughout the play. The General himself goes through severe moments of depression. He would be a fool if he did not feel the weight of the world on his shoulders, if he were unconscious of man's fate.

A third character makes her presence known: a ravishing pin-up. She too knows many terrifying secrets. There is, then, a kind of joust between the three characters. The play can be labeled tragic because of the themes it treats. Yet one laughs a lot.

Q. The theatre is no *pensum* for you. On the contrary, it's a joy. Does this mean that you are averse to what is commonly referred to as the "new theatre"?

A. There are many types of new theatres. Some are stylish and some will disappear tomorrow. I do not believe in avant-garde theatre because it is transformed too quickly into rear-garde theatre. I believe in good or bad theatre. What is merely a cerebral exercise or a theatrical escapade is doomed from the very beginning.

Q. Do stage sets play an important role in your theatre?

A. Yes and no. I think it again depends upon the play. When a play has nothing to say, then the dramatist or director must resort to intricate decors. When a play is profound in meaning and eternal in quality, no decors are even necessary. Shakespeare, Jonson, Aeschylus, etc. need no sets at all. Sets are frequently used to distract spectators from the essential weakness of the text. Yet, in some plays — particularly in comedy — sets frequently become a necessity. In *The Unknown General*, for example, the kitchen has become transformed into an atomic-proof armored kitchen. The General enters from the ceiling. Décor then plays an important role in this drama. In *And At the End There Was a Bang* the stage sets are also important. A column was featured on stage upon which the hero, a second or third century stylite, stands. You recall that there were three Saint Simeons who spent their lives standing on a column. As a matter of fact, **Buñuel** made a picture of just such a man.

There are other plays, however, where sets are of no import. It is the play *per se* which must excite, reverberate and stimulate audiences. Sets are always secondary unless they are absolutely intrinsic to the text itself.

Q. Are you working on something now?

A. I am always writing plays. What interests me in the creating of new works. It brings me happiness. I enjoy the labor involved, the long hours of solitude and meditation, the fulfillment as well as the joy that the creative act brings me.

We wish to thank the editors of *Drama and Theatre* for permission to reprint the above interview (Vol. II, no. 1).

## *REZVANI*

*Interviewer's Note:*

Born in Iran of a Persian father and a Russian mother, Rezvani was brought to Paris early in his life. He lived there until the Liberation (1945), when he suddenly left the Saint-Germain-des-Prés section of the city and retired with his wife to the south of France. It is from this region that his novels: *Lulu's Years, The Voice of America* (1966); and his plays: *The Remora, Body, The Brain* (1970), *Captain Schelle and Captain Eçço* (1971), *The Camp of the Golden Cloth* (1972), etc., were written.

Rezvani could be called a Renaissance man since he is equally at home in the theatre, in the novel, and in the pictorial and musical arts. His plays have added something new to the theatre: a disquieting and poetic feeling, rung in a strident note. His biting satire and his corrosive humor succeed in provoking both audiences and readers, and enticing them into new realms. And it is there that he holds them tightly in his grasp.

Q. Could you tell us something about your father? He was a dancer, wasn't he?

A. My father was a man of the theatre. He was a director, a theatrical manager, an actor in Teheran in the 1920's.

He later became a dancer and performed almost everywhere with his second wife. He was — it seems — one
of the last artists to be able to perform the traditional
Iranian dances. He even wrote a book in French in
which he speaks of the Babylonian origin of both the
theatre and the dance (the mysteries of Marduk, Mazda,
Mithra, etc.). My father throughout his life defended —
and passionately — the following theses: the theatre
originated on the Iranian plateau; and Dionysos was
venerated in Persia and India, long before the arrival
of Alexander the Great, and that this Greek god was of
Indo-Iranian origin. My father also became famous as
both a magician and a seer (*Magus*). I have related
all the details concerning my father in my book, *The
Years of Light,* published by Harcourt Brace in New
York. Despite this mountebank father of mine, I was
not really attracted to the theatre.

Painting was all-important to me. I have been a
painter for over twenty years. (With one exception.
In 1947 I wrote a play, but promptly lost the manuscript.) So I was a painter. I could really say an
"artist-painter" because my paintings were aesthetic
renditions. They were "beautiful" and were an expression of my conceptions of art during that period
of my life. Now, however, I reject those ideas. I
believed sincerely and naïvely at the time that tenderness, silence, goodness, sensuality, etc. permitted
one and helped one to overcome and confront the
harshness of life. And this passive attitude of mine
led me to become more and more isolated. I had many
exhibits, right and left in fact, like all painters.
But I always refused to play the usual gallery-game.
Soon I felt myself smothering in a series of airless
galleries. Outside of Picasso, a painter who was
always *engagé,* artists are all muzzled. In any event,
I felt that my situation as a painter was making me
more and more mute and asocial. Rather than strug-

gle, I remained silent. My silence consisted in merely
nodding my head — acquiescing. For twenty years I
lived outside of the political and social world. I
had "retired from the world," so to speak, and lived
in the south of France with my wife (where we still
live today). It was like a retreat from the harsh
realities of the world — a dive into an exceptionally
beautiful area where nature dominates. (I tell about
our departure from Paris in my play, *The Remora*.)
**Little by little, after having cut myself off from every-
thing, I began writing.** Songs (words and music first)
just to amuse myself. They filled the silences in
my life. These songs, however, became very popular
after a while. They were sung in the film *Jules and
Jim*, directed by Truffaut and in J. L. Godard's movie,
*The Mad Pierrot*. To make a long story short, my
songs filled my overflowing need for verbal expression.
And then, one day, my **song-writing** seemed too limited
a field for me. The "frame" burst, so to speak, and
from a song erupted my first theatrical work: *The
Immobile*. This was followed by two other plays,
*The Remora* and *The Brain*. These three plays were
conceived as a theatrical triptych based on the theme
of "intrusion." They were, as far as I was concerned,
*indivisible*.

The theme of *The Immobile* is autographical in a
way (let us say as far as my feelings are concerned),
in that it expresses a kind of distressing anticipation.
The heroes (who could be the same as those of *The
Remora* but fifty years ahead of their time) are two
pitiful old men, appalled by the world they live in and
who survive only because of their total love for each
other. By divesting a couple of their usual attributes
(youth, beauty, etc.) I have tried to trap *love* in the
raw. My two heroes have withdrawn from life — and
this for over forty years. They live enclosed in a
wretched-looking apartment (the same type in which

the young couple in *The Remora* lived). One of the old men composes a miniature pocket opera, as he calls it. The theme: intrusion. In fact he writes a stylized version of *The Remora* (*The Remora* had not yet been written). **The Immobile, then, is a kind** of parody of the theatre in the theatre. The voice in this work is of primary importance because throughout the play the old man, Bob, imitates the joyous and crystalline voice of children with his own rattle or raspinglike voice. This play could also be looked upon as a kind of anti-Tristan and Isolde story. It goes against **the archaic puritanical tradition and theme of** love **sanctified because it is unfulfilled and ends in violent death. My heroes have lived their entire lives in the ambiance of love, togetherness, happiness,** and we surprise them in this play at the end of each trajectory, as much in love, as close to each other and as happy as before — definitely senile.

Q.   What about the two other plays?

A.   After having completed *The Immobile,* I finished the other two panels of my triptych: *The Remora* and *The Brain.* I hoped to see these three plays produced together in a kind of long six-hour séance. Naturally, no one took this "folly" of mine seriously. The three were consequently produced separately.

The second play, *The Remora* (I discuss this play's genesis in my novel *Lulu's Years*), is the story of a young couple. They're madly in love. They live in the politically and socially decadent post-war atmosphere. They are members of a generation which was too young to understand and realize what was happening at the time of the Liberation. (This was the case of my generation.) These adolescents of the Liberation period found themselves caught between **three possibilities:**

1. Attempt to become integrated. This is Karlos' case in *The Remora*. (The word "remora" comes from the Greek meaning "too late"; it is also a parasitical fish which attaches itself to another fish.) Karlos becomes a type of social parasite. He lives from the crumbs handed to him by his elders. For him — a person who sees himself a writer—life amounts to becoming a journalist for the Lazareff paper syndicate. Karlos "collaborates." He "nibbles to the right and to the left."

2. Become a member of the Communist party. This is Clovis' case. Clovis wants to change the world. He believes in social justice and wishes most ardently to accomplish a "Thorough International Housecleaning." He is, in other words, a narrowminded person, and certainly a Stalinist.

3. The luck of falling in love. This is Charles' case. He meets Lulu. They love each other madly. They are carefree, selfish; they refuse to have children because they love each other and are totally at odds with the society in which they live. Finally, they flee. Those who follow are left the job of working out society's problems. We will see how their successors solve the question of confronting them — and in a violent manner.

My third play, *The Brain,* is a musical farce, and a social one too. A novel I wrote, *Voice of America,* changeable? In *The Brain,* after a certain accident, changeable? In *The Brain* after a certain accident, the head of a thief (from the lower classes) is grafted onto the body of an aristocratic banker. The imprisoned thief awakens and finds himself in the body of a

man representing a class that he has always hated.
He expresses utter disgust at being where he is, etc.
His problems are solved in this play by means of a
scalpel, the death penalty, and finally a sub-machine.
I don't want to reveal any more details.

These three plays should be performed in a rather
free way, interwoven with each other. The directing
should be broad, farce-like, with plenty of fantasy.
The spectators should, as we say, bring their sand-
wiches with them.

Q.   What are your ideas as far as directing is concerned?

A.   Every author has certain ideas concerning the directing of his plays. I also have mine too. When I write
my novels, for example, I can actually see parts of
scenes unfolding before me. But because of the way
we live — the fact that I spend twelve months out of
the twelve here in the country — far from the theatre,
I am not tempted to take part or to attend any productions of my works. Nevertheless, I believe that a
play must be virtually rewirtten once the actors and
director begin to work on it. But I repeat, I am not a
man of the theatre. If I write plays it's because it's
the only way I can express myself. Directing is
really not my problem.

What is of import at this point is to be able to
"drive" my painting, my novel writing, my playwriting,
my music, as one does a team of horses. I am furiously
against all specialization. I refuse all cultural taboos.
We are capable — all of us — of writing, painting, etc.
We are all poets. All we have to do is run the risk
of living a little, of letting ourselves go and rejecting — completely — the conception of the civil servant,
or, in other words, living the limited existence of a
routine life.

Q. Do you have any theories concerning acting?

A. If an actor merely practises his profession and has no callouses on his hands, he's dead as far as I am concerned. It he does not know how to use a hachet, a pen, ten or more musical instruments, if he does not know how to cook a bit, to feel involved in the organized slaughter being carried out today by a group of international political "directors", if an actor remains rigidly constricted within the narrow confines of his artistic conceptions, he becomes a kind of *homme de métier* and, in this case, he holds no interest for me. I am convinced that theatre must come from the streets and perhaps never leave them.

The idea of enclosing oneself in a building, in a hall, after having paid an entrance fee, appears hollow to me and utterly without significance. I believe that the theatre may be a substitute for action — until the day action becomes a substitute for the theatre. We are on the verge of vast social upheavals. For the moment we are becoming liberated, and we are rushing back into the ambiguous world of Art.

Art is life and one without the other cannot exist. Art must be the profound *expression of our lives;* otherwise it's merely an intellectual exercise, devoid of any kind of significance. The day unity is established between art and life the theatre will no longer have any *raison d'être.* One will not have to replace the other. We will no longer need priests, nor shamans, nor gurus, nor sorcerers of any kind. Our acts will fashion reality.

Q. Who are your theatrical ancestors, that is, the dramatists who have influenced you most profoundly?

A. If I became a playwright, it was just by chance, as I said before. It was a kind of necessity probably which drove me to it. Neither actors nor directors attracted me to the theatre — certainly not the stifling nature of the theatre with its clusters of red velvet seats always present in elegant theatrical edifices.

I know almost nothing about the theatre — whether classical or modern. And if I speak of Shakespeare, it would be merely out of a kind of laziness on my part since I have read only *King Lear*, *Hamlet* and *Measure for Measure* (for which I designed the sets a long while back). I remain indifferent to Ionesco's theatre. I reject Beckett's. I remember having reacted very deeply, when I was a child, to a *guignol* performance. Artaud alone overwhelmed me with his ideas on the theatre.

Q. Are you attracted to politically oriented theatre?

A. I believe that everything we do is political. Even when we refuse to take part in politics, it's a means (perhaps the most criminal) of engaging in politics because we let things happen. The theatre is political. Even a boulevard play is a political act. It sides with power because it invites us not to pose any questions; it invites us to digest everything served to us in the theatre rather than to question. Personally, I believe only in a critical kind of theatre, that is, theatre which is necessarily politically oriented. One of my plays features two captains: Captain Schelle and Captain Eçço.

Q. What would be the physical aspect of your ideal theatre: a theatre in the round, out of doors, etc ?

A. I require no formal kind of edifice. Any type of expanse where people can gather would suit my purposes. Any place where five or six people or more could come together, where ideas could circulate, would suffice.

The police have understood the possibilities — the dramatic ones — of groups gathering together. They therefore forbade the right to assemble. They were afraid of a theatre which would free itself from their control. Let the container be round, cubical, triangular; it's the contents which count. Arsenic remains arsenic in any kind of vial.

Q. Does the dream play a role in your theatre?

A. The theatre *is* a dream one shares.

Q. You use several theatrical techniques: satire, irony, etc. Can you tell us how you use these techniques and to what end?

A. If humor is omitted from a play, we become animals once again. Satire is a marvelous weapon since it provokes laughter. Laughter, as you know, frequently strikes far more powerfully than anything else, particularly since there is no weapon created which can offset it (unless you actually suppress the person physically). On the other hand, irony does not attract me. I find nothing pleasant about irony. In general, the one who indulges or manipulates this technique gives the impression of being arrogant, superior to others. Or else he impresses me as being despairing. You need a great deal of humor to make irony palatable and lots of wit and intelligence.

Q. It seems to me that sound effects assume the role of protagonists in your dramas. Is this true?

A. Yes. They have. I pay a great deal of attention to noise. In *The Immobile*, for example, the window is open at a certain point and everyone falls flat on the floor. Why? Because the noise coming in from the

outside is just too strong. In the triptych, *The Immobile, The Brain* and *The Remora,* noise plays a
dominant role since the main theme is that of intrusion. Noise is an intrusion against which there is
no defense. Yes, certainly in these plays sound
effects do become protagonists — and antagonists.

Q.   Do you consider yourself as part of the "new novel"
group, along with such writers as Nathalie Sarraute,
Michel Butor, etc.?

A.   No. I'm not at all attracted by the "new novel." In
general I don't like modern French literature. The
French novelists, for the most part, are formalists.
They want to add beautiful cultural objects to their
world. They are almost all from the bourgeoisie and
in general their work reflects nothing but a kind of
nostalgia.... The only modern French novelists I
admire are Céline and Genet: both sons of the people.
      Unlike the "new novelists," my novels are not
objects. They do not attempt to achieve any kind of
formal perfection. On the contrary, my plays and my
novels are born from events. They develop, stop, and
finally take on whatever direction they choose. They
never end. I have never written a novel from which a
play could not be drawn, or at least the outline for a
play. I must point to the fact that my work is stylized
to a certain degree; this is in order to give the play
or the novel as a whole more humanity and warmth.
      In conclusion, I should like to say once again
that I am against any kind of specialization, whether
it be artistic or social. I believe in the pluridi-
mensional man: free, creative, an artist of life.

We wish to thank the editors of *Drama and Theatre* for permission to reprint the above interview (Vol. 9, no. 3).

ACTORS

## MARIE BELL

*Interviewer's Note:*

Paul Claudel called Marie Bell's performance in *The Satin Slipper* "unforgettable." About her portrayal in Racine's *Phaedra,* Jean Cocteau wrote: "One would like to immobilize Mme Bell, turn her into a statue and paint her unceasingly until her death. Her voice, her superb gestures have destined her for the great repertory roles . . ." Marie Bell began her career as a dancer at the Opera. She then studied at the Conservatory in Paris and after completing her training, joined the Comédie-Française. In 1953 she left the Comédie-Française and decided to "fly on her own wings." She acted in such plays as **Antony and Cleopatra** by **Shakespeare**, **The Balcony** by Jean Genet, *The Good Soup* by Félicien Marceau, *The Misanthrope* by Molière, and *Sometimes Violins* by Françoise Sagan, to mention but a few. Marie Bell, who owns the **Théâtre** du Gymnase on the Boulevard **Bonne Nouvelle,** has become a manager-actress. She has toured in the great capitals of the world: London, Moscow, Athens, New York . . . . In the movies she has been seen in such classics as *The Great Game, Dance Card, The Good Soup.*

When asked how she prepares roles such as Phaedra, Berenice, Mme Irma, etc. she answered: "One must know how to look out upon life, upon humanity as a

whole, upon people as individuals... An actor must have
loved and suffered, known jealousy and learned gen-
erosity .... He must have *lived* all these things in order
to be able to express them.''

Q.   You once said that Genet and Claudel were comparable
     in terms of their writing style and their deeply re-
     ligious approach to life. Could you clarify this state-
     ment?

A.   As far as their writing is concerned I really cannot see
     vast differences between these two writers.  The
     poetry, the strength, the power of their words, and
     the rhythms and musicality of their sentence structure
     are comparable.  They both use words in the broadest
     of senses and they have the courage to go to the ex-
     treme. They push, they pound, they mould their words.
     Their language is hard, brutal; their images are flam-
     boyant, visceral, painful and searing.
          Had these two writers met they might not have
     liked each other... and yet, I'm really not so sure of
     this. Genet greatly admires Claudel.  Though Claudel
     was a very Catholic writer — Genet must have been a
     believer at one point in his life.  His writing is mys-
     tical...

Q.   How did you come to play the role of Dona Prouhèze
     in Claudel's *The Satin Slipper?*

A.   Claudel came to see me in my dressing room one Sun-
     day afternoon after a matinee and said to me: ''Made-
     moiselle, I would very much like you to play the part
     of Dona Prouheze. You of course know my play *The
     Satin Slipper?*'' I answered that I did not know his
     play.  He laughed very heartily when I confessed my
     ignorance because it is very rare for an actress to
     dare to admit that she has not read something.  Then

he told me he would have the manuscript sent to me
immediately and would call me the following day.
I received the manuscript at home and read the play.
When he telephoned the next day I told him that I had
read *The Satin Slipper,* that it was very beautiful,
but that I did not understand a thing. At this point,
he burst out laughing. He came to see me a few days
later and read the play to me. When Claudel reads he
has a way of phrasing his sentences which is unique.
We understood each other perfectly. And I must say
that to have played the part of Dona Prouhèze was one
of the greatest joys of my career.

Q.   How did you visualize or understand this complex
character, willing to sacrifice all of her earthly joys
in order to win her reward in heaven?

A.   The role came to me as Claudel read his play aloud.
You know he was a prodigious actor: exuberant,
funny, witty. When reading he would actually play
the part of Dona Prouhèze for me. He was not very
young at the time, but the manner in which he portrayed her helped me understand the many ambiguities
in her character. He might not have been capable of
playing on the stage, but Claudel was very gifted
nevertheless. He was also a marvelous director and
technician of the theatre. Gestures were always of
extreme importance to him, as was diction, of course.

Q.   How did you prepare the roles of Racine's *Phaedra* and
*Bérénice?*

A.   I gave these two roles a great deal of thought before
I attempted to portray them. When I was eighteen
years old I thought I could act Racine's Phaedra and
Berenice. I was so wrong. One must have suffered a
great deal and have lived before one can portray such

women.    To understand a personality — someone
else's — cannot be learned cerebrally.    Experience
is the only teacher.    The emotions and feelings one
seeks to express on stage must have been lived.

*Q.*  Did you use **Stanislawski's** method to prepare *Phaedra?*

*A.*  No.  I use no method.  One does of course recall past
experiences.    Perhaps one does not think of them
consciously, but one's unconscious frequently brings
forth certain events or sensations which enable one
better to understand the part being portrayed.  I proceed by *instinct*.  I *throw* myself into the roles I play.
There is, naturally, a great deal of preparation: gestures, costumes, the *mise en scène* ...  When I take
on a part I either find my character's soul and humanity
immediately or I never find it.  Now take Phaedra's
death scene ...  I *found* just the right way to portray
her death — my death — at the very first rehearsal.
I have never touched this scene since.  I don't know
why or how I found it, I just did ....

*Q.*  You live the characters you play.  This is contrary to
Diderot's way as described in his *Paradox on the
Comedian.*

*A.*  Yes.  I believe I do.  If one has not lived the actual
events involved, one has at least seen others experience them.    During the German occupation of
France, for example, one just had to look about to
observe the suffering of others.  Such pain remains
with you; it is unforgettable.  When I act, I play out
my suffering and my pain.  It is my way of ridding
myself of heartaches.  Acting has become a physical
and emotional necessity for me.  The theatre has a
healing effect for me.

Q. What are the actual techniques involved in preparing a role?

A. I have no techniques. I read and reread the play in question. I cannot learn a text as others do, that is, act by act. I have to learn my part from the very first line to the last without any breaks and right away. I cannot learn fifteen lines now and twenty the following day. When "I know" my lines I find my "character's" personality almost immediately — then I integrate it into the ensemble.

Q. Do you ever change your interpretation during rehearsals?

A. Sometimes. If I have a director who tells me that he would like me to play a certain line one way, I do it. If something bothers me, however, I tell him. I tell him how I would like to see the line acted. I might be wrong. Sometimes I'm right. In *Phaedra*, for example, she says at the end of Act II:
  Et Phèdre, au labyrinthe avec vous descendue,
  Se serait avec vous retrouvée ou perdue ...
When I rehearsed these lines I discovered that the words "retrouvée" and "perdue" we so different — as different as the sixth floor and the ground floor. And so, I let a few moments elapse between the two words. The effect on the audience was devastating. It seemed to intensify my character's anguish. But you've got to find these things out for yourself.

Q. Since you played in *Antony and Cleopatra* could you compare Shakespeare and Racine from the actress' point of view?

A. Both Shakespeare and Racine have *grandeur*, depth, and majesty. Their characters are human and alive.

They are many-faceted and so respond to my personality. But Shakespeare is a more masculine writer than Racine. There are few great women's parts in Shakespeare whereas Racine's plays have many marvelous feminine roles. Racine *knew* the woman's heart.

Q. Would you say that Racine is modern? Can he still appeal today?

A. Racine is one of our most modern authors. Were he writing *Phaedra* or *Bérénice* today, he would not change a line. And I believe he knew how to speak of love better than any other author. Dramatists today really don't know how to speak of real love — *l'amour passion*.

   Racine knew women: he knew their hearts. Corneille, on the other hand, is a writer who appeals more to men. When a Racine play is produced today, it is played with a modern twist. In fact *Phaedra* and *Bérénice* have been played in modern dress. Racine belongs to no period. He is universal and each epoch interprets his creations in a different manner.

Q. Do you prefer classical or modern roles?

A. I love them both. I like what *will* take place. The role I prefer is the one I *shall* act — the one which *will* come into being.

Q. What kind of training should an actor have today?

A. Acting today presents serious problems. Actors are no longer taught diction. They slur their words; they do not know how to articulate. Audiences do not understand what they are saying. I don't really know

why actors are so sloppy diction-wise. Perhaps it is
due to television, movies, and radio. I'm not certain.
I think that modern plays are easier to perform than
classical ones. I must say, however, that there are
very few great actors left who are capable of performing Shakespeare or Racine. The era of great acting,
I believe, has vanished. Today, an actor must work
on television as well as in the theatre in order to earn
a living. The techniques in these fields are different.
Consequently, he does not have sufficient time to
devote to the theatrical arts. The moment the actor
places the word "money" before the word "art," he
is lost.

I started dancing and acting at the age of seventeen. I was what is commonly alluded to as a *rat de
l'opéra*. This training was very helpful to me. Dancing should be taught to all children. It helps them
walk and move about gracefully. I earned three francs
fifty centimes a day. There were many days, however,
when I went without food. It was not important to me
because I loved my *métier*. Others also suffered pangs
of hunger: Dullin, Artaud, Barrault..... Now actors
want to dress well, they want to go to bars... True
passion for the theatre perhaps no longer exists. We
are living in strange times, indeed.

Real acting cannot be learned. Diction, stance,
etc. ... can, of course. Acting is an instinct. Moreover, as I said before, an actor must not only observe
the world around him, he must partake of life in all of
its manifestations. It is ridiculous to try to teach
actors where and when to use certain gestures. These
should come naturally to him. Gestures, movement,
grace, for example, play an enormous part in both
Genet and Claudel's plays. An actor must *feel* his
way. In tragic plays, for example, I tell my actors
that they must never touch each other on stage — they
must never have any physical contact. The minute an

actor touches another, the illusion he is trying to
create vanishes, every-day reality steps in. In great
roles, one must never touch another person on stage.
I can say, for example, to my beloved: "Je vous
adore," and these words will assume gigantic proportions because of the way I say them and the feelings I inject into them. Yet, if I touch the person in
question as I am saying these words, the majesty of
the feelings involved diminishes considerably.

Q.  What gave you the idea of producing *The Balcony?*

A.  I produced Genet's play because I was warned by my
compatriots not to do so. I was advised to steer clear
of his work. It was dangerous, they told me. This
attitude annoyed me. Since Genet is a great writer,
I felt that there should be no problem in producing a
great work. I asked Peter Brook to direct *The Balcony* and I played the part of Madame Irma. She amused
me greatly. The stage settings were ultra-lavish.
    I have the impression that Americans understand
Genet better than we do. I don't know why this should
be. In France people feel that he is a man riddled
with complexes. He has some, of course. Who
doesn't? There are few in France today — if any —
who write as well as he does. And he is fearless.
His characters have magnitude — they are *enormous* —
like your skyscrapers.

Q.  Do you know Genet well?

A.  Yes. He is a good friend of mine. When we are together we spend out time insulting each other and
arguing. But you know that when people love each
other they always say disagreeable things. I see Genet
when I'm on tour — in London, Athens .... When you
make an appointment with Genet and you only have

fifteen minutes to spend with him, the fifteen minutes turn into four hours. You cannot detach yourself from him. He is dangerous; he casts a spell on you; he magnetizes you. He has a way of understanding things, life — a very special way — and after talking with him you begin to wonder: Is he right? or am I?

Q.   Did Genet attend the rehearsals for *The Balcony?*

A.   I asked him not to come. I know him and he gets into tempers. Had he attended the rehearsals he would have wanted to change everything.

Q.   Do you enjoy having a permanent company?

A.   I don't have one. I have my own troupe of actors and every five or six years I change my actors. I do this because after a while an actor develops bad habits. It's like a marriage. When one gets married one thinks it is for good. One no longer tries to act one's best or to expend any great effort along these lines. One becomes lax. Of course, if I don't have an actor to fill a particular part, I can always hire one from the outside.

Q.   You have acted in the movies, television and in the theatre. What are the difference between these media?

A.   There is a world of difference. First of all, I dislike television. I have the distinct impression that some- one is looking at me through a key hole when playing on television. In the theatre we have the play, the actors, the director and the audience. In the movies there is the scenario, the director who is master after God, and the operator. The actor comes sixth in line. When making a movie you are at the mercy of the machine. You are a package. I played the part

of Marie-Paul in both stage play and the film version
of Félicien Marceau's *The Good Soup.* In the theatre,
it is instinct which counts. You feel the audience,
you feel it following you into your world of illusion
and you know when your audience is with you and
when it isn't. In the movies you are put in a box for
six months and you have no idea whether the film will
be good or bad. When making a picture you arrive at
the studio at 8:00 in the morning. You are made up.
The director arrives. He tells you to stand near the
window, how to lift the telephone receiver... It's
just marvelous! The movies give you a good rest.
Films amuse me. Actually, anyone can become a
movie actress providing the director is good. Few can
become great theatrical performers.

Q. Did you know Louis Jouvet?

A. **Yes, and I admired him greatly.** He did not have a very
melodious voice but he was a great actor. When he
opened or closed a door you knew immediately that
someone was there. There are actors who open and
shut a door and there is really nothing striking about
such an action. Jouvet had what we call *présence.*
He was like a fakir. A fluid would emanate from him
and flow from his soul, from his very **being outward,**
into the audience, enveloping it within its grip.

## MICHEL ETCHEVERRY

*Interviewer's Note:*

Even before Michel Etcheverry received his diploma from the Paris Conservatory for Dramatic Arts (1947), he became a member of the Louis Jouvet acting company (1945-1951), portraying such roles as the pharmacist in Jules Romains' *Knock*, the King in Giraudoux's *Ondine*, the Commander in Molière's *Don Juan*, and the notary in his *School for Wives*. After Jouvet's death, however, Michel Etcheverry free-lanced, acting in such works as Sartre's **The Devil and the Good Lord, Pygmalion,** and the **Diary of Anne Frank**. A sociétaire at the Comédie-Française since 1964, he has not only pursued his acting career in both classical (Molière, Corneille, Racine, Musset, Beaumarchais, etc.) and modern (Gide, Valéry, Claudel, Ionesco, Montherlant, etc.) repertories, but has also branched out in the directing fields, creating the *mises en scènes* for works by Strindberg, Giraudoux, Musset and others. A favorite on television, he has incarnated the exciting figures of King Lear, Augustus (in *Cinna*) and Ulysses (in *The Trojan War Will Not Take Place*).

An indefatigable artisan of the theatre, Michel Etcheverry works his roles through to perfection, devoting hours and weeks of intense study to them if necessary. He is a believer in depth analysis of the roles to be portrayed and of the play as an entity unto itself; he considers indispensable a familiarity with the times in which the author lived, and the literature and the art of the period as well. Ethical and honorable in his approach to the theatre, imbued with the vigor and fire necessary for fascinating portrayals, Michel Etcheverry can be called a true artist of the stage.

Q.  Can you tell us something about your early training?

A.  I don't think that my background or my training was vastly different from that of other professional actors. I began with amateur companies. I went to the Ecole Normale and the Conservatoire in Paris. I enjoyed working in the theatre. I cannot say that I was born to play one type of role or another; that I was either made for comedy or for tragedy. I think one works oneself into parts and into plays. I've enjoyed my trade or should I say my trades: acting, directing and teaching. They fascinate me and amuse me at the same time.

Q.  You studied acting at the Conservatoire and you also became a member of Louis Jouvet's acting company. Were there differences between these two companies and their views on the theatre?

A.  My memories of the years I spent with Jouvet have blotted out almost everything else. They were marvelous. It would take me a long time to explain the differences between what I had learned at the Conservatoire and what I experienced with Jouvet and his troupe. One of the main differences probably resides in the fact that with Jouvet an actor was part of a collective or group. An actor trained at the Conservatoire has a tendency to look upon himself as a *soloist*. He works on a scene. He cuts his partner's lines if he considers them to be too long. He can steal the scene and really do anything he wants. He is the center, the focal point, of everything he undertakes. He considers himself as does a violin or piano virtuoso and spends years preparing for this role. Such an attitude seems very unfortunate to me. What these people seem to forget is that most of the would-be piano and violin virtuosos end up by playing in an orchestra. It is just this *sense of the orchestra* which I learned from Jouvet. To work together, in a **group. Everyone, after all, depends** upon the next one in an acting company: actor, director, electrician, stage manager, etc.... It's a collective undertaking. Now, the avant-garde theatrical groups speak of the theatre as a "collective creation." They believe they have created something new and original in the theatre. Not at all. In Jouvet's time we were doing just this. Today, many of the new directors reject the written word and want to create something totally **spontaneous and unwritten.**

Q. You are now a full-fledged member of the Comédie-Française. Could you go into detail concerning the differences in techniques between those of the Comédie-Française and of Louis Jouvet's troupe?

A. Tremendous differences. First of all Jouvet was the sole director of his troupe. He was looked upon as our master, as a God. He was the boss in all senses of the word. He could hire, fire, decide upon the play, cast it, etc. His authority was clear and simple. We were aware of this fact the minute we set foot into his theatre. At the Comédie-Française, the situation is quite different. The Comédie-Française comprises thirty "sociétaires" or **"owners,"** if you wish. We have a **six-member** committee — I am one of them — which decides upon the repertoire and casts the plays as well. This kind of division of labor or community type of governing policy creates an entirely different atmosphere. We are sixty-four actors and actresses at the Comédie-Française. In Jouvet's troupe there were a dozen or so. Jouvet used to perform the same play — or perhaps two of them — all year long. At the Comédie-Française, we rotate the plays. One night I might play one role with one half of the company; the following evening, another, with the other half. . . .

Q. You must have problems casting a play?

A. We do. Sometimes it's quite a delicate situation. First of all the troupe is large and though the actors know that at one time they may play the lead, the next time they must be prepared to play a minor role. The situation is quite clear cut when we invite an out-side director to create the *mise en scène* for one of our plays. In this case, he is the master and selects whom he wishes. When Jean-Marie Serreau directed **Ionesco's *Hunger and Thirst,*** he had *carte blanche.* But when we ourselves direct a play — the question of personality, of friendship — very delicate situations — arise.

Materially speaking, we are quite well off. We have at our disposal funds from the government, a vast library, research assistants, costumes and fine technical equipment, etc. We also have what many directors want so desperately: time. We can spend four to six months, or more if necessary, rehearsing a play. We rehearsed Molière's *The Miser* for four months.

Q. Since the Comédie-Française is a government sub-sidized theatre, do you find yourself hampered in any way? Does the government intervene, politically speaking? Does it prevent you from producing certain works?

A.   No.  We have complete freedom.  But something interesting happened a few years ago at another govern-
ment-subsidized theatre, the Théâtre National Populaire.   The government stepped in and prevented
Armand Gatti's anti-Franco **play**, *The Passion of
General...* from being performed.   The play condemned a leader of state with whom France had political ties.  It would seem rather paradoxical to me
if the government would grant eight or nine million
francs to a theatre and have that same theatre turn
right around and spit on that very government...
If, for example, a government subsidized theatre would
produce a play condemning **Nixon,**   how would Americans react?  Or, another example, if an employee of
Renault were to be interviewed and he declared that
the Renault cars were the worst possible and that
Citroën manufactured the best, he would certainly be
fired the next day.  Let him go to Citroën if the cars
they make are superior.  The same can be said of the
Gatti situation.  To produce a play which might inter-
fere with government policy or tend to create un-
pleasant relations, politically speaking, is not in
order.  I think the government's action was logical and
the right one.  If a private producer were to direct
Gatti's play it would be perfectly fine; it would be a
personal venture and not a governmental one.  Another
question now comes to mind.  Why hasn't anyone else
produced Gatti's play?  Because it just happens that
the play is a poor one.  No private producer would risk
it.  The play is a typical thesis play.  It is not at all
**dramatic.  It was not well conceived; it has no depth
or poetry to it.**

Q.   You have played both classical and modern roles.
Could you tell us how you look upon these various
parts?  how you prepare for them?

A.   Let's take the seventeenth-century author, Corneille, as
our first example.   I played the part of Emperor
Augustus in *Cinna*.   Actually, the play analyzes or
reveals the evolution — the spiritual ascension — of
one man, Augustus. **In the beginning of the drama, you**
recall, he is described by the two young people as a
sanguinary tyrant... a cruel individual.   When he
finally appears on stage, you see a man in his fifties
who has really reached the end of his rope. He wants
to retire.   The power which he had sought to acquire
throughout his life now hurts him.   He wants to leave
his frenetic life, retire and find peace both without
and within his being.   Yet, he feels bound to remain
as a ruler because he feels that should he abdicate,
chaos would reign in his kingdom.

Augustus, therefore, evolves throughout the play.
From a material being, firmly entrenched in the things
of this world, he ascends the ladder and becomes a
more spiritual and complete man.   He renounces his
wordly goods and his acquisitions.   What makes this
character unique is the fact that he is able to tran-
scend, to go beyond what had formerly preoccupied
him.   He rises above the flesh, so to speak, and opts
for something eternal.   He can achieve such a state
through pardon.

**The actor, of course, must memorize** his role.
Those of us who have been trained in classical theatre find little difficulty in memorizing such parts,
though they may be considered extremely lengthy.
After the memory work — or during that period — one
cannot cut these things up.   The actor must try to
understand the play as a whole, the character in all
of its nuances.   The actor is not a creator of characters — Corneille, Molière, Racine are.   The actor
must try to approach this person into whose flesh he
wants to insinuate himself, and try to incarnate him
as best he can. Sensitivity, understanding, intuition —

all of these elements play a part in the portrayal.

Q.  Can you describe a modern play in which you acted, and
the difficulties involved in such a production?

A.  Ionesco's *Hunger and Thirst,* which I consider one of
the finest modern works. Granted it is a bit long and
a bit involved at times, it is yet quite extraordinary.
We were faced with certain technical problems. First
and foremost, Ionesco's language. Whereas classical
theatre is memorized with ease, Ionesco's vocabulary
is quite different. It's terribly difficult to learn his
lines by heart. This may be due to his special way
of thinking, and the rhythm of his language. Classical
works are clear, direct, precise. There were other
problems also.
   I played the part of Brother Tarabas. I greeted
the visitors as they entered the monastery. I use the
word monastery, but Ionesco does not specify the
locale which is not a monastery, he says, nor a hospital .... We just don't know what it is or where it is.
The spectator can consider it what he wishes. It
could be hell for that matter. At any rate, guests
arrive at what we call a monastery, for convenience's
sake. They are treated with the utmost gentleness
and kindness. They are fed, clothed, and their feet
washed. They are even entertained. A kind of short
play is enacted before them. Two characters arrive
in cages: one is called Brechtoll (there is certainly
an allusion to Brecht since Ionesco despises him).
The other is a Christian. The former says that God
does not exist, the latter that he does. The monks
impose a fast upon both of them. They will be given
food only if they recant. Days pass. Finally, as they
cannot bear their condition any longer, the Christian
finally admits that God does not exist and the atheist
confesses that he does. Both then have perjured them-

selves.  They renounce what they had so firmly believed in.  Ionesco wants to prove that theories alone
are of no value.  After the end of the performance, the
visitor on the scene is asked to do a favor in return
for the kindness he has experienced at their hands.
He agrees.  They ask him to serve at table.  He does
so.  No sooner does he serve the monks around the
table than the first ones served have already finished
and he must begin serving them all over again.  The
pace speeds up at the play's finale and you see him
running frantically from one side of the table to the
other as Brother Tarabas keeps saying "continue...
continue ...." The end is a whirlwind of activity!

One has the impression that his servitude will
last eternally.  The role of Brother Tarabas is one of
my favorite parts.  Again, I must say that the technical
aspects of a play must of course be mastered; but so
should its deeper meanings.  These must be brought
out and revealed subtly to the audience.

I have no pre-conceived notions concerning the
theatre.  A lot depends upon the director.  If he is a
good director, the role emerges and grows by itself.
To incarnate a role is a slow process.  It must gestate,
like a baby; grow within and then burst forth in all of
its newness and beauty.

Q.   You also act on television.  Is there a conflict between
these two media?

A.   The techniques are different, certainly.  The eyes and
the ears have to be trained in varying manners.  For
example, on television a microphone is hidden some
place in our costume.  This permits us to talk very
softly, to whisper if we must.  Our acting, perhaps
**because of this, can be more sincere, more** truthful.
On the stage, however, we have no microphone on our
person and if we do speak in very low tones no one in

the audience will hear us.   We have to project our
voices outward.   The entire vocal techniques are different.   The play's tempo also varies as does the
climate and the entire atmosphere and point of view.

Q.   What are your impressions of contemporary theatre?

A.   There is an enormous amount of activity going on.   We
have grave problems because we have few *great*
authors.   We have many promising ones.   At least
that's what people say.   But let's remember that
Corneille was thirty-four years old when he wrote his
first masterpiece, *The Cid.*   All these promising
authors are now in their forties and fifties.   I am still
waiting for a masterpiece.   This dirth of great writers
may be due to the troubled times in which we are
living.   Perhaps out of the *pot pourri* we have today
in the theatre (the theatre of improvisation, of nudity,
of eroticism, of derision, of panic, etc.) some genius
will appear — soon!

We wish to thank the editors of *Drama and Theatre* for permission to reprint the above interview (Vol. 9, no. 2).

*AMIDOU*

*Interviewer's Note:*

A native of Morocco, Amidou played Saïd in Roger
Blin's production of Genet's *The Screens* (1966) at the
Odèon in Paris. Amidou studied at the Conservatoire and
acted in several films directed by Claude Lelouch, including *To Be a Crook*. After Blin saw *To Be a Crook* he
invited Amidou to read for *The Screens*. (The following
interview was conducted by Claude Avrane.)

Q. How did you meet Genet?

A. One day Blin brought Genet to the theatre where I was
   rehearsing with Barrault for *Numance* by Cervantes.
   Blin told Genet he wanted me to play Saïd. Then I
   went away with Genet for eight days. He did not —
   absolutely did not — want to talk about the theatre.
   Nor did he want to hear me read the role. We just
   had our little breakfasts and dinners. And we talked.
   After eight days he said, "Yes, I think you can play
   Saïd."

Q. Tell me about those eight days.

A. What I can tell you is this: the real Genet is exactly

the Genet of his books. The way he drinks coffee ...
the way he talks ... you really have to hang on to
every word he says in order to follow him. He's
fascinating. I couldn't leave him for a second. I
was afraid the first two days. He has such extreme
simplicity. He's a man with whom you can have real
human contact, but he's not human. It's not that he's
inhuman: he's more than human. I can't find the right
words to express what I feel.

Q. Did he ask you questions?

A. Yes. All the time. And what interested him most was
my sports training — particularly judo. We spoke
about Algeria.

Q. Did he come to many rehearsals?

A. Towards the end he came all the time. At first he
didn't want to spoil things, so he stayed away. He
has great confidence in Blin. Genet said that, aside
from himself, Blin understands his plays best. After
he watched a rehearsal, Genet said, "Well, I never
realized I had written something so beautiful." This
was meant particularly for Blin and his *mise en scène*.
Blin's directing is quite special — and disconcerting.
He doesn't give much direction, yet at the end of a
day's work we seem to know everything. He lets the
actors do what they feel in the character. But he lets
us improvise only if it is in the spirit of the sentence.
Then he erases everything that's peripheral to the
character. He explains what has to be explained; then
we work within that frame.

Genet said, in the beginning, that he didn't like
the way the actors walked. He told us that we always
moved as if we were going someplace. When we're on
stage, he said, we should act as if we were nowhere.

For example, it took us two weeks to use the word "heaven" without gesturing. The word "heaven" is enough by itself; hands are not necessary. "He's coming this way," Genet said, "should be said without turning the head." Often if the person says someone is coming from the left, Genet would assume that the character was coming from the right. Just as "heaven" can be anywhere, so a person could be coming from any direction. This kind of non-movement gives the impression of unlimited space. Another example: when I call my mother, I call her from the garden side. And when I asked why she came from the opposite direction, Genet said that the theatre was an unlimited space.

There are some beautiful things one can learn from Genet: how to talk and walk. He wants no useless gestures. I'm from the south and I use my hands when I talk. I worked with Blin for three months to master this. Blin, like Genet, believes the word to be essential and not the gesture. *The Screens* is a poetic text, but it does not have to be spoken poetically. Speak it simply and the lyricism will be there.

Q.  Did Genet ever speak to you about the role?

A.  Yes. He repeated the same thing all the time. "Go and practice your judo and you will know how to play Saïd. You will discover his character." I asked him why. "You'll understand what I mean later. Right now, the only thing I insist on is that you study your judo." I discovered later that he wanted me to experience a certain kind of concentration. In both karate and judo you develop an "attitude" as you wait expectantly. Saïd is like that. When I say, "Attention! C'est une couleuvre qui passe," I assume this kind of attitude, an attitude which must last about two seconds. Everything Saïd says should be said with

utmost concentration, with this "attitude" of expect-
ancy.

I asked Genet why Sáïd says "vous" to his
mother. "To create a certain rapport between mother
and son; to give the mother a certain importance — a
crushing importance. She's the one who decides about
your marriage, your conduct, your cowardliness."
Many people feel that *The Screens* is crude. But
Genet says, "Beauty must emerge from dirt. Why
should beauty only emerge from beauty?" I discussed
this with him and he told me: "You must force beauty
out of ugliness and you cannot beat around the bush."

Q. If you were to describe Genet to someone who didn't
know him, what would you say?

A. He is secretive. He doesn't talk much. But he is
there, and nothing escapes him. He hates only one
thing — amiability, *la complaisance*. He says what
must be said and that's all. He has his own ideas.
He is silent for one or two seconds; then he speaks
and what he says has but one meaning. He gets right
to the point. "You'll play the character like this.
This is the way I see him. You'll start over again."

Q. Does your background affect your playing?

A. I feel the role of Sáïd very deeply. So deeply that I
weep when he weeps, I suffer when he suffers. I am
so deeply involved in this character that even if the
greatest star on earth came on stage I would feel
nothing because I am totally enclosed within Sáïd's
personality. I am now playing opposite Renaud,
Barrault, Casarès, in a role I would not have dreamed
of playing four years ago. I feel comfortable with
these stars. It's as if I were going to see my real
mother. I am more afraid of Casarès after rehearsals

than when I am actually working on stage.

Q. Are the relationships between the characters cruel?

A. It's not cruelty, but a form of love with Genet. Saïd
likes his wife, Leila, and yet both in the text and in
the mise en scène they act cruelly toward each other.
Genet touches us through this harshness of his. His
cruelty is a kind of humanity. He is sincere, not
soft.

Q. How do you feel Leila's ugliness?

A. It is real, tangible. She has become a mask. It is up
to each spectator to feel her ugliness personally.
This ugliness is something insurmountable.

Q. Do you have Arab mannerisms when you act?

A. Yes. But both Genet and Blin did not encourage them.
I try to be more French. For example, when I say
"Aïn Sefra," I say it with a French accent.

Q. In the stage directions, Genet says: "The acting: to
be extremely precise. Very taut. No useless gesture. Every gesture must be *visible*."

A. Such directions are very difficult. When you do what
Genet and Blin tell you to do you realize how weighted
with meaning each word and movement becomes.
The personality of the character does not budge.
That's why judo was so important: concentration,
constancy, impassivity, patience. Blin always makes
us repeat our work whenever it isn't clear. He insists
on discipline.

Q. Can you explain Saïd's description of the Place

Léopardi in Verona in the eleventh scene?

A. Sáïd says, "I saw you on Place Léopardi in Verona, one day, around 4 o'clock in the morning, under dove's shit, and naked." (This reference was cut in the English translation.) No one understands why Sáïd says this. The day before yesterday I sat next to Genet and said to him: "I'm preoccupied about my costume. In the first scene I go off stage because I'm going to get married. At that time I'm wearing a jacket, a pair of trousers, and a shirt. After that I go to prison. I go over the mountains. I steal, I see many, many things. And all this, in the same costume!" Genet looked at me and smiled. Then he said, "You're not going to get married. You're not going to prison. You're not going any place." I asked: "Then this is the way Sáïd went to Place Léopardi?" Genet laughed. "Yes, that's it."

Q. What about the Algeria of the play?

A. It's not Algeria, except in one tremendous scene, that of the Cadi. Genet gives us his special interpretation of Algeria. But the relationship between colonists and natives is perfect — there, he hit the bull's eye. If countries have rebelled it is not because of European governments, but because of the Blankensees. The Blankensees have crushed and destroyed any kind of relationship between the natives and the colonists.

Q. Are the characters in *The Screens* dead or alive at the same time?

A. You are not dead for Genet. We pass from one stage to another. When one character dies he bursts through a screen and says: "Well, well! What do you know! That's it! . . . And they make such a fuss about it!"

Death is just another phase of existence for Genet.

Q. Would you have preferred to do *The Screens* in an open-air theatre?

A. No. The open-air theatre — the sky, the singing of the birds — disconcerts me. I prefer the stage. I feel better in a theatre where I cannot see the audience, and where a ramp separates me from the audience.

Q. Was Genet nervous before the opening of *The Screens?*

A. He is not easily excited. He seems almost uninterested. He came to rehearsals almost to soothe his conscience. What he has written belongs to the past.

Q. Genet is always interested in the difficult things in life?

A. He loves to talk about sports, automobiles, whatever is difficult. He considers all sports in this light: difficult yet effective gestures. He said to me, to illustrate this, "Pour the coffee, but don't drink it." My gestures always seem to inhibit me. I'm a slave of my involuntary gestures. Even my way of speaking. When I say, "Attention" I must say, "Ah ... tention." That's the way Genet wants it.

I thought I would have great difficulty understanding and learning the text. The day I was given the text to read for the first time I understood nothing. I began declaiming it à la Sarah Bernhardt. I went to see Genet. I said, "Please be kind. Read this text for me." He read it as though he were saying, "Why don't you go eat a banana."

Reprinted in part from *The Drama Review* (Vol. 11, No. 4, Summer, 1967).

## DANIEL IVERNEL

*Interviewer's Note:*

Daniel Ivernel earned his reputation as an actor in Dyer's *The Staircase*, Anouilh's *Becket*, and Sagan's *The Piano on the Grass*, as well as in classical dramas. Born in Versailles of a Norman father and an Austrian mother, Ivernel was trained by such greats as Charles Dullin and Jean Vilar. Ivernel is an "instinctual" actor who does not adhere to cerebrally constructed rules and regulations, but rather listens to his "inner voice." He first experiences the role he is to portray from within; and only afterward is he able to exteriorize the personality he seeks to portray, making of it a living and vibrant creature.

Q. Can you tell us something about your training in the theatre?

A. I was a student first at the Conservatory in Versailles and then in Paris. M. Brunot, an actor at the Comédie-Française, was my teacher at the Conservatory in Paris. After three years of arduous training at the Conservatory, I passed my examinations and then my career began. During my student years, however, I played bit parts at the Comédie-Française.

Q.  Was the theatre your first and only love?

A.  No.  You may find what I'm going to say rather strange,
    but when you think about it closely, it seems to make
    sense.  I was educated in a parochial school before
    going to the Conservatory.  I wanted to be a priest.
    Then — suddenly — and very naturally, I developed a
    passion for the theatre.  The priesthood and the the-
    atre have something in common: show.  Both are ab-
    normal careers.  As a priest you give yourself to God;
    as an actor, you sacrifice yourself to your art.

Q.  Was your début in the theatre a difficult one?

A.  Actually not.  After graduating from the Conservatory,
    I acted in Georges Neveu's *Theseus' Voyage*.  I was
    not the only one making his début in 1944.  There was
    also Maria Casarès and Michel Auclair — today very
    famous actors as you know.  I played the part of a
    Greek coward who was forever plagued by fright.
    Right after this production, I performed under the
    aegis of that remarkable director Charles Dullin, in
    Calderón's *Life is a Dream* — a momentous and un-
    forgettable production.

Q.  Dullin was a theatrical genius.  He had been trained
    by another brilliant man of the theatre, Jacques
    Copeau, who founded the Vieux-Colombier Theatre in
    Paris in 1913.  They were men devoted exclusively to
    their art, and to their troupe.  You could say that both
    Dullin and Copeau were monks or priests of sorts.
    Their lives centered around their theatre.  Can you
    tell us something about the environment in Dullin's
    troupe?

A.  First comes the play — that is, the text.  Secondly,
    the actor.  Dullin was not one to scoff at the written

word as some theatrical directors do today. The text
was the discipline, the food with which the actors
nourished themselves. **The actors had to be initiated,
then,** into the wonderful world of the text. Dullin was
never one to imprison his actors or the production
itself in stage sets. Sets were used as accoutrements
as well as symbols. Frequently, however, a play
might be more forceful, and its impact more breath-
taking without sets. Sometimes a piece of wood or a
bit of plaster served perfectly to create illusion.

Dullin made use of curtains in a masterful way.
I must say that I personally like to use curtains on
stage. I despise doors — that is, the opening and
closing of doors in the theatre. There is nothing as
deadly as opening or closing a door on the stage. I
might add while talking about décors, that I also dislike proscenium-type stages, that is, an enclosed
stage so popular during the Renaissance in Italy and
in France. These theatres were built before the advent
of electricity. Since we are fortunate today in being
able to delineate a face by means of spotlights, we
can show off whatever part of the theatre we desire.
These old fashioned theatres should no longer be
used.

Dullin was a creator-type. When he staged a play
it was from the inside out; the text, the character, the
mood, the atmosphere were all built up virtually
simultaneously. The impact on the audience was for-
midable.

Jean-Louis Barrault, also trained by Dullin, has
written about the monastic atmosphere of this group.
So has Antonin Artaud.

Q. You have also acted at the Théâtre National Populaire
headed at that time by Jean Vilar. Can you tell us
something about his techniques?

A.    There were many similarities between his way of
directing and Dullin's.    Both men considered the
beauty and splendor of the written word of primordial
importance.    Vilar also used curtains.    No doors.
Remember that the TNP stage was and is vast. It's
almost like playing out of doors.    This spaciousness
gives the actor a lot of lee way and infinite possibilities in interpreting his role.    Frequently, one
emerges on stage in total darkness.    Suddenly, a dim
light is focused upon you and you are transformed.
You are the character you are portraying.    Vilar continued in the Copeau-Dullin tradition; that is, he did
away with 19th-century rococco sets and the realistic,
slice of life theatre that another famous director
André Antoine, had fostered.

Q.    Vilar directed you in Alfred de Musset's *Lorenzaccio*
at the Avignon Summer Theatre Festival.    Can you
describe this production?

A.    Musset was a nineteenth-century romantic. He saw life
as a series of bursts of passion.    Gérard Philippe
played the young Lorenzaccio and I portrayed the
vice-ridden and corrupt Alexander de Medicis.    It's
difficult for me to tell you how I saw my character.
I am not one of those actors who can analyze his
roles or explicate the various steps taken in assuming
a part portrayed.    I have heard many actors discuss
their roles — how they could or would like to play
them, etc.    Then, when I saw them, their creations
were entirely different.    Perhaps I am a bit super-
stitious because each time I try to analyze a role I
play it badly.    The moment I am incapable of describing it, that means it's in me.

Q.    Then what is your favorite role?

A. I don't have favorites. I have liked seven or eight parts which I suppose I could call my favorites. The role of Alexander in *Lorenzaccio*; Nero in Racine's *Britannicus*, Becket in Anouilh's play by the same name; Henry VIII in **Thomas More,** the Prince in *Life is a Dream*.

Q. Since you do not like to discuss your roles, could you tell us the problems — if any — involved in portraying a classical or modern role?

A. One of the big differences between classical and modern theatre is the fact that the classical dramatist is dead. Because of this fact he cannot participate in the creation of his production. This may seem obvious to you. But let's look at some of today's productions. Modern actors and directors can see anything and everything in classical drama. *Britannicus*, for example, can be played as a fascist, republican or communist work. Each character can say his lines as he or as the director sees fit. The slant then, is entirely subjective. There are, as a matter of fact, certain directors in France today who are remaking Molière, Racine, Shakespeare — to suit the modern tempo.

When Marguerite Jamois, Raymond Jérôme and I played *Britannicus*, we play this drama like a crisis or an experience in hysteria. Throughout the drama Nero could opt for evil or for good. It was played in the manner of a Hitchcock film — a type of gangster or cloak-and-dagger drama. But Hitchcock, I must say — never succeeded in creating the same kind of inexorable suspense that Racine injected into his tragedy. The waiting, the anguish, became something quite horrendous for modern spectators. Would Nero take the beautiful Junie for his own? Would he have his half-brother Britannicus killed? Would his

mother, Agrippina, intervene? Would she in turn be
done away with?

Of course, the most dramatic of all tales is
*Oedipus Rex*. It's the story of a boy who seeks his
own destiny and who discovers that he has killed
his father and slept with his mother. No crime picture
**or murder mystery that Hitchcock could dream up could**
compare with this ancient Greek tale of horror and
woe.

Modern roles are, of course, less intricate. The
author may intervene in the interpretation.

Q.   Did you work with other directors outside of Dullin
and Vilar?

A.   Yes. Albert Camus. He had a tremendous talent for
directing. In fact, he was the kind of director who
effaced himself before his actors. What I mean is
that he directed his actors without their realizing he
was even there. This is an admirable trait. The
actor gains in confidence since he thinks he is actually creating a role and not being bullied into portraying
it a certain way.

In the movies I have made, I can say that the
same thing is true about Renoir's and Buñuel's techniques. They never block the actor by screaming at
him. To create a mental block in an actor — as so
many directors do — is to spell the actor's end. You
must realize that the actor's psyche is fragile. He is
a sensitive being and if a director begins screaming
at him on stage, he can become petrified. If a director
shouts at me, he turns me off. It's finished. I can't
portray a thing. No director after this can extract
anything from me. Moreoever, if a director begins to
scream at an actor, it is an indication of his own
impotence.

**Buñuel** and Renoir never scream. Nor did Vilar

and Dullin. They all made us feel that we had discovered our parts, that we were in effect the creators
of the spectacle and not they. At the end we frequently said: "Yes, that's the way I saw my part. I
found it myself..." Yet, they are the ones who suggested it.

Q.   You also played in Georg Büchner's **play**, *Danton's
     Death* (1810).   Can you describe the production?

A.   Yes. It's the most beautiful play ever written on the
     French Revolution. It's comparable in certain ways
     to the story of Hamlet — but a **forty-year-old** Hamlet.
     It's a play dealing with remorse: the kind Stalin might
     have experienced after having put so many innocent
     people to death. The plot deals with Robespierre's
     battle with Danton.
         It must be recalled that Danton had always wor-
     shipped truth. In fact he had devoted his life to his
     people and to his country. He represents the positive
     aspects of the French Revolution. He confronts
     Robespierre, an equally great man, who incarnates
     the destructive-idealistic element of the Revolution.
         Danton did not like the Reign of Terror. If he
     did give way to it for a while it was because he felt
     that the people could rid themselves of their aggres-
     sions by means of it and that it would prevent a
     national and international blood bath. Danton de-
     plored the September Massacres. Yet, on the other
     hand, he was the one to ask for a Revolutionary Tri-
     bunal to be organized. No sooner had he advocated
     such a step, than he was considered a moderate — a
     dangerous man, a foe of the Revolution. Moreover,
     Danton believed in clemency. So did Robespierre,
     for that manner, but each one wanted to decide on the
     way in which "clemency" was to manifest itself.
         Danton said throughout that Revolution demands

sacrifice, complete sacrifice. Each person must know what is at stake if he advocates such a course. It is no wonder that Danton cried out in 1787: "Misfortune to those who make revolution because the price is a terrible one."

You must take into consideration that *Danton's Death* was written in 1810, a very romantic era. The characters are idealistic. They have faith in the future and speak of a wonderful state free of cruelty and pain. But Büchner also brought out the sadistic and horrendous acts of which man was and is capable.

*Danton's Death* was written by a German, a young man who understood only too well the Hamlet-aspect of the situation. This kind of play could only be written by a young man, just as Lorenzaccio was written in 1833, when Musset was only twenty-three years old. Young men have the courage to express their fiery ideas and to fight for them. Musset's hero, Lorenzaccio, had the strength necessary to kill the dictator, Alexander de Medicis. The young have the courage, the fervor, the idealism. They lack, however, the experience of life and its wisdom.

You can understand why the role of Danton so fascinated me.

Q.  You have also acted in Françoise Sagan's *The Piano on the Grass*. You played the part of the Drunkard.

A.  Yes. I'd rather not talk about the play *per se*, but about its authoress. Françoise Sagan reminds me in certain ways of Marcel Proust. Not, of course, in terms of her writing style, but in the manner in which she views her contemporaries. Sagan sees the types that flock to St. Tropez in the south of France and she judges them. Proust also judged the society of his day: Paris, Deauville, etc. Those who go to St. Tropez today are immensely rich people — the Onassis

types. They have created a legendary world for themselves; they are examples of degradation, vice and
dissoluteness. Sagan senses *death* and *decay* in these
beings.    They become mythical figures under her
scrutiny.

*The Piano in the Grass* tells the story of a very
wealthy woman who had married several men, including
an oil king.  At forty years of age she calls a meeting
of her former lovers.    They gather together — and
voilà!

Q.   Can you tell us something about Anouilh's method of
     creating his plays?

A.   Anouilh has a peculiar way of writing.  He leaves his
     office or home at noon and some time later—a day,
     a week, a month or so — he hands me a play. "Here",
     he says, "I've just written *Becket*.  Read it.  Have
     fun.  It will amuse you."  When he gave me the play
     to read I was scheduled to perform in another work.
     I was so captivated by his drama that I turned the
     offer down and devoted my energies to *Becket*.

Q.   How did he come to write such a play?

A.   He told me that he was reading the life of Henry II
     of England during a short train trip.  He found it ex-
     citing at the time.  The next thing I knew, *Becket* had
     become a reality!

## Index of Names and Titles

(Last names of authors and theatre directors appear in
parentheses following titles of works and names of theatres.)

313

314

315

318

319

320

321

322